Discovery
*A Comparison between English and
American Civil Discovery Law with
Reform Proposals*

DISCOVERY

*A Comparison between English and
American Civil Discovery Law with
Reform Proposals*

JULIUS BYRON LEVINE

CLARENDON PRESS · OXFORD
1982

Oxford University Press, Walton Street, Oxford OX2 6DP
London Glasgow New York Toronto
Delhi Bombay Calcutta Madras Karachi
Kuala Lumpur Singapore Hong Kong Tokyo
Nairobi Dar es Salaam Cape Town
Melbourne Auckland
and associate companies in
Beirut Berlin Ibadan Mexico City

Published in the United States by
Oxford University Press, New York

British Library Cataloguing in Publication Data

Levine, Julius Byron
    Discovery.
    1. Evidence, Documentary—England
    2. Civil law—England
    3. Evidence, Documentary — United States
    4. Civil law — United States
    I. Title
    344.207'72   KD7512

    ISBN 0-19-825368-0

Typeset in Baskerville 10/12 (VIP)
by Syarikat Seng Teik Sdn. Bhd., K.L.
Printed in Great Britain
at the University Press, Oxford
by Eric Buckley
Printer to the University

To my mother Celia G. Levine, my father Lewis Lester Levine, my sisters Judith S. Brody and Ida-Joyce Levine, my brothers Robert A. Levine and Frederick E. Levine, my children Rachel A. Levine and Sarah L. Levine, my wife Susan, my sister-in-law Tobie G. Levine, and my brother-in-law Morton A. Brody.

Preface

A book about discovery in Anglo-American civil cases addresses a major inroad in the adversary system of adjudication. A
purely adversary system would not compel one party before
trial to provide an opposing party with evidence and other
information about the case. The law of discovery does just this.
Unless discovery is used, surprising evidence would be presented at trial far more frequently; and surprising evidence
would mislead the judge or jury all too frequently to the wrong
factual decision. Likewise, unless discovery is used, important,
at times even decisive, evidence sometimes would not be presented at trial; and compromise settlements would be reached
on terms reflecting the litigants' ignorance. In all these ways a
purely adversary system obstructs doing justice and finding the
truth. By removing the obstruction, discovery enhances the
probability that the truth will be found and justice done.

Discovery in civil cases is well entrenched in English and
American law. However, the mechanisms and scope of discovery in each country differ. Whether the quality and quantity of
Anglo-American discovery are ideal or desirable is the question
this book grapples with. The question is a timely one. There
has not been a critical study of English discovery of the quality
of Wigram's *Points in the Law of Discovery* (2nd edn., London)
since 1840. Since the major modifications of American federal
discovery in the Federal Rules of Civil Procedure of 1938, there
has been a degree of complacency in America with little, if any,
re-examination of first principles.

My examination of discovery has been financed in part by
the Rhodes Scholarship Trust and the Boston University
School of Law under Deans Paul M. Siskind, Austin T. Stick-
ells, Richard E. Speidel, and William Schwartz. I am grateful
to them. My appetite for procedural law was whetted by the
inspiring teaching of Professor James H. Chadbourn of the
Harvard Law School. The late Professor R. N. Cross, then of
All Souls College, and Leonard Hoffman, then of University
College, guided my study at the University of Oxford of the

English law of discovery. I must add my most sincere thanks to Valorie Mulholland, Sonia Zecher, Jamila Dphrepaulezz, and Sändra Wilfong for their cheerful typing, to my brother Attorney Frederick E. Levine for many helpful contributions, and to the law students who have been my research assistants, Peter Kitson, Jeanne LaFlamme, Philip Hertz, Douglas Kowal, John Boylan, Peter Foulkes, Emily Donovan, Sanford Victor, William Wertheimer, Gerald Heupel, and John Guppy.

When the text or notes do not contain the full citation to cases, books, rules, articles, and the like, the reader will find the full citation in the Table of Cases, Table of Statutes and Rules of Court, or the Bibliography. The major discovery rules of both countries are given in the Appendix.

February 1980
Boston, Massachusetts, U.S.A.   J.B.L.

Contents

TABLE OF CASES   xi

TABLE OF STATUTES AND RULES OF COURT   xxix

1. INTRODUCTION   1

A. Intended Benefits of Discovery   1
    1. *Evidence of Benefits*   3
    2. *Evaluation of Discovery*   5

B. Differences between English and American Discovery Mechanisms   8

2. INTERROGATORIES   12

A. Requirement of Leave of Court; Method of Objecting   12

B Answers Ascertainable from Records   15

3. DOCUMENTS   17

A. Documents under F.R.C.P. 34; R.S.C. 1965, 0.24   17
    1. *American Mechanisms for Production upon Request*   17
    2. *Contrast between English and American Discovery*   18
    3. *Extent of Discovery*   25
    4. *Proposed Reform of Discovery in American Courts*   28

B. Documents under F.R.C.P. 45   31
    1. *Mechanics for Production*   31
    2. *Two Successive Discovery Mechanisms*   34
    3. *Relationship between Person and Documents Subpoenaed*   36
    4. *Production from Parties under F.R.C.P. 34 is Preferable*   37

4.	REAL AND PERSONAL PROPERTY	40
A.	Proposed Reform of Discovery	40
B.	Examples of Enlightened, Flexible Inspection Orders	40
C	Exchange of Experts' Reports	41
D.	Inspection of Methods of Operation in England	42
5.	ADMISSIONS OF DOCUMENTS AND FACTS	45
6.	ORAL EXAMINATIONS OR DEPOSITIONS	61
7	MEDICAL EXAMINATIONS	68
8	RESTRICTION OF DISCOVERY BY 'OWN CASE' RULE	75
A.	Application of the Rule in England	75
	1. *'Fact-Evidence' Rule*	75
	2. *Definition of 'Own Case'*	76
B.	Prohibition of Discovery of Witnesses in England	76
C.	Disadvantages of English 'Own Case' and Fact-Evidence' Rules	76
	1. *'Fishing'*	84
D.	F.R.C.P. 26 (b) (1)	84
	1. *Restriction on Discovery of Witnesses by 'Own Case' Rule*	85
	2. *Discovery of American Contentions*	87
E.	Discovery of Information Impeaching Credibility	93
9.	DISCOVERY FROM NON-PARTIES	95
A.	General Rule against Discovery from Non-Parties in England	95
	1. *Exception for Member or Officer of a Corporate Party*	95

2.   *Exception to Determine whom to Sue*   95
3.   *Exception of Banker's Books Evidence Act 1879,*
      s.7   95
4.   *Exception for Real Plaintiff in Interest*   96
5.   *Exception for Documents and Property in*
      Personal-Injuries Cases   96

B.   Proposed Reform of English Civil Discovery   97

C.   Suggested Extension and Improvement of
      American Discovery   103

10. ANALYTIC SUMMARY OF DISCOVERY LAW
      REFORM PROPOSALS   112

11. EPILOGUE: ANTICIPATED OPPOSITION TO
      EXPANDING AMERICAN DISCOVERY   115

NOTES   123

BIBLIOGRAPHY   154

APPENDIX: MAJOR DISCOVERY RULES   161

SUMMARY OF CONTENTS   201

INDEX   205

Table of Cases

'T' before a chapter-note number indicates that the case is cited in the text preceding the note.

A.	Chapter-Note
Abel Investment Co. v. *U.S.* 53 F.R.D. 485 (D.C. Neb. 1972)	2–18
ACF Industries, Inc. v. *Equal Employment Opportunity Commission* 439 U.S. 1081	11–42
Adams v. *Lloyd* 3 H. & N. 351 (1858)	8–6
Ex parte Aiscough 2 P. Wms. 591 (1730)	4–20, 7–6, 7–32, 7–33, 7–37
Alexander v. *Rizzo* 52 F.R.D. 235 (E.D. Pa. 1971)	5–22
Alfred Crompton Amusement Machines Ltd. v. *Customs & Excise Commissioners* [1974] A.C. 405	3–35, 3–36, 3–45
Allhusen v. *Labouchère* 3 Q.B.D. 654 (1878)	8–103
Allright, Inc. v. *Yeager* 512 S.W.2d 731 (Texas Court of Civil Appeals 1974)	8–93, 8–94, 8–97
Alltmont v. *United States* 177 F.2d 971 (3rd Cir. 1949)	3–11
Alma-Schuhfabrik AG v. *Rosenthal* 25 F.R.D. 100 (E.D. N.Y. 1960)	T3–73
Amos v. *Herne Bay Pavilion Promenade & Pier Co. Ltd.* 54 L.T. 264 (1886)	9–2, 9–5
Andresen v. *Maryland* 427 U.S. 463 (1976)	3–73
Anzaldo v. *Croca* 478 F.2d 446 (8th Cir. 1973)	1–5
Arnott v. *Hayes* 36 Ch.D. 731 (1887) (CA) ...	9–12, 9–48
Ashley v. *Taylor* 37 L.T. 522 (1877), see 38 L.T. 44 (1878)	8–6, 8–74

Chapter-Note

Aste v. *Stumore* 13 Q.B.D. 326 (1883) 6–44
Atlanta Fixture & Sales Co., Inc. v. *Bituminous Fire & Marine Ins. Co.* 51 F.R.D. 311 (N.D. Ga. 1970) 2–15
Atty.-Gen. v. *Clapham* 10 Hare App. II 69 (1853) 5–72
Atty.-Gen v. *Corp. of London* 2 Mac. & G. 244, 2 H. & Tw. 1, 19 L. J. Ch. 314 (1849) ... 8–1, 8–10, 8–74
Atty.-Gen v. *Gaskill* 20 Ch.D. 519 (1882) (CA) 8–5
Atty.-Gen. v. *Lambe* 11 Beav. 213, 17 L. J. Ch. 154 (1848) 8–3
Atty.-Gen. v. *Newcastle-Upon-Tyne Corp., No. 1* [1897] 2 Q.B. 384 (CA) 8–11, 8–12
Atty.-Gen. v. *Thompson* 8 Hare 106 (1849) 8–2
Aveling v. *Martin* 17 Jur. (P.I.) 271 (1853) .. 5–55

B.

Baker v. *Newton* [1876] W.N. 8 8–103
Balfour v. *Farquharson* 1 Sim. & St. 72, aff'd., sub nom. *Farquharson* v. *Balfour* Turn. & R. 184 (1822) 5–55
Balls v. *Margrave* 3 Beav. 448 (1841) 9–1
Barlow v. *Bailey* 1870 W.N. 136 8–5
Barreca v. *Penn. R.R. Co.* 5 F.R.D. 391 (E.D. N.Y. 1946) 8–105
Batley v. *Kynock* L.R. 19 Eq. 90 (1870) 8–5
Baugh v. *Delta Water Fittings, Ltd.* [1971] 3 All E.R. 258 .... 7–8, 7–38
Bayley v. *Griffiths* 1 H. & C. 429 (1862) 8–10
Beegle v. *Thomson* 2 F.R.D. 82 (N.D. Ill. 1941) 3–62, T3–63
Ex parte Bellet 1 Cox 297 (1786) 4–20
Bellwood v. *Wetherell* 1 Y. & C. 211 (1835) .. 8–10
Benbow v. *Low* 16 Ch.D. 93 (1880) 8–6, 8–8, 8–18, 8–21, 8–42
Bennett v. *Griffiths* 3 El. & El. 467 (1861) 4–6, 4–7, 4–8
Bennitt v. *Whitehouse* 28 Beav. 119 (1860) 4–6, 4–7, 4–12
Berkeley v. *Standard Discount Co.* 13 Ch.D. 97 (1879) 9–7

Chapter-Note

Berry v. *Haynes* 41 F.R.D. 243 (D.C. Fla. 1966) 1–3, 1–6

Berry v. *Keen* 26 Sol. J. 312 (1882) (CA) 9–2

Bettison v. *Farringdon* 3 P. Wms. 363 (1735) . 8–1, 8–26, 9–33

Bidder v. *Bridges* 29 Ch.D. 29 (1884), rev'd. on unclear grounds, 29 Ch.D. 46 (1885) . 8–6, 8–12, 8–54

Bifferato v. *States Marine Corp. of Delaware* 11 F.R.D. 44 (S.D. N.Y. 1951) 3–33

Bird v. *Malzy* 1 C.B. (NS) 308 (1856) 5–1

Bligh v. *Benson* 7 Price 205 (1819) 8–18

Blue Chip Stamps v. *Manor Drug Stores* 421 U.S. 723 (1975) 11–8

Boddie v. *Connecticut* 401 U.S. 371 (1971) 1–54, 5–76

Bogatay v. *Montour R.R. Co.* 177 F.Supp. 269 (W.D. Pa. 1959) 8–107

Boldt v. *Sanders* 111 N.W.2d 225 (Minn. 1961) 8–110

Bolton v. *Corp. of Liverpool* 3 Sim. 467 (1831), aff'd., 1 Mg. & K. 88 (1833) 8–10

Bough v. *Lee* 29 F.Supp. 498 (S.D. N.Y. 1939) 3–72

Boyd v. *Petrie* 20 L.T. 934, 17 W.R. 903 (1869) 8–10

Brennan v. *Engineered Products, Inc.* 506 F.2d 299 (8th Cir. 1974) 8–63, 8–65, 8–68, 8–71

Briggs v. *Morgan* 2 Hag. Con. 324 (1820) 7–4

British Xylonite Ltd. v. *Fibrenyle Ltd.* [1959] R.P.C. 252 4–21

Broadway & Ninety-Sixth St. Realty Co. v. *Loew's Inc.* 21 F.R.D. 347 (S.D. N.Y. 1958) 1–3, 1–6

Brookes v. *Prescott* [1948] 2 K.B. 133 8–11

In re Brown 4 Bro. C.C. 91 (1792) 4–20

Brown v. *Moore* 3 Bligh 178 (1816) 4–22

Brown v. *United States* 276 U.S. 134 (1928) .. T3–23, T3–24, T3–66, T3–70

Brown v. *Wales* L.R. 15 Eq. 142 (1872) 8–3

Buden v. *Dore* 2 Ves. Sen. 445 (1752) 8–1

Chapter-Note

Burchard v. *Macfarlane* [1891] 2 Q.B. 241
   (CA) 9–2, 9–3, 9–49
Burrell v. *Nicholson* 1 Myl. & K. 680 (1833)   8–3
Burstall v. *Beyfus* 26 Ch.D. 35 (1884) (CA) .   9–2
Bustros v. *White* 1 Q.B.D. 423 (1876) 9–37, 9–46

C.

Causten v. *Mann Egerton Ltd.* [1974] 1 All E.R.
   453   7–40
Cayley v. *Sandycroft Brick, Tile & Colliery Co.*
   33 W.R. 577 (1855)   8–74
Central News Co. v. *Eastern News Telegraph Co.*
   53 L.J.Q.B. 236 (1844)   9–24
Chaddock v. *British South Africa Co.* [1896] 2
   Q.B. 153 (CA)   9–6
Chagas v. *United States* 369 F.2d 643 (5th Cir.
   1966)   5–60
In re *Chapnick* 6 F.R. Serv. 45b, Case 1 (S.D.
   N.Y. 1942)   3–68
Clarke v. *Clarke* [1899] W.N. 130   5–46
Clarke v *Martlew* [1972] 3 All. E.R. 764 ....   7–11, 7–40
Close v. *Sanderson & Porter* 13 F.R.D. 123
   (W.D. Pa. 1952)   8–75
Coca Cola Co. v. *Dixie-Cola Labs., Inc.* 30
   F.Supp. 275 (D.C. Md. 1940)   1–5
Combe v. *City of London* 4 Y. & C. Ex. 139
   (1840)   8–10
Combe v. *Corp. of London* 15 L. J. Ch. 80
   (1845) 8–3, 8–10
Commissioners of Sewers of City of
   London v. *Glasse* L. R. Eq. 302 (1873) 8–1, 8–10
Communist Party of United States v. *Subversive
   Activities Control Board* 254 F.2d 314 (D.C.
   Cir. 1958)   8–105
Compagnie Financière Du Pacifique v. *Peruvian
   Guano Co.* 11 Q.B.D. 55 (1882) (CA) 9–37, 9–46
Conley v. *Gibson* 355 U.S. 41 (1957) 3–29, 8–88,
                                                                         8–91

Chapter-Note

Consolidated Rendering Co. v. *Vermont* 207 U.S.
541 (1908) T3–23, T3–24,
                                                                                                    T3–70
Coomer & Son v. *Hayward* [1913] 1 K.B. 150   9–24
Coster v. *Baring* 2 C.L.R. 811 (1854)   8–3
Couch v. *United States* 409 U.S. 322 (1973) ...   3–73
Coxe v. *Putney* 26 F.R.D. 562 (E.D. Pa. 1961)
....   1–3
Crofts v. *Peach* 1 Webs. Pat. Cas. 268 (1837)   8–5

D.

Dalgleish v. *Lowther* [1899] 2 Q.B. 590 (CA)   8–6, 8–8, 8–17
Daniel v. *Ford* 47 L.T. 575 (1882)   8–104
DaSilva v. *Moore-McCormack Lines, Inc.* 47
F.R.D. 364 (E.D. Pa. 1969)   8–105
Davenport v. *Jepson* 1 N.R. 307 (1862) 4–13, 4–22
Davers v. *Davers* 2 P. Wms. 410 (1727) 8–1, 9–1
Daw v. *Eley* 2 H. & M. 725 (1865) 8–6, 8–15
Dawson v. *Dover and County Chronicle, Ltd.* 108
L.T. 481 (1913) (CA)   8–11
Demeulenaere v. *Rockwell Mfg. Co.* 13 F.R.D.
134 (S.D. N.Y. 1952)   3–68
Democratic National Committee v. *McCord* 356
F.Supp. 1394 (D.C. D.C. 1973) T3–27
Derby Commercial Bank v. *Lumsden* L.R. 5 C.P.
107 (1870)   8–10
Dineley v. *Dineley* 2 Ath. 394 (1742)   9–8
Dinsel v. *Penn. R.R.* 144 F.Supp. 880 (W.D.
Pa. 1956)   9–69
Doe I. Morris v. *Roe* 5 L. J. Ex. 105, 1 M. &
W. 207, 1 Tyr. & G. 545, 1 Gale 367
(1836)   9–1
Dow Chemical Co. v. *Monsanto Chemicals Ltd.*
[1969] F.S.R. 504   4–21
Duke of Bedford v. *Macnamara* 1 Price 208
(1814)   8–10
Dummer v. *Chippenham* 14 Ves. 245 (1807) ...   9–1, 9–25
Dusek v. *United Air Lines* 9 F.R.D. 326 (N.D.
Ohio 1949)   8–83

E.

Eaddy v. *Little* 235 F.Supp. 1021 (E.D. S.C. 1964)   8–105

Eade v. *Jacobs* 47 L. J. Ex. 74, L.R. 3 Ex.D. 335, 37 L.T. 621, 26 W.R. 159 (1877) (CA) 8–6, 8–8, 8–16, 8–26

Earl of Lonsdale v. *Curwen* 3 Bligh 168 n. (1799) 4–8, 4–9

Earl of Suffolk v. *Howard* 2 P. Wms. 177 (1723) 8–1, 8–26

Earp v. *Lloyd* 3 K. & J. 548 (1857)   8–3

East India Co. v. *Kynaston* 3 Bligh 153 (1821)   5–55, 5–69, 5–79

Edmeades v. *Thames Board Mills, Ltd.* [1969] 2 All E.R. 127 ....   T7–9, 7–9, 7–10, 7–12, 7–13, 7–14, 7–15, T7–16, 7–19, 7–20, 7–21, T7–22, T7–24, T7–25, T7–27, 7–31, 7–38, 7–41

Edwards v. *Wakefield* 6 E. & B. 462 (1856) ...   8–6, 8–74, 8–90

Egremont Burial Board v. *Egremont Iron Ore Co.* 14 Ch.D. 158 (1880)   8–30

Elder v. *Charter* 25 Q.B.D. 194 (1980) 9–13, 9–24

Ellenwood v. *Marietta Chair Co.* 158 U.S. 105 (1895)   9–67

Ennor v. *Barwell* 1 De G.Y. F. & J. 529 (1860) 4–11, 8–5

Essgee Co. v. *United States* 262 U.S. 151 (1923)   3–60

Eyre v. *Rodgers* 40 W.R. 137 (1891)   9–9

F.

Farrer v. *Hutchinson* 3 Y. & C. 692, 9 L. J. Ex. Eq. 10 (1839, 1840)   5–55

Chapter-Note

Feingold v. *Walworth Bros.* 144 N.E. 675
(N.Y. 1924) 5–67

Fenton v. *Hughes* 7 Ves. 287 (1802) 9–1, 9–25, 9–29

Finch v. *Finch* 2 Ves. Sen. 491 (1752) 8–103

Firkins v. *Lowe* 13 Pri. 193 (1824) 8–1

Fisher v. *United States* 425 U.S. 391 (1976) ... 3–73

Flitcroft v. *Fletcher* 11 Exch. 543 (1856) 8–74

Flower v. *Lloyd* [1876] W.N. 169 4–13

Fong Sik Leung v. *Dulles* 226 F.2d 74 (9th Cir.
1965) 9–69

Foundry Equip. Co. v. *Carl-Mayer Corp.* 11
F.R.D. 108 (N.D. Ohio 1950) 3–11

403–411 East 65th Street Corp. v. *Ford Motor
Co.* 27 F.Supp. 37 (S.D. N.Y. 1939) 3–65, T3–69,
T3–71

Franklin v. *Daily Mirror Newspapers*, Ltd. 149
L.T. 433 (1933) (CA) 1–60

Freed v. *Erie Lackawanna Railway* 445 F.2d
619 (6th Cir. 1971) 5–53, 8–93

Friend v. *London, Chatham & Dover Ry.* L.R. 2
Ex.D. 437 (1877) 7–8

G.

Garand v. *Edge* 37 W.R. 501 (1889) (CA) 9–24

G.F. Heublein & Bro. v. *Bushmill Wine &
Prods.* Co. 2 F.R.D. 190 (M.D. Pa. 1941)   1–5, 1–8

Gibbons v. *Waterloo Bridge Co.* 5 Price 491
(1818) 9–1, 9–25

Gillam v. *A. Shyman, Inc.* 22 F.R.D. 475
(D.C. Alaska 1958) 3–55, 3–78

Goldlaw, Inc. v. *Shubert* 25 F.R.D. 276 (S.D.
N.Y. 1960) 3–37

Goldman v. *Mooney* 24 F.R.D. 279 (W.D. Pa.
1959) 5–28

Goodman v. *Hobroyd* 15 C.B. (NS) 839 (1864)   8–10

Gordon, Wolf, Cowen Co., Inc. v. *Independent
Halvah & Candies, Inc.* 17 Fed. Rules Serv.
34.621, Case 1 4–23

In re Grand Jury Subpoena Duces Tecum 72
F.Supp. 1013 (S.D. N.Y. 1947) 3–72

Chapter-Note

Greyhound Lines, Inc. v. *Miller* 402 F.2d 134
   (8th Cir. 1968)   1–5
Griebart v. *Morris* [1920] 1 K.B. 659 ....   8–11, 8–16
Griffin v. *Archer* 2 Anstr. 478 (1794) 1–57, 9–43

H.

Hall v. *Truman, Hanbury & Co.* 29 Ch.D. 307
   (1885)   8–6
Hammond Packing Co. v. *Arkansas* 212 U.S.
   322 (1909) 5–61, T5–61,
                                                               5–63, 5–65,
                                                               5–66, T5–68
Harris v. *Aldrit* 2 Chitty's Reports 229 (1814)
     9–1
Harrison v. *Prather* 404 F.2d 267 (5th Cir.
   1968) 3–55, 3–78
Hart v. *Montefiore* 30 Beav. 280 (1861)   5–72
Hartsfield v. *Gulf Oil Corp.* 29 F.R.D. 163
   (E.D. Penn. 1962) 8–80, 8–91
Heathcote v. *Fleete* 2 Vern. 442 (1702)   9–8
Heatley v. *Newton* 19 Ch.D. 326 (1881) (CA) .   1–2, 9–2, 9–34
Heaton v. *Goldrey* (1910) 1 K.B. 754 (CA) ...   1–60
Hennessy v. *Wright* (No. 2) 24 Q.B.D. 445, 4
   T.L.R. 662 (1888) (CA) 8–6, 8–13
Herbert v. *Lando* 441 U.S. 153 (1979) 11–1, 11–36,
                                                               11–37, 11–40,
                                                               11–41, 11–56
Hersom v. *Bernett* [1954] 3 All E.R. 370   9–9
Hewitt v. *Piggott* 5 Car. & P. 75 (1831) 3–44, 9–37,
                                                               9–46
Hickman v. *Taylor* 329 U.S. 495 (1947) 1–5, 1–10,
                                                               1–63, 1–65,
                                                               T3–67, T3–72,
                                                               8–105
Hills v. *Wates* 43 L.J.C.P. 380 (1874)   8–3
Hoffman v. *Postill* L.R. 4 Ch. App. Cas. 673
   (1869)   5–1
Holland Am. Merchants Corp. v. *Rogers* 23
   F.R.D. 267 (S.D. N.Y. 1959)   3–33

Chapter-Note

Hovey v. *Elliott* 167 U.S. 409 (1897) T5–61, T5–63,
T5–68, 5–69,
5–74, T5–75,
T5–76
How v. *Best* 5 Madd. 19 (1820) 9–1, 9–25
Howard v. *Beall* 23 Q.B.D. 1 (1889) 9–12
Huffman v. *Boersen* 406 U.S. 337 (1972) 5–76
Humphries v. *Penn. R.R. Co.* 14 F.R.D. 177
(N.D. Ohio 1953) 9–60
Hungerford v. *Goring* 2 Vern. 38 (1687) 8–3

I.

Imperial Land Co. v. *Masterman* 29 L.T. 559
(1873) 3–45
Ingilby v. *Shafto* 33 Beav. 31 (1863) 8–6, 8–74, 8–90
Ironmonger & Co. v. *Dyre* 44 T.L.R. 579
(1928) (CA) 9–11
Ivy v. *Kekewick* 2 Ves. Jun. 679 (1795) 8–1

J.

James Nelson & Sons Ltd. v. *Nelson Line Ltd.*
[1906] 2 K.B. 217 (CA) 9–13
Jenkins v. *Bushby* 35 L. J. Ch. 400 (1866) 8–2, 8–10
John Walker & Sons, Ltd. v. *Henry Ost & Co.*,
Ltd. (1970) R.P.C. 151 (CA) 8–101
Johns v. *James* 13 Ch.D. 370 (1879) 8–6, 8–74
Jones v. *Jones* 3 Mer. 161 (1817) 5–72

K.

Katz Exclusive Millinery, Inc. v. *Reichman* 14
F.R.D. 37 (W.D. Mo. 1953) 8–75
Kearsley v. *Philips* 10 Q.B.D. 465 (1883)
(CA) 8–5
Kerr v. Rew 5 My. & Cr. 154, 9 L.J. (NS)
152 (1840) 9–39, 9–41
Kettlewell v. *Dyson* 18 L.T. 285 (1868) 8–6, 8–74
Kirkland v. *Morton Salt Co.* 46 F.R.D. 28
(N.D. Ga. 1968) 3–11

Chapter-Note

Knapp v. *Harvey* [1911] 2 K.B. 725 .... 1–46, 8–16,
8–29, 8–56,
8–57, 8–74

Knight v. *Marquess of Waterford* 2 Y. & C. 23
(1835) 8–10

Korman v. *Shull* 184 F.Supp. 928 (W.D.
Mich.), app. dismissed, 310 F.2d 373 (6th
Cir. 1960) 3–67

Kynaston v. *East India Co.* 3 Sw. 248 (1819),
aff'd., 3 Bligh 153 (1821) 4–5

L.

Lane v. *Willis* [1972] 1 All E.R. 430 .... 7–11, 7–23,
7–38, 7–40

Leach v. *Greif Bros. Cooperage Corp.* 2 F.R.D.
444 (S.D. Miss. 1942) 1–7

LeBarron v. *LeBarron* 35 Vermont 365 (1862) 7–4

Lee v. *Angas* L.R. 2 Eq. 59 (1866) 9–49

Lee v. *Electric Products Co.* 37 F.R.D. 42 (N.D.
Ohio 1963) 2–17

Lethbridge v. *Cronk* 23 W.R. 703 (1875) 3–45

Leumi Financial Corp. v. *Hartford Accident &
Indemnity Co.* 295 F.Supp. 539 (S.D. N.Y.
1969) 8–80, 8–86,
8–93, 8–99

Lewis v. *Marsh* 8 Hare 97 (1849) 8–5

Lind v. *Isle of Wight Ferry Co.* 8 W.R. 540
(1860) 8–3

Lowndes v. *Davies* 6 Sim. 468 (1834) 8–1

Lumb v. *Beaumont* 27 Ch.D. 356 (1884) 4–11

Lyell v. *Kennedy* (No. 1) 8 A.C. 217 (1883) .. 8–5, 8–11

Lyon v. *Tweddle* 13 Ch.D. 375 (1879) 8–74

M.

Maitland v. *Rodgers* 14 Sim. 92 (1844) 5–55

Manchester Fire Ins. Co. v. *Wykes* 33 L.T. 142,
23 W.R. 884 (1875) 9–1, 9–25, 9–39

Margeson v. *Boston & Maine R.R.* 16 F.R.D.
200 (D.C. Mass. 1954) 8–107, 8–109

Chapter-Note

Marriott v. *Chamberlain* 17 Q.B.D. 154 (1886)
(CA) 8–6, 8–8, 8–16

Marshall v. *Feeney* 2 J. & H. 313 (1861) 5–1

Marshall v. *Goulston Discount (Northern) Ltd.*
[1967] 1 Ch. 72 (CA) 3–46

Martin v. *Long Island Railroad Co.* 63 F.R.D.
53 (E.D. N.Y. 1974) 8–23, 8–107,
8–109

Martin v. *Nederlandsche Amerikaansche
Stoomvaart Maatchappij* 8 F.R.D. 363 (S.D.
N.Y. 1948) T3–38

Mayor of London v. *Levy* 8 Ves. 398 (1803) ... 9–1, 9–8, 9–25

McCargo v. *Hedrick* 545 F.2d 393 (4th Cir.
1976) 5–52

McElroy v. *United Air Lines, Inc.* 21 F.R.D.
100 (W.D. Mo. 1967) T8–92

McLean v. *Prudential Steamship Co., Inc.* 36
F.R.D. 421 (E.D. Va. 1965) 3–62, 9–56

Minet v. *Morgan* L.R. 8 Ch. App. Cas. 361,
21 W.R. 467 (1873) 8–1

Mitchell v. *Watson* 361 P.2d 744 (Wash.
1961) 5–67

Moline v. *Tasmanian Railway Co.* 32 L.T. 828
(1875) 9–24

Monarch Liquor Corp. v. *Schenley Distillers
Corp.* 2 F.R.D. 51 (N.D. N.Y. 1941) 3–10, 3–13

Montecatini Edison v. *Rexall Drug & Chemical
Co.* 288 F.Supp. 486 (D. Del. 1968) 8–86, 8–94

Moor v. *Roberts* 2 C.B. (NS) 671 (1857) 8–6, 8–74

Morgan v. *Alexander* L.R. 10 C.P. 184, 44
L.J.C.P. 167 (1875) 9–24

Morgan v. *Seaward* 1 Webs. Pat. Cas. 167
(1835) 4–22

Morse v. *Buckworth* 2 Vern. 433 (1703) 9–8

Mort v. *A/S D/S Svendborg* 41 F.R.D. 225
(E.D. Pa. 1966) 8–107

Mullen v. *Mullen* 14 F.R.D. 142 (D.C. Alaska
1953) T3–38

Murphy v. *Ford Motor Co. Ltd.* [1970]
(Unreported) 7–17, 7–31

Chapter-Note

Murray v. *Walter* Cr. & Ph. 114 (1839)   3–41

N.

Nash v. *Layton* [1911] 2 Ch. 71 (CA) 3–46, 8–7,
                                                     8–51, 8–52,
                                                     8–53, 8–55

National Hockey League v. *Metropolitan Hockey
    Club, Inc.* 427 U.S. 639 (1976) 5–62, 5–75,
                                                     T5–76, 5–77,
                                                     T5–78, 11–42

Newman v. *Godfrey* 2 Bro. C.C. 332 (1788) ..   1–57, 9–43
Newmark v. *Abul* 196 F.Supp. 758 (S.D. N.Y.
    1952) 3–62, 9–56
Nicholl v. *Jones* 2 H. & M. 588 (1865) 9–37, 9–46
Norwich Pharmacal Co. v. *Commissioners of
    Customs & Excise* [1973] 2 All E.R. 943
    (House of Lords) 9–9, 9–25, 9–44

0.

O'Donnell v. *Breuninger* 9 F.R.D. 245 (D.C.
    D.C. 1949)   1–5
O'Rourke v. *Darbishire* [1920] A.C. 581 ....   5–7, 9–37, 9–46
Orr v. *Diaper* 4 Ch.D. 92 (1876)   9–8
Ortwein v. *Schwab* 410 U.S. 656 (1973)   5–76
O'Shea v. *Wood* [1891] P. 286 (CA) 9–2, 9–24
Osram Lamp Works, Ltd. v. *Gabriel Lamp Co.*
    [1914] 2 Ch. 129 (CA) 9–37, 9–46
Owen v. *Nickson* 3 El. & El. 602 (1861)   8–26

P.

Paterson v. *Chadwick* 1 W.L.R. 890 (1974) ...   9–18
Penfold v. *Pearlberg* [1955] 3 All E.R. 120   9–24
Penn-Texas Corp. v. *Muralt Anstalt No. 2*
    [1964] 2 Q.B. 647 (CA) 9–2, 9–48
Perry v. *Phosphor Bronze Co. Ltd.* 71 L.T. 854
    (1894) (CA)   9–10
Phillips v. *Phillips* 40 L.T. 815 (1879)   8–104
Pickett v. *Bristol Aeroplane Co. Ltd.*
    (unreported)   7–28

Chapter-Note

Pierce v. *Pierce* 5 F.R.D. 125 (D.C. D.C.
1946) 1–5
Piggott v. *Anglo-American Telegraph Co.* 19
L.T. 46 (1869) 4–12, 8–5
Plummer v. *May* 1 Ves. Sen. 426 (1750) 9–1, 9–25, 9–38
*Plymouth Mutual Cooperative and Industrial
Society, Ltd.* v. *Traders' Publishing Assoc.,
Ltd.* [1906] 1 K.B. 403 (CA) 8–11
Pollock v. *Garle* [1898] 1 Ch. 1 (CA) 9–11
Portugal v. *Glyn* 7 Cl. & Fin. 466 (1840) 1–4, 1–57,
9–13, 9–28,
9–39, 9–41,
9–42, 9–43

Potter v. *Metropolitan District Ry. Co.* 28 L.T.
231 (1873) 8–15
Potts v. *Adair* 3 Swans. 265 (1793) 1–6, 9–34, 9–35
Potts v. *Whitmore* 8 Beav. 317 (1845) 5–55
Pressley v. *Boehlke* 33 F.R.D. 316 (W.D. N.C.
1963) T8–92
Preston v. *Carr* 1 Y. & J. 175 (1826) 8–1, 8–15
The Princess of Wales v. *The Earl of Liverpool* 1
Swan. 114 (1818) 5–72, 8–1

R.

Radio Corp. of America v. *Rauland Corp.* [1956]
1 All E.R. 549 .... 9–2, 9–37, 9–46
Reade v. *Woodrooffe* 24 Beav. 421 (1857) 9–48
Regina v. *Inhabitants of Llanbaethly* 2 E. & B.
940 (1853) 9–31
Reid v. *Powers* 28 Sol. Jour. 653 (1884) 9–24
Republic of Liberia v. *Roye* 1 App. C. 139
(1876) 5–58
Rew v. *Hutchins* 10 C.B. (NS) 829 (1961) 5–1
Richards v. *Maine Central R.R.* 21 F.R.D. 595
(D.C. Me. 1957) 8–63
Rishdon v. *White* 5 T.L.R. 59 (1888) 9–24, 9–47
Rishton v. *Grissel* 14 W.R. 789 (1866) 3–45
In re Rivièra 79 F.Supp. 510 (S.D. N.Y. 1948)
.... 3–72

Chapter-Note

Rochdale Canal Co. v. *King* 15 Beav. 11 (1852)
.... 3–19

Rockett v. *John J. Casale, Inc.* 7 F.R.D. 575
(S.D. N.Y. 1947) T3–38

Roe v. *Wade* 410 U.S. 113 9–86

Rogers v. *Tri-State Materials Corp.* 51 F.R.D.
234 (N.D. W.Va. 1970) 6–7, 8–80, 8–94

Ross v. *Longchamps, Inc.* 336 F.Supp. 434
(E.D. Mo. 1971) 2–18

Rowell v. *Pratt* [1938] A.C. 101 9–30

Ruiz v. *Hamburg-American Line* 478 F.2d 29
(9th Cir. 1973) 8–93, 8–97

Rutter v. *Chapman* 8 M. & W. 388, 1 Dowl.
(NS) 118, 11 L. J. Ex. 178 (1841) 5–3

S.

S. v. *S.* [1970] 3 All E.R. 107 .... 7–4, 7–18,
7–24, 7–28,
7–29, 7–39

St. Paul Fire & Marine Ins. Co. v. *King* 45
F.R.D. 521 (W.D. Okla. 1968) 8–63

Saunders v. *Jones* 7 Ch. D. 435 (1877) 1–2, 8–74

In re Saxton [1962] 1 W.L.R. 859 .... 3–43, 4–15

Schlagenhauf v. *Holder* 379 U.S. 104 (1964) . 7–1, 7–22,
9–72, 9–73,
9–85, 9–86

Schwimmer v. *United States* 232 F.2d 855 (8th
Cir.), cert. denied, 352 U.S. 833 (1956) .. 3–72

Scott v. *Walker* 2 El. & Bl. 555 (1853) 8–10

Scovill Mfg. Co. v. *Sunbeam Corp.* 357 F.Supp.
943 (D. Del. 1973) 8–76

Sebright v. *Hanbury* [1916] 2 Ch. 245 9–9

Seuthe v. *Renwal Products, Inc.* 38 F.R.D. 323
(S.D. N.Y. 1965) 3–65, 4–1

Shaftesbury v. *Arrowsmith* 4 Ves. 66 (1798) 8–1

Shaw v. *Smith* 18 Q.B.D. 193 (1886) (CA) .. 9–24

Shawmut, Inc. v. *American Viscose Corp.* 12
F.R.D. 488 (D.C. Mass. 1952) 5–16

Chapter-Note

Shelak v. *White Motor Co.* 581 F.2d 1155 (5th
Cir. 1978) 8–93, 8–97,
11–54

Sherwood v. *Lord Lonsdale* L.R. 5 C.P.D. 47
(1879) 8–103
Shrader v. *Reed* 11 F.R.D. 367 (D.C. Neb.
1951) 8–61
The Shropshire 38 T.L.R. 667 (1922) (CA) ... 8–6, 8–74
Sibbach v. *Wilson & Co., Inc.* 312 U.S. 1
(1941) 1–62, 7–41,
9–70, T9–75,
9–76, 9–77,
9–78, 9–79,
9–80, 9–81,
9–82, 9–83,
9–84, 9–86

Sientki v. *Haffner* 145 F.Supp. 435 (S.D. N.Y.
1956) 3–65, 3–66
Sierocinski v. *E.I. DuPont de Nemours & Co.*
103 F.2d 843 (3rd. Cir. 1939) 8–75, 8–88,
8–91

Smith v. *Central Linen Service Co.* 39 F.R.D.
15 (D.C. Md. 1966) 3–11
Smith v. *Duke of Beaufort* 1 Hare 507, aff'd., 1
Phil. Ch. R. 208 (1843) 8–3, 8–10
Smith v. *Great Western Ry. Co.* 6 El. & Bl. 405
(1856) 2–13
*Société Internationale Pour Participations
Industrielles et Commerciales*, S.A. v. *Rogers*
357 U.S. 197 (1958) 3–37, 5–59,
T5–61, 5–63,
5–64

South Staffordshire Tramways Co. v. *Ebbsmith*
[1895] 2 Q.B. 669 (CA) 9–11, 9–12,
9–48

Spiers & Pond, Ltd. v. *'John Bull', Ltd* 85
L.J.K.B. 992 (1916) (CA) 1–60
Stainton v. *Chadwick* 3 Mac. & G. 575 (1851) 8–3

Chapter-Note

Starr v. *National Coal Board* [1977] 1 All E.R.
243 .... 7–16, 7–17,
                                                        7–26, 7–28,
                                                        7–30, 7–31

Stoate v. *Rew* 11 W.R. 595, 14 C.B. (NS) 209
(1863) 8–6, 8–74
Stone v. *Marine Transp. Lines, Inc.* 23 F.R.D.
222 (D.C. Md. 1959) 8–107
Stone v. *United States* 167 U.S. 178 (1897) 9–67
Storey v. *Lord George Lennox* 1 Keen 341, 6 L.
J.Ch. (NS) 99, aff'd., 1 My. & Cr. 525.
(1836) 8–3
In re Strachan [1895] 1 Ch. 439 (CA) 8–18, 8–23,
                                                        8–28, 8–30
Straker v. *Reynolds* 22 Q.B.D. 262 (1889) 9–24
Stroud v. *Dracon* 1 Ves. Sen. 37 (1747) 8–10
Sutherland (Duke) v. *British Dominions Land
Settlement Corp., Ltd.* [1926] 1 Ch. 746 ...... 1–2, 1–6, 1–7,
                                                        8–90

T.

Taylor v. *Rundell* Cr. & Ph. 104 (1841) 3–41, 3–42
Teller v. *Montgomery Ward & Co.* 27 F.Supp.
938 (E.D. Pa. 1939) 1–5
Temperley v. *Gye* 6 El. & Bl. 380 (1856) 9–1
Terrell v. *Standard Oil Co. of N.J.* 5 F.R.D.
146 (E.D. Pa. 1945) 3–11
Theaker's Case Cro. Jac. 686 (1625) 4–20, 7–7, 7–32
Thomason v. *Leiter* 52 F.R.D. 290 (N.D. Ala.
1971) 2–15
Tobe Deutschmann Corp. v. *United Aircraft
Prods.* 15 F.R.D. 363 (S.D. N.Y. 1953) 1–6
Tomlinson v. *Lymer* 2 Sim. 489 (1829) 8–1
Tooth v. *Dean and Chapter of Canterbury* 3 Sim.
49 (1829) 1–57, 9–43
Tudor Accumulator Co. Ltd. v. *China Mutual
Steam Navigation Co. Ltd.* [1930] W.N. 200
(CA) T4–17
Turquand v. *Guardians* 8 Dowl. 201 (1840) ... 7–35
Tyler v. *Drayton* 2 Sim. & St. 309 (1825) 8–1

U.

Union Bank of London v. *Manby* 13 Ch.D. 239
(1879) 9–9

Union Pacific Ry. Co. v. *Botsford* 141 U.S. 250
(1891) 9–69, 9–86,
9–87

United Sheeplined Clothing Co., Inc. v. *Nat'l.
Broadcasting Co., Inc.* 11 F.R. Serv. 2d
34.13, Case 8 (S.D. N.Y. 1968) 3–33, 8–75

United States v. *American Optical Co.* 2 F.R.D.
534 (S.D. N.Y. 1942) 3–25, 3–26

United States v. *Becton, Dickonson & Co.* 30
F.R.D. 132 (D.C. N.J. 1962) 2–17

United States v. *Dioguardi* 361 F.Supp. 954
(S.D. N.Y. 1973) 9–69

United States v. *Guterma* 24 F.R.D. 134 (S.D.
N.Y.), rev'd., 272 F.2d 344 (2nd Cir.
1959) T3–73

United States v. *International Business Machines
Corp.* 66 F.R.D. 215 (S.D. N.Y. 1974) 8–105

United States v. *Kelsey-Hayes Wheel Co.* 15
F.R.D. 461 (E.D. Mich. 1954) 5–16

United States v. *Kras* 409 U.S. 434 (1973) 5–76

United States v. *National Broadcasting Co., Inc.*
65 F.R.D. 415 (D.C. Cal. 1974), appeal
dismissed, 421 U.S. 940 (1975) T3–40, T3–46

United States v. *Proctor & Gamble Co.* 356 U.S.
677 (1958) 1–49

United States v. *Sisson* 297 F.Supp. 902 (D.C.
Mass. 1969), appeal dismissed, 399 U.S.
267 (1970) 1–53

United States v. *62.50 Acres of Land, More or
Less* 23 F.R.D. 287 (N.D. Ohio 1959) 8–105

United States v. *Taylor* 100 F.Supp. 1016
(W.D. La. 1951) 5–18

United States v. *216 Bottles* 36 F.R.D. 695
(E.D. N.Y. 1965) 8–63

United States v. *United States Alkali Export
Ass'n.* 7 F.R.D. 256 (S.D. N.Y. 1946) 3–26, T3–26

Chapter-Note

W.

Walker v. *Fletcher* 3 Bligh 172 (1804) 4–8, 4–9, 4–10, 4–14

Walsh v. *Conn. Mutl. Life Ins. Co.* 26 F.Supp. 566 (E.D. N.Y. 1939) 5–16

Watson v. *Cannon Shoe Co.* 165 F.2d 311 (5th Cir. 1948) 8–98

Webster Motor Car Co. v. *Packard Motor Car Co.* 16 F.R.D. 350 (1954) 8–61

Welsbach Incandescent Gas Lighting Co. v. *New Sunlight Incandescent Co.* [1900] 2 Ch.1 9–6

Whaley v. *Brancker* 10 Jur. (NS) 535 (1864) . 4–12

Wharton v. *Lybrand, Ross Bros. & Montgomery* 41 F.R.D. 177 (E.D. N.Y. 1966) 8–105

Willis & Co. v. *Baddeley* [1892] 2 Q.B. 324 .. 9–13, 9–14, 9–15

Willoughby's Case Cro. Eliz. 566 (1597) 4–20, 7–7

Wilson v. *Church* 9 Ch. Div. 552 (1878) 9–2, 9–5, 9–6

Wilson v. *Raffalovich* 7 Q.B.D. 553 (1881) (CA) 9–13

Wilson v. *United States* 221 U.S. 361 (1911) .. 3–60

Wirtz v. *Hooper-Holmes Bureau, Inc.* 327 F.2d 939 (5th Cir. 1964) 8–65

Wirtz v. *Local 169, Hod Carriers' Union* 37 F.R.D. 349 (D.C. Nev. 1965) 3–67

Wych v. *Meal* 3 P. Wms. 310 (1734) 9–32

Wynn v. *Humberston* 27 Beav. 421 (1858) 5–72

Z.

Zielinski v. *Philadelphia Piers, Inc.* 139 F.Supp. 408 (E.D. Pa. 1956) T8–92

Zolla v. *Grand Rapids Store Equipment Corp.* 46 F.2d 319 (S.D. N.Y. 1931) 1–3, 1–8

Zumbeck v. *Biggs* 82 L.T. 654 (1900) 9–48

Table of Statutes and Rules of Court

'T' before a Chapter-Note number indicates that the statute or rule is cited in the text preceding the note.

	Chapter-Note
Administration of Justice Act 1970	
ss.32, 33	T9–64
s.32(1)(2)	T9–17, 9–18, 9–53
s.32(4)	9–17
s.33(1)	9–19
s.33(2)	9–20
Banker's Books Evidence Act (42 Vict. c.11) 1879	
s. 7	T9–10
Civil Evidence Act 1968, s.16(2)	T8–5, T8–18, T8–46
Common Law Procedure Act 1854, s.46	9–24
Contempt of Court Act, s.15, r.12 (1830)	5–55
Court of Chancery Procedure Act 1852	
ss.18, 20	T3–19
s.19	5–73
The Evidence Act 1851, s.6	8–1
s.2	9–27
Family Law Reform Act 1969	
s.21–(1)	7–41
s.23	7–41
Federal Rules of Civil Procedure of 1938 (F.R.C.P.)	T1–1, T5–4, 5–73, T6–9, T8–87, T9–54, T9–60, T9–66, T9–68, T9–69, 9–69, T9–70, T9–74, T9–85, 9–85, T9–86, T11–1, T11–16, T11–52, T11–54

Chapter-Note

1970 Amendments to the F.R.C.P. T1–38, T1–40,
                                               T1–45, T1–48,
                                               T2–3, T2–14,
                                               3–10, 3–13,
                                               T3–27, T3–49,
                                               T3–58, T8–75,
                                               T8–76, 8–79,
                                               T8–94, T9–61,
                                               T11–7, T11–33,
                                               T11–34
1980 Amendments to the F.R.C.P. 11–33, T11–35,
                                               11–35, T11–48,
                                               T11–52

F.R.C.P. 1   1–50
          5(a)(b) T3–31
          6(a)(b)   3–79
          8(a)(2) T8–87
          8(e)(2) T8–80, T8–81
          11 ....   T8–81
          14(a)(b)..........................   T9–68
          15(b) T5–51, T8–97,
                                               8–97, T8–98,
                                               T8–99, T8–100,
                                               8–100, T8–103
          16 ....   5–51, T5–52,
                                               8–65
          26–37   5–73
          26–37 and 45 ....   T1–2
          1970 Amendment
             to F.R.C.P. 26 ....   T8–64
          26(a) T3–4, T8–72,
                                               T9–59, T9–60
          26(a)(c) T2–1
          26(b) T3–9, T3–12,
                                               T3–20, 3–20,
                                               T3–21, T3–56,
                                               T5–4
          26(b)(1) 3–14, T3–20,
                                               5–29, 5–47,
                                               T8–60, T8–63,

Chapter Note

	T8–68, 8–68, T8–71, 8–71, T11–1, T11–41, T11–47, T11–42, T11–52
26(b) (1) (2) (3)	T3–14, T3–20, 3–20, T3–24, T3–25, T3–64
26(b) (4)	3–20, 3–64
26(b) (4) (A) (i)	T8–64
26(b) (4) (A) (ii)	3–64
26(b) (4) (A) (ii), (c)	8–64
26(b) (4) (B)	3–64, 4–16
26(c)	2–16, T3–15, T3–25, T3–57, T9–56, 10–1, T11–41, 11–41, T11–42, T11–47, T11–52
26(e)	5–23, T8–72, T8–73, 8–73, T8–94, 8–94, T11–1
26(e) (1) (A)	T8–72
26(e) (2)	T8–72, 8–98
26(f) (added in 1980)	1–55, 11–41, T11–42, 11–42, T11–52
28–32	T6–3, 6–24
28	3–75
28(a)	T3–53
30	T3–20, T3–31, T3–53, T3–66, T9–69
30(a) (c)	T9–55
30(b)	T3–62
30(b) (1)	3–77
30(b) (5)	T4–1
30(b) (7) (added in 1980)	6–6

Chapter-Note

30(c)	3–31, T3–53, 3–75, 3–76, T9–56
30(d)	T9–56, T11–42, T11–47, T11–52
30(e)	3–32, T9–56
30(f)(2)	T9–56
31	T3–20, T3–31, T3–53, T3–66, T9–69
31(a)	T3–53, T3–62, 3–77
31(a)(b)	T3–53, 3–75
31(b)	3–31, 3–32, T3–53, 3–76
1946 Amendment to F.R.C.P. 33	2–1
1970 Amendment to F.R.C.P. 33	T3–80, T8–76, T8–77, T8–81, T8–83, T8–86, T8–90, T8–92, T8–94
1970 Amendments to F.R.C.P. 33 and 37	T2–2
1970 Amendments to F.R.C.P. 33(a) and 37(a)(2) (3) (4) ...	T2–5, T2–7
F.R.C.P. 33	T2–1, T2–4, T3–66, T3–81, 6–18, T8–78, T8–81, T8–92
33(a)	T2–1, T2–2, 8–78
33(b)	T8–72, T8–78, 8–79, T8–81, T8–97, T8–98, T8–100
33(c)	T2–14, T2–15, T2–16, T2–17, T3–1, T11–1

Chapter-Note

1970 Amendments
to F.R.C.P. 34 .... T3–1, T3–3,
T3–9, T3–12,
T3–21, T3–22,
T3–24, T3–26,
T3–28, T3–67,
T3–68, 3–70

F.R.C.P. 34 .... 2–17, T3–1,
T3–6, T3–11,
T3–13, T3–14,
T3–20, 3–20,
T3–21, 3–21,
T3–22, T3–23,
T3–24, T3–26,
3–27, 3–28,
T3–30, T3–31,
T3–32, 3–37,
T3–38, T3–40,
T3–48, T3–49,
T3–50, T3–52,
T3–63, T3–67,
T3–68, T3–69,
T3–70, 3–70,
T3–72, T3–73,
T3–74, 3–74,
T3–79, T3–80,
T4–1, T4–2,
T4–3, 4–16,
T5–54, T5–55,
T9–59, T9–60,
T9–62, T9–63,
T11–1

34(a) T3–1, 3–1,
T3–20, 3–20,
T3–25, T3–33,
3–56, 3–79,
9–54

34(a)(2) T4–23

34(a)(b) T3–43

34(b) 3–3, T3–4,

Chapter-Note

	T3–8, T3–9, T3–12, T3–15, T3–20, T3–21, T3–24, T3–30, T3–80, T4–1, T11–1
34(c)	T9–61, T9–65, T9–66
35	T7–1, T7–4, T9–71, T9–75, T9–79, 9–79, T9–83, T9–84, T9–85, 9–85, T9–87
1970 Amendments to F.R.C.P.	
35(a)	9–69
F.R.C.P. 35(a)	7–24, 9–69, T9–71, T9–74
35(b)	T4–16, 4–16, 7–40
35(b)(1)	T4–16, 9–71
35(b)(2)	T4–16, 7–40
35(b)(3)	T4–16
1970 Amendments to F.R.C.P.	
36	T5–17, T5–19, T5–22, T5–42, T5–43, T8–76, T8–81, T8–83, T8–84, T8–90, T8–92
F.R.C.P. 36	T5–4, T5–15, T5–27, T5–30, T5–53, T5–54, T5–55, T5–61, T8–81, T8–82, T8–83, T8–100
36(a)	T5–4, T5–15, 5–15, T5–17, T5–18, 5–18, T5–19, T5–22,

Chapter-Note

	T5–30, T5–32, T5–33, T5–34, T5–59, T8–72, 8–79, T8–81, T8–83, T8–97, T8–101
36(b)	5–23, T5–24, T5–53, T8–82, 8–97, T8–100, 8–100
36(b) (2) (A)	5–33
37	8–73, T9–80, 11–41, T11–42, 11–42, T11–47, T11–52
37(a)	T3–4, T3–5, T3–15, T3–20, T3–25, T3–26, T4–1
37(a) (2)	T2–9, T3–4, 3–57
37(a) (2) (3) (4)	T2–2
37(a) (4)	T3–4, T3–26, T5–18
37(a) (4), (b) (2), (d)	5–31
37(b)	5–60
37(b) (1)	9–79
37(b) (1) (2) (C) (D) (E)	5–56
37(b) (2)	T3–26, T3–59, T3–60, T5–32, T5–59, T5–61, T5–75
37(b) (2) (i) (ii) (iii) (before 1970 amendment)	T9–82
37(b) (2) (iv) (before 1970 amendment)	T9–76, T9–79, 9–79
37(b) (2) (A)	5–33, 5–57
37(b) (2) (A) (B) (C) (E)	T9–87

Chapter-Note

37(b) (2) (B) (C) 5–58
37(b) (2) (C) T5–67
37(b) (2) (D) 5–59, 7–41
37(b) (2) (D) (E) T9–87
37(c) T5–31, 5–31,
                                              T5–34, T5–41,
                                              5–59, T5–60

37(d) T5–60, 5–60
45 .... 3–27, T3–53,
                                              T3–56, T3–60,
                                              T3–62, T3–63,
                                              T3–67, T3–68,
                                              T3–70, T3–71,
                                              T3–72, T3–73,
                                              T3–74, 3–74,
                                              T3–75, T4–1,
                                              4–2, T4–3,
                                              4–16, T5–54,
                                              T5–55, T9–55,
                                              T9–60, T9–68,
                                              T9–69, T11–1
45(a) T3–60, T3–61
45(a) (b) (c) (d) (f) T3–53
45(a) (b) (c) (e) (f) T3–53
45(b) T3–57, T3–61,
                                              T3–66, 3–80
                                              T11–42,
                                              T11–47,
                                              T11–52
45(c) 3–55, 3–78
45(d) T3–60, T3–62,
                                              T3–63, T3–64,
                                              T3–72, T3–73,
                                              T3–74, T4–1,
                                              T9–59, T9–70,
                                              T11–1, T11–42.
                                              T11–47,
                                              T11–52
45(d) (1) T3–57, T3–58,
                                              T3–60, T3–61,

Chapter-Note

T3–62, T3–63,
T3–66, T3–80,
3–80, 9–54,
T9–55, T9–58,
T9–59

45(d) (1) (f)	T9–68
45(d) (2)	T3–63, 9–55
45(d) (b)	T3–63
45(d) (f)	9–44
45(e)	T3–62
45(f)	T3–59, T9–60, T9–68, T9–74
83	1–55
84	3–3, 5–27, 8–87
Mass. Gen. Laws. ch. 233, ss.24–63	6–17
1975 Amendment to s.24	6–17
Mass. Gen. Laws. ch. 231, ss.61–7	6–18
1975 Amendment to s.61	6–18
1974 Massachusetts Rules of Civil Procedure	6–17, 6–18
1975 Amendment to s.61	6–18
1974 Massachusetts Rules of Civil Procedure	6–17, 6–18
Rules 28–32	6–24
Rule 33	6–18
Massachusetts Rules of the Supreme Judicial Court 3:15, ss.1–5, 8, 9	6–24
Rules Enabling Act	T9–75, T9–78, T9–85, 9–85, T9–86
1883 Rules of Supreme Court (R.S.C.)	3–41, T9–14
Order (O.) 19, rule (r.) 6	8–90
O.19, r. 7	8–90
O.31, rr. 13A, 13B, 19A–(3)	3–45
O.37, r. 7	9–24
O.50, r. 3	T4–17, T4–18, 9–24
1893 Amendment to R.S.C. 1883, 0.31, rr.12, 18	T3–16

Chapter-Note

1965 R.S.C.	T3–16, T3–18, T3–19, T3–41, T3–48, 8–5
O.7, rr.1, 2	9–21
O.18, r. 12(1)	8–90
r. 12(3)	8–90
Orders 24, 26, 27, and 29	T1–2, 5–73
O.24	T3–1, T3–15, T3–19, T3–20, T3–35, T5–10, T5–46, T5–47, 5–51, T8–24
r. 1–(1)	T3–1, T3–33
r. 1–(2)	T3–16
r. 2–(1)	3–41, T5–50
rr. 2–(1), 5	T3–16
rr. 2–(1), 9	T3–63
r. 2–(2)	T3–18
r. 2–(5)	T3–16
r. 2–(7)	T3–16
rr. 3, 8, 11, 13–(1)	T3–19
r. 7A	T9–21
r. 7A–(1) (2) (4)	9–21
r. 7A–(3)(b)	9–22
r. 7A–(3)(b), (6)(b)	9–50
r. 7A–(5)	9–23
r. 7A–(6)(b)	T9–24
rr. 8, 13–(1)	9–48
r. 9	T3–16, 3–41
rr. 9, 11	T3–43
r. 11(2)	3–41
r. 11(3)	3–41
r. 16–(1)	T5–59
r. 16–(1)(2)	5–56
r. 16–(2)	T5–59
O.25, r. 1–(1)	2–11
r. 4	T5–51
r. 6–(3)	5–56
O.26, r. 1	T2–1
r. 1–(1)(b)	T2–2

Chapter-Note

r. 1–(1) (2) (3) T2–8
r. 1–(3) T2–12, 2–12,
                                       T2–13, T2–16,
                                       9–48
r. 1–(4) T8–103, 8–106
r. 2 .... T9–4, 9–6
r. 3 9–4
r. 4 .... T2–8, 2–8
    r. 5 6–1
    r. 6–(1) (2) 5–56
    r. 6–(2) T5–59
O.27 .... T5–46, T5–59
    r. 2 .... 5–4, T5–5,
                                          T5–26, T5–54
    r. 2–(1) T5–9, 5–10
    r. 2–(2) T5–24
    r. 4 .... T5–5, 5–25
    r. 4–(1) T5–25
    r. 4–(1) (a) T5–12
    r. 4–(1) (b) T5–12, T5–15
    r. 4–(1) (2) T5–10, T5–11,
                                          5–54
    rr. 4, 5 .... T5–24
    r. 5 .... 5–25, T11–1
    r. 5–(1) T5–4
    r. 5–(1) (2) (3) 5–10, 5–11
O.29 4–21
    rr. 2–(1) (2) (4) (6),
        3–(1) (2) (3) T4–3
    r. 2–(1) (2) 9–24
    r. 3–(1) 9–24
    r. 3–(1) (2) 9–24
    r. 7A T9–21, T9–68
    r. 7A–(2) (3) 9–21
    r. 7A–(3) 9–22
    r. 7A–(5) 9–23
    r. 7A–(7) T9–24
O.38, r. 13 .... 9–24, 9–48
O.62, r. 3–(5) 5–9
    r. 3–(5) (6) T5–32

	Chapter-Note
O.103	4–21
r. 26(2)(f)	4–21
48 Stat. 1064 (1934)	9–75
Statute Law Revision and Civil Procedure Act (46 & 47 Vict. c. 49) 1883	9–24
Supreme Court of Judicature Acts 1873 & 1875	T1–1, 5–73, T8–1, T8–4, T8–7, T8–11, T8–12, T8–15, T8–18, T8–56, T9–9
28 U.S.C. s.331	1–13
s.2072 (1948)	9–74

1

Introduction

The principal trial court in England is the Supreme Court of Judicature; the Divisions of this Court which handle the most significant civil cases are called collectively the High Court. The principal trial courts in the American federal judicial system are the United States District Courts. By virtue of the English Supreme Court of Judicature Acts 1873 and 1875, and the Federal Rules of Civil Procedure for United States District Courts (hereafter denoted F.R.C.P.) of 1938, the previously separate courts of equity and common law have been merged into the single High Court in England and United States District Court in America. Today the discovery available in civil cases in these Courts does not differ according to whether the nature of the case is legal or equitable.

A great deal of important civil litigation in America does not take place in the American federal courts but in the independent courts of the fifty States. However, the proposals for reform and comparisons in this book about American federal law almost always apply to the laws of the American States as well. This is because since 1938 more than 80 per cent of the States have revised their civil discovery law substantially along the lines of federal discovery law.[1]

The law of English and American federal civil discovery is largely, but not entirely, codified. The chief codifications are the American F.R.C.P. 26–37 and 45 and the English Rules of Supreme Court 1965 (hereafter denoted R.S.C. 1965), Orders 24, 26, 27, and 29, both of which are in the Appendix.

A. INTENDED BENEFITS OF DISCOVERY

English authorities have recognized several ways in which discovery may be beneficial by providing parties with information bearing on litigation. For instance, it enables them to make a more accurate evaluation of the strengths and weaknesses of their own case and that of their opponent. As a result of such enlightened evaluations English authorities believe that the parties may reach compromise settlements or agree to narrow the issues, or that one side may concede defeat.[2] American federal authorities too have pointed out these benefits of discovery.[3]

Another benefit from discovery, according to English authorities, is that it may permit a party to expose as false or misleading evidence which otherwise would surprise him at trial, when he would have neither the time nor opportunity to demonstrate its unreliable nature. As early as 1840 Lord Wynford formulated this benefit as follows:

> It is of very little use to get hold of any facts in Court, unless you have a knowledge of those facts beforehand, in order to use them advantageously at the time of trial ... [A] bill of discovery is much better in many cases than the examination of a witness. In the examination of a witness the answers may come upon you by surprise, but by means of a bill of discovery you have the whole examination in your possession, and you have an opportunity of thinking of it before it is used in Court ...[4]

American federal authorities likewise have envisaged eliminating surprise at trial as one of the benefits of discovery.[5]

The third and most obvious benefit from discovery is that it may provide, or lead to, evidence a party presents at trial, as both English and American federal authorities have recognized.[6] The party might not come upon this evidence at all were it not for discovery. Even if he could acquire it by other means, such means might be more expensive and time-consuming than discovery.[7] If by questioning witnesses or from subpoenas duces tecum a party were to learn of evidence for the first time at the trial, rather than by discovery before trial, the lack of time to consider and prepare is likely to render the presentation of the evidence at trial less effective and efficient than it might be.[8] This lack of time is especially acute when trial is by jury, as it is frequently in American federal civil cases but infrequently in English civil cases.[9] If counsel does not have the time and quiet in which to fathom the full significance of evidence, the jury or judge probably will fail to do so as well. The upshot is not insignificant, for it may well be injustice.

Since an intended benefit of discovery in both the American federal and English legal systems is to eliminate surprise and to promote adjudication in the light of all relevant facts rather than in various degrees of darkness,[10] discovery is intended to blunt some of the rough edges of the adversary system. That is, discovery in both legal systems is an antidote to the 'sporting theory' of justice.[11]

1. EVIDENCE OF BENEFITS

There has been no sophisticated empirical study of English discovery. American federal discovery during 1962 and 1963 was the subject of such a comprehensive study.[12] The Advisory Committee on Rules for Civil Procedure, under the auspices of the American federal Judicial Conference,[13] engaged the Columbia University Project for Effective Justice to determine the effects of American federal discovery by a national field-study.

To obtain the necessary data, the study used two methods. A questionnaire was sent by mail to attorneys in cases recently terminated in thirty-seven districts...Personal interviews were conducted with attorneys in cases recently terminated in six districts. The interview sought to elicit more details...The self-administered questionnaire was twenty-two printed pages in length and could be answered in about thirty minutes...[14] The intent of the questionnaire was a stratified probability sample of private civil cases terminated in United States District Courts...The principal categories [of civil cases] taken for sampling...were personal injury,...breach of contract,[15]...anti-trust, copyright-patent-trademark...[16]

The interview questionnaire was eighty-three pages, and the average interview lasted one and one-half hours...The sample design for the interviews was stratified and judgmental; no selections were made by true probability methods...[17]

The incomplete response pattern to the national mail questionnaire seems to result in a body of data weighted toward the cases with greater activity [i.e.]...the larger cases[18]...The data can resolve some of the controversies about discovery by testing whether some of the predicted gains...occur often or rarely.[19]

This sophisticated empirical study considered the extent to which discovery has brought about the three benefits both English and American federal authorities have expected from discovery.

One such benefit is eliminating or curtailing surprise at trial. The study concluded that 'lawyers are *not* less likely to be surprised if they have discovered.'[20] On the other hand it found that 'lawyers are surprised *more* often if their adversaries have discovered.'[21]

If discovery is related to creating greater surprise, the process must be indirect. A lawyer cannot surprise his adversary with the facts secured from discovery, since he got them from the adversary or — when...[from] nonparty witnesses — in the presence of the adversary. Surprises occur more often from the lawyer's contentions than from his evidence. Discovery may reduce surprise due to evidence but increase it due to the new ideas inspired by the discovered facts. Therefore discovery may have several unexpected side effects by stimulating lawyers' thinking about possible new contentions;...it increases surprise among some lawyers while reducing it among others.[22]

The second benefit expected from discovery is providing or leading to evidence presented at trial. The field study learned that this benefit has materialized. From discovery litigants learn of new witnesses, obtain new evidence, and become alerted to new issues.[23]

[T]he parties made use of the antecedent discovery, by actually presenting the products in evidence, in 77 per cent of the cases [which reached trial][24]...In three-fourths of the[se]...cases the lawyers said that if they had not been able to avail themselves of discovery, they would simply not have obtained the evidence uncovered.[25]

But the study found no evidence that the presentation at trial of evidence obtained by discovery is more efficient and effective than the presentation of evidence first found at the trial itself.[26]

The third category of benefits expected from discovery are those that enable the parties to make a more accurate evaluation of their cases, with the results of compromise settlements, narrowed issues, and concessions of defeat. The study unearthed no positive evidence that discovery promotes the latter two results.[27] Nor did it find that it promotes settlement.[28] But, after setting forth evidence that cases in which there was discovery reached trial 19 per cent of the time while those in which there was no discovery reached trial only 10 per cent of the time, Professor Maurice Rosenberg, the director of the Project for Effective Justice which conducted the study,[29] admonished,

I want to caution that those figures cannot be taken as proof positive. The non-discovery cases are probably different from the others in respects that materially affect their potentiality for reaching trial. There is evidence that I shall not now explicate that cases without discovery are not normal cases in respects other than their apparant above-average tendency to settle before trial. Since the non-discovery and the discovery cases are not entirely comparable, we cannot confidently ascribe their different traits of durability to the presence of discovery.[30]

The study learned, however, that in settlement negotiations the parties use the new evidence, witnesses, and issues revealed to them by discovery.[31] William A. Glaser of the Columbia University Bureau of Applied Social Research thinks such information renders parties less amenable to settlement.[32] On the other hand, Professor Rosenberg has concluded that discovery 'is improving...very probably the quality of the settlement process, according to the heavily preponderant weight of the evidence from the field survey'.[33] The Advisory Committee on Rules of Civil Procedure likewise understood this study to show that discovery 'makes for a fairer...settlement'.[34]

Glaser must be positing either that the parties are unrealistic or that information obtained by discovery does not hurt the case of the discovering party. Because parties sometimes discover information which weakens their cases,[35] this information leads them, if they are at all realistic, to be willing to settle on terms more favourable to their opponents. This is especially so since their opponents have the same information, for they either provide it or also receive it from non-parties.[36] Without discovery, parties might not learn of information which hurts them: non-parties might refuse to give it to them; and their opponents might prefer to reserve it until trial, when surprise might multiply its justified effect. Without discovery, too, parties might well not learn of information which helps them; surely their opponents would be extremely unlikely to volunteer it to them. Hence, if discovery does not engender a larger number of settlements, it nonetheless improves the quality and fairness of settlements by enabling parties to learn of information which both hurts and helps them before deciding on what terms they will settle.

2. EVALUATION OF DISCOVERY

The American federal empirical study discussed in the preceding subsection found no evidence that discovery narrows the issues or eliminates or curtails surprise at trial from unanticipated contentions. Discovery in American federal litigation terminating in 1962 and 1963, which the study investigated, failed to remove surprise from the arsenal of practitioners of the 'sporting theory' of justice. Most American federal lawyers were such practitioners; they were 'still motivated to conceal as much as possible, particularly evidence or witnesses that will have a dramatic effect at trial'.[37] However, this persistence of surprising contentions and failure to narrow the issues in

American federal cases should not be understood to reflect an inherent deficiency of discovery. These findings were made before the 1970 amendments to the F.R.C.P., at a time when many American federal courts were holding that contentions were not subject to discovery.[38] At that time American federal practice required only the most general pleadings and did not provide for a bill of particulars.[39] One can hardly imagine a better combination of pleading and discovery characteristics to encourage surprising contentions at trial.

The 1970 amendments to the F.R.C.P. would appear to make contentions discoverable. But, as discussed in detail in Chapter 8, Section D2, the Advisory Committee Note to these amendments would not limit parties at trial to the contentions revealed in their answers to interrogatories. For discovery to realize the benefits of eliminating or curtailing surprise and narrowing the issues at trial, the American federal courts must reject this position of the Advisory Committee, as argued in Chapter 8, Section D2.[40]

The empirical study of American federal discovery confirmed that discovery provides or leads to evidence presented at trial which otherwise often would not be uncovered. But this study also found that the presentation of irrelevant evidence at trial is positively correlated with discovery.[41] Professor Rosenberg feels, nonetheless, that providing parties with evidence to be presented at trial which otherwise would have been beyond their reach 'is the most serious and weighty possible endorsement of the basic efficacy of the Federal discovery system'.[42]

Discovery seems to entail additional time, money, and inconvenience, not only through presentation of irrelevant evidence at trial, but also through the procedures incident to seeking and giving discovery.[43] Yet the empirical study of American federal cases found that in most cases the time, money, and trouble entailed by discovery are not excessive.[44] This study suggested also that there may be a negative correlation between settlements and discovery, as has been seen; and settlements are, of course, more economical to all concerned than trials.

Despite these diseconomies of discovery, the American federal Advisory Committee on Rules of Civil Procedure did not, upon receipt of the results of the empirical study which it had commissioned, propose the abolition or curtailment of discovery. Instead it recommended its continuation and expansion by the 1970 amendments to the F.R.C.P. The Committee's reason for doing so was that 'discovery frequently provides evidence that would not otherwise by available to the parties and thereby makes for a fairer trial or settlement'.[45] It should not be overlooked that, owing to the reluctance of wise trial lawyers to ask on cross-examination questions whose answers they cannot confidently predict, discovery is usually the only means by which a party may secure evidence decisive in his favour but known only to his opponent; it thus blunts that rough edge of the adversary system which approves a party's concealment of 'awkward facts'[46] which his opponent does not ask him for at trial.[47]

The United States Supreme Court adopted the Advisory Committee's recommendation of the continuation and expansion of discovery by promulgating the 1970 amendments to the F.R.C.P. It did so without explanation. But one member of that Court on another occasion remarked that the most important benefit achieved by discovery is 'assuring that right and justice shall have the most favorable opportunity of prevailing in cases that are tried . . .'.[48] Another member of that Court on a different occasion similarly had remarked, 'Modern instruments of discovery . . . make a trial less a game of blindman's buff [*sic*] and more a fair contest with the basic issues and facts disclosed to the fullest practicable extent'.[49] Hence the United States Supreme Court, like the Advisory Committee, undoubtedly endorsed discovery in 1970 in the light of the findings of the empirical study that discovery fosters just adjudication, even if dilatory and expensive.

If discovery may not at once foster the 'just, speedy and inexpensive determination of every action',[50] it is far better that discovery be available to permit such speed and economy as is consistent with justice than that it be curtailed in order to have such injustice as is consistent with speed and economy.[51] Even in this day of docket congestion a sociologist has acknowledged, '[I]n some fields, policy can be based on the preponderance of events. But this is not true of judicial administration: justice must be done not only in the majority of cases but in every possible case.'[52] If justice is not done because discovery is unavailable, disrespect for the law will be encouraged. Yet,

[the rule of] law cannot be adequately enforced by . . . courts supported merely by the police. . . . [It requires] men disciplining themselves to obey the law they respect . . .[53] [I]t is . . . the injection of the rule of law that allows society to reap the benefits of rejecting what political theorists call the 'state of nature'.[54]

Given the paramount goal of promoting the just adjudication of disputes, efforts must nevertheless be made to minimize the diseconomies entailed by discovery and disclosed by the empirical study of American federal discovery. The mechanisms and scope of discovery law should be shaped to economize on time and money, provided that this is not done at the expense of justice.[55]

B. DIFFERENCES BETWEEN ENGLISH AND AMERICAN DISCOVERY MECHANISMS

Section A shows that the intended benefits of discovery in the English and American federal civil legal systems are the same. As these are two busy common-law jurisdictions with a common heritage, *a priori* one would expect them to use generally the same mechanisms for bringing about discovery. This does not turn out to be so.

In England, as will be seen, interrogatories and inspection of real and personal property are available by court order; oral depositions and physical and mental examinations of parties and discovery from non-parties by any method are generally unavailable; admissions of facts may be sought by request; while disclosure and production of documents must be made by each party to his opponent, who need not even request them; and such disclosure of documents automatically is deemed a notice to admit their genuineness. On the other hand, in the American federal system, as will be seen, interrogatories, inspection of real and personal property, oral depositions, production of documents, and admissions of documents and facts are all available by extrajudicial request; physical and mental examinations may be ordered by the court; and discovery is available generally from non-parties by oral deposition and extrajudicial subpoena.

What is the rationale for the differences in methods of discovery in the two systems? Surely the goal of just adjudication alone is not the explanation, for it is fortuitous whether a mechanism available in one system but unavailable in the other will be indispensable for the court in any given case to ferret out the true state of the facts on which its decision depends. In one case a document required to be disclosed by the English system but not requested in the American federal system will

prove decisive. Yet in another case, evidence obtained by following up a non-party's information, available before trial in
the American federal system but unavailable in the English,
will prove crucial. In any given case the midwife to truth may
be, and may only be, any one or more of the mechanisms of
discovery.[56]

The American federal mechanisms of discovery comprehend
all sources of information bearing on litigation. The absence in
general of three of these mechanisms — physical and mental·
examinations, oral depositions of parties, and discovery from
non-parties — in the English system is remarkable. The English
have explained the absence of two of them on grounds of super-
vening social policy. They have said that the peace and privacy
of non-parties should not be disturbed by the litigation of
others.[57] They have felt that the liberty of the subject exempts
him from a responsibility to submit to a physical or mental
examination.[58] But the absence of the third mechanism, oral
depositions, especially while interrogatories are available to
reach the same sort of information, suggests that economizing
on time and money has occupied a high place in the English
scheme of priorities. In arguing that England should add oral
depositions to its discovery mechanisms, Chapter 6 draws on
the conclusion, in the empirical study of American federal discovery by the Project for Effective Justice, that the oral deposition is the most productive mechanism of discovery. This study
demonstrates that to economize on time and 'money by the
absence of oral depositions is to pay a heavy cost in terms of
lost benefits. While oral depositions may well be more expensive than interrogatories,[59] they seem to score significantly
higher on a cost-benefit analysis.

In any event, the apparently high value placed by the English on minimizing delay and expense probably also explains
why the English system requires court orders for interrogatories
and inspections of personal and real property. This requirement saves time and expense when the court declines to make
the order sought and when a party fails to seek it owing only to
the delay and expense of applying for it. The requirement
wastes both, however, when the court makes the order. At least
in respect of interrogatories in England, the net effect may well
be to save time and money by diminishing the quantity of discovery.[60]

The American federal system, by contrast, is not so devoted

to this interest in economy as to deny discovery altogether by oral depositions and to diminish it by requiring court orders for its other methods (except physical and mental examinations).[61] It does, however, recognize this interest by making all of its mechanisms except physical and mental examinations available by the most economical devices, namely, extrajudicial request or subpoena. The American federal exception of requiring a court order for physical and mental examinations reflects a social policy like the English concern for the liberty of the subject—concern for the 'privacy of the person' and 'the sensibilities of people or even their prejudices as to privacy'.[62]

The English system departs from devotion to economy, and devotes itself instead fully to promoting just adjudication, in its documentary discovery. It requires each party to disclose and produce his documents to his opponent, who need not even request them (see Chapter 3, Section A2). It thus is more expensive and dilatory than the American federal documentary discovery by extrajudicial request. It thus too does not rely on the 'sporting instincts' of the litigants to lead them to use this tool for resolving disputed factual questions accurately. It requires them to use it in society's interest of achieving justice. Yet the English system uses this procedure of automatic, mandatory discovery only for documents (and, incidentally, admissions of their genuineness). It probably subjected documents to this procedure because of its interest in economy, for they, of all sources of information, are usually amenable to this procedure with the least expense and inconvenience. In view of the American federal system's relative lack of devotion to the interest of economy, its failure to use this concept must be ascribed to the obstinate magnetism of the 'sporting theory' of justice.

It should be noted that English documentary discovery nudges the adversary system to perform in practice as it is thought to perform in theory. The theory is that vigorous lawyers battling as adversaries thoroughly investigate and analyse a case so that each may present at trial all information helpful to his side.[63] In American practice, owing to indolence, incompetence, or the heavy demands on the time of busy trial lawyers, they may neglect to serve a request for documentary discovery. The English documentary-discovery mechanism, on the other hand, weds adversary theory to practice, for it facilitates thorough investigation of an adversary's documents by eliminating the need to serve a request in order to see the documents.

At the same time, the English documentary mechanism does not inhibit the lawyers' adversary function. Under this mechanism a party still may resist disclosure and production of documents on any of the traditional grounds, including the at least conditional privilege for materials a lawyer has prepared in readiness for trial, called 'legal professional privilege' in England and 'work product privilege' in the United States. Although this privilege is beyond the scope of this work, it is appropriate here to note that it makes some relevant information unavailable and thereby limits the degree to which discovery may promote just adjudication.[64] The purpose of this privilege is to avoid 'demoralizing' effects on the adversary function of lawyers in two senses.[65] First, an adversary who may sit back and secure by discovery the fruits of his opponent's trial-preparation efforts will be discouraged from independently investigating and analysing the case. Second, an adversary who will be required to turn over the fruits of his investigative and trial-preparation labours to his opponent may well decide not to exert such labours, since their fruits may prove more helpful to his opponent than to himself.[66]

Interrogatories

A. REQUIREMENT OF LEAVE OF COURT; METHOD OF OBJECTING

F.R.C.P. 33 regulates interrogatories. The most salient difference between this Rule and the English practice is that interrogatories in American federal courts are available without leave of court (compare F.R.C.P. 33(a) with R.S.C. 1965, 0.26, r. 1). Nor is the frequency of service of American federal interrogatories limited, unless the party interrogated obtains for good cause a court order against successive sets (F.R.C.P. 26(a)(c)).[1] The interrogated party may object to particular interrogatories, in which event the reasons for objections are stated in lieu of answers (F.R.C.P. 33(a)). The party signs his answers under oath, as in England; his lawyer signs his objections (ibid.; R.S.C. 1965, 0.26, r. 1–(1)(b)). If the American federal interrogating party decides to press the questions to which there are objections or, in his view, incomplete or evasive answers, the burden is on him to move for a court order compelling answers (F.R.C.P. 33(a), 37(a)(2)(3)(4)).

Before the 1970 amendments to F.R.C.P. 33 and 37, when an interrogated party objected to an interrogatory he was required to serve with his objection a notice of the court hearing he had scheduled on his objection for the earliest practicable time.[2] In fact, before 1970, interrogatories had given rise to a higher proportion of objections and motions, and so court intervention, than any other American federal discovery mechanism.[3]

Nevertheless, in reviewing approximately thirty years' experience under F.R.C.P. 33, the Advisory Committee on (Federal) Rules of Civil Procedure in 1967 did not propose that the English practice that interrogatories are available only with leave of court be adopted. Instead the Committee attributed excessive objections and motions spawned by interrogatories to the following reasons: time-periods that were too short for filing answers and objections; the want of sanctions against a party who made unjustified objections; the requirement that the party interrogated schedule a hearing on his objection when he filed it; and the lack of compulsory joinder of hearings on objections and motions for further answers.[4] Accordingly 1970 amendments to F.R.C.P. 33(a) and 37(a) (2) (3) (4) were directed to these ills.[5]

These amendments do nothing directly to encourage the party serving interrogatories to improve his questions. Yet

common complaints are that the adversary sends more questions than are justified by the nature of the litigation, that he poses inept and ambiguous questions, that he asks for more information than he is entitled to learn, that he asks loaded and tripping questions...[6]

F.R.C.P. 33(a) and 37(a) (2) (3) (4), as amended in 1970, do, however, indirectly discourage such interrogatories by allocating to the party serving them the burden of moving for a court order compelling answers to questions objected to or not answered; and by imposing on an unsuccessful moving party or his attorney the cost of his opponent's reasonable expenses incurred in opposing the motion, including attorney's fees,[7] unless the motion was substantially justified.

It was probably wise not to try to cure the ills of American federal interrogatories by following the English example of requiring leave of court to serve them. This requirement surely does not minimize court intervention. Under the English practice, leave of court must be sought for proposed annexed interrogatories, even when the party interrogated has no objection to them (R.S.C. 1965, 0.26, r. 1–(1) (2) (3)). Furthermore, if he has objections, he presents them at the very hearing which his opponent's application for leave makes necessary (see R.S.C. 1965, 0.26, r. 4; I. Jacob et al., *Supreme Court Practice 1979*, 126/ 4/1, pp. 452–3). Hence the party interrogated is not discouraged from objecting by the expense, delay, and inconvenience of a separate hearing on his objections. Nor do these considerations encourage the interrogating party to accede to the objections. The inevitability of court intervention runs counter to extrajudicial interrogatory practice. Moreover, under the English practice the party interrogated may object, on the ground of privilege, after leave to serve the interrogatory has been granted.[8] Hence in cases in which privilege is invoked, there may be two instances of court intervention under the English practice but only one under the American federal practice.

Nor does the requirement of leave of court *per se* improve the quality of the interrogatories. A party disposed to ask unjustified, inept, and tripping questions, and able to serve them directly on his opponent, seldom would be less likely to ask such questions if he had to secure court leave. Moreover, even if the court denied leave, it undoubtedly would permit him to amend his questions and seek leave anew, as English masters customarily do. Without the necessity of leave of court, his opponent might object to the offending questions. By either method, the burden to improve the quality of the questions would be on their proponent—in one case, by seeking leave to file amended interrogatories, in the other, by testing the objection with a motion to compel answers under F.R.C.P. 37(a) (2) or by serving a revised set of interrogatories on his opponent. On the other hand, if the proponent would be embarrassed to have his defective questions come to the knowledge of the court or if the court *sua sponte* would detect some defects which his opponent would overlook, requiring leave of court would improve the quality of his interrogatories *pro tanto*. But neither contingency is very realistic in an age of overcrowded dockets which make it

next to impossible for a judge to make himself acquainted, upon an interlocutory application made amid the hurry and confusion of his chambers, with the bearing [or lack of bearing] of particular questions on the perhaps complicated matters in dispute...[9]

Even if a 'protracted case' is assigned to a single judge or master who does become familiar with the complicated matters in dispute,[10] the immense stakes in such litigation will make it extremely unlikely that the interrogated party will fail to detect defective questions.

Requiring leave to serve interrogatories therefore would be extremely unlikely either to improve the quality of questions or to minimize court intervention; however, it would preclude the benefits of discovery in the following marginal case: the proponent feels that his opponent voluntarily will give him some answers and that the benefit he would obtain from the answers to his interrogatories, for which the court would give him leave, would not outweigh his burden in securing such leave.[11] In addition, where, as in England, leave is not granted automatically in the absence of sound objections, but is granted only if the interrogatories satisfy the test that they are 'necessary either for disposing fairly of the cause... or for saving costs' (R.S.C. 1965, 0.26, r. 1–(3)), then the requirement of leave also would preclude the benefits of discovery in those cases in which the court did not find the test satisfied.[12]

B. ANSWERS ASCERTAINABLE FROM RECORDS.

An interrogatory may ask for information which may be secured only by poring over voluminous documents accessible to the party interrogated. Rather than compelling him to do so, the English R.S.C. 1965, 0.26, r. 1–(3) requires the court 'in deciding whether to give leave... [to] take into account any offer made by the party to be interrogated... to produce documents relating to any matter in question'.[13] The rationale is to relieve the party interrogated of the burden of investigation and shift it to his opponent who desires the information. On the same rationale F.R.C.P. 33(c) was added by the 1970 amendments to F.R.C.P.[14]

F.R.C.P. 33(c), however, is ill drafted in two respects to realize its rationale. First, its terms make it a sufficient answer to an interrogatory to afford the interrogating party opportunity to inspect specified records from which the answer may be ascertained, if *inter alia* 'the burden of... ascertaining the answer is *substantially the same* for the party serving the interrogatory as for the party served...'(emphasis added). The condition that the burden be 'substantially the same' satisfies the drafters' intention that the option to produce records instead of answering the interrogatory should not be available when ascertaining the answer would be substantially more burdensome for the interrogating party than for his opponent.[15] This condition, however, is not fulfilled when the burden on the interrogating party would be substantially less than that on his opponent; yet this is an *a fortiori* case for the option to produce records compared to the case spelt out in the rule—when the burden is 'substantially the same' for both parties. Given the rationale for the rule, this condition in the rule should have been drafted as follows: 'where... the burden of... ascertaining the answer is *not substantially greater* for the party serving the interrogatory than for the party served...' Despite the unskilful drafting, one would hope courts will construe this condition as it is suggested it should have been drafted. To refuse to do so will be to frustrate the purpose of F.R.C.P. 33(c).

A second respect in which its language is too narrow for its purpose is that the option only applies to 'the *business* records *of the party*'(emphasis added). If in a tort action for alienation of affections the defendant is asked in an interrogatory for the dates of love letters sent to him by the plaintiff's former wife, and if defendant answers that he offers to let plaintiff's counsel inspect and make copies or compilations of the hundreds of such love letters stored in an old dresser in his attic, it appears that this answer would not be sufficient since the love letters are not 'business records' as F.R.C.P. 33(c) requires. If F.R.C.P. 33(c) had said 'records' or 'documents' alone, as does the English R.S.C. 1965, 0.26 r. 1–(3), rather than 'business records', defendant might have shifted to plaintiff the burden of perusing a myriad of musty letters.[16] Furthermore, if the United States in a hypothetical action against Daniel Ellsberg to recover the Pentagon Papers should ask him in an interrogatory to describe by colour each of the Pentagon Papers, would it be a sufficient answer under F.R.C.P. 33(c) for him to offer to let the United States Attorney inspect and make copies or compilations of the tens of thousands of such papers stored in safe-deposit boxes? Are they 'business records'? Even if they are, are they his business records — 'the business records of the party' (F.R.C.P. 33(c)) — especially if the United States' complaint alleges that the Pentagon Papers belong to it and Ellsberg's answer alleges that they belong to his former colleagues at the Rand Corporation? If they are neither 'business records' nor 'records of the party', then the answer is insufficient under F.R.C.P. 33(c).[17] As we shall see, courts have been vexed enough to construe the phrase 'documents which are in the possession, custody or control of the party'[18] (e.g. F.R.C.P. 34(a); R.S.C. 1965, 0.24, r. 1–(1)). It compounds the confusion for F.R.C.P. 33(c) to say only 'records of the party'.

Documents

A. DOCUMENTS UNDER F.R.C.P. 34; R.S.C. 1965, 0.24

1. AMERICAN MECHANISMS FOR PRODUCTION UPON REQUEST

The 1970 amendments to F.R.C.P. 34 made production of documents available upon request.[1] Previously an American federal party seeking to inspect his opponent's documents had to move for a court order for production, which would not be granted unless the moving party showed good cause for it.[2] Since the 1970 amendments, a party seeking to inspect his opponent's documents need merely serve a request on him. The request must list[3] the individual documents or categories of documents

and describe each... with reasonable particularity. The request shall specify a reasonable time, place and manner of making the inspection...

The party upon whom the request is served shall serve a written response within 30 days... The court may allow a shorter or longer time. The response shall state, with respect to each... [document] or category, that inspection... will be permitted as requested, unless the request is objected to, in which event the reasons for objection shall be stated. If objection is made to part of ... [a document] or category, the part shall be specified. The party submitting the request may move for an order under Rule 37(a) with respect to any objection to or other failure to respond to the request or any part thereof, or any failure to permit inspection as requested. F.R.C.P. 34(b)

If the motion under Rule 37(a) is granted, the opponent will be required to pay the moving party's reasonable expenses of the motion, including attorney's fees, unless his opposition was substantially justified; if the motion is denied, the moving party is subject to the same sanction (F.R.C.P. 37(a)(4)).

On the face of it, the last sentence in F.R.C.P. 34(b) quoted above suggests that, if the response to the request objects to the time, place, or manner of making the inspection specified in the request, then the sole course available for the party requesting production of the documents is to move under F.R.C.P. 37(a)(2) for an order of the court compelling production in accordance with the request. But two other courses are available. The requesting party under F.R.C.P. 26(a) may file another request which differs from the first only by modifying the specified time, place, or manner of making the inspection, so as to accommodate to the reasons for objection to the inspection stated in the response to the first request. Alternatively, the requesting party may seek an informal agreement with his opponent as to the time, place, or manner of production.[4] Such agreements probably will be frequent, since each side otherwise risks the sanction of paying the other's expenses occasioned by a Rule 37(a) motion;[5] indeed, when F.R.C.P. 34 required a showing of good cause and a court order, well over half of the productions of documents were by informal agreement.[6] In any event, the requesting party should be successful in avoiding an objection to the time, place, or manner of production if his request simply specifies 'at a time and place and in a manner convenient to' his opponent.[7] This information should satisfy F.R.C.P. 34(b)'s requirement that 'the request shall specify a reasonable time, place and manner of [production]', given the intent 'to have the rule operate extrajudicially'.[8] For the same reason the opponent who responds to this request that he will permit the production 'as requested' (F.R.C.P. 34(b)) should be held obligated to notify the requesting party reasonably promptly of the time, place, and manner convenient to him.

2. CONTRAST BETWEEN ENGLISH AND AMERICAN DISCOVERY

Before the 1970 amendments to F.R.C.P. 34 a party might secure production of documents under this rule only if he showed the court *inter alia* that his opponent had the possession, custody, or control of designated documents which related to matters within the scope of discovery as defined by F.R.C.P. 26(b).[9] If he did not have this information, he had to try to get his opponent to disclose it to him by another American federal discovery step — interrogatory, deposition upon oral examination, or deposition upon written interrogatories.[10] If he thus succeeded in gaining disclosure about documents, production of the documents did not automatically follow; he was required to take the additional step of a motion to the court to order production under F.R.C.P. 34.[11] Hence, before the 1970 amendments to F.R.C.P. 34, two separate discovery steps were necessary to obtain both disclosure and production of documents.

These amendments eliminated the requirements that the party seeking production of documents show that they are in his opponent's possession, custody, or control and within the scope of discovery as defined by F.R.C.P. 26(b). But they did not eliminate the requirement of designating the documents; instead they amplified it to require that 'the request...describe each...[document] and category [of documents] with reasonable particularity' (F.R.C.P. 34(b)).

Does this requirement of describing documents or categories of documents 'with reasonable particularity' mean that two separate discovery steps remain necessary to obtain disclosure and production of documents, or is production[12] available directly under F.R.C.P. 34 for a party who knows nothing about what discoverable documents his opponent may have?[13] This is to ask, if a party's F.R.C.P. 34 request describes the category of documents he seeks as 'all documents which constitute or contain matters within the scope of F.R.C.P. 26(b) (1) (2) (3)',[14] if his opponent's response objects to this request for the reason that the request does not describe the category of documents with reasonable particularity, and if the requesting party moves for an order under F.R.C.P. 37(a) compelling production in accordance with the request, should this order be made?

Note that this question assumes that the sole reason for objection stated in the response is that the request does not describe the category of documents with reasonable particularity. Because F.R.C.P. 34(b) provides that 'the response shall state...the reasons for objection', a court should not refuse to make the order in question on the ground that it would place an undue burden on the opponent or annoy, embarrass, or oppress him. If this were so, the opponent should have so stated in his response or moved for a protective order under F.R.C.P. 26(c).

The order in question would not be unworkable. It would be tantamount to the English R.S.C. 1965, 0.24, with the exception that this Order is self-executing. This Order provides the following scheme of documentary discovery for typical cases: within fourteen days after the close of pleadings both parties must serve on each other a list of relevant documents now or previously in their possession, custody, or power[15] (0.24, rr. 2–(1), 5) and an affidavit verifying the list if notified to do so by the other party (r. 2–(7)); when each serves his list, he must also serve a notice stating a time and a place where the documents he does not object to produce may be inspected (r. 9). This scheme does not apply in several instances, such as, if the parties otherwise agree (r. 1–(2)), and if a party who objects to giving discovery applies for and the court makes an order to the contrary—the court must do so if it is of the opinion that discovery is not 'necessary either for disposing fairly of the action or for saving costs' and otherwise may do so at its discretion (r. 2–(5)).

Thus automatic, mandatory discovery goes forward even if not in fact necessary either for disposing fairly of the action or for saving costs. The court is not authorized on its own motion to deny or limit discovery which is not so necessary. It must, and may, do so only if a party objects to giving discovery. In this way the R.S.C. 1965 have acknowledged that the requirement added to R.S.C. 1883, 0.31, rr. 12, 18 in 1893[16] that the court disallow documentary discovery not necessary for either purpose has had miniscule, if any, effect.[17] R.S.C. 1965, too, thus recognize that any possible effect of such a duty on the court would not justify the expense and delay which such court intervention would cause to a scheme which is otherwise self-executing.

The scheme also does not apply to defendants in actions arising out of vehicular accidents (r. 2–(2)). Presumably this exception was made because such a defendant ordinarily has no or few relevant documents.[18] Even if so, it appears ill advised. If he has no relevant documents, it would be but a trifling burden on him to file a list or affidavit saying so. The expense would be equally inconsequential. No delay would result, since defendant would comply with the scheme during the same time within which plaintiff must do so in any event. On the other hand, if defendant does have relevant documents, perhaps even decisive documents, plaintiff, and perhaps ultimately the trial court, will be denied the light they shed on the case unless plaintiff suspects their existence and so goes to the trouble and expense of applications for court orders under the procedures for exceptional cases described just below. To remit plaintiff to such a position is invidious in view of the obligation on him automatically to disclose and produce his relevant documents to defendant.

In the exceptional cases to which the general Order 24 scheme of automatic, mandatory discovery does not apply and in instances in which a party does not comply with his duty of automatic disclosure and production or in which a party has objected to production and the other party wishes to contest the objection, R.S.C. 1965, 0.24, rr. 3, 8, 11, 13–(1) require two applications and court orders for disclosure and production; and the court is not to order either except so far as is necessary for either saving costs or disposing fairly of the action. It is regrettable that in cases falling outside the general scheme of Order 24 the R.S.C. 1965 fail to provide for disclosure and production of documents by a single application and order, as was done under the English Court of Chancery Procedure Act, 1852, SS. 18, 20.[19]

These exceptions notwithstanding, the general scheme of R.S.C. 1965, 0.24, requiring automatic, mutual, mandatory disclosure and production of documents, strikes a bold blow in the cause of the informed conduct and adjudication of litigation. This scheme has the salutary effect of encouraging legal practitioners to consider documentary discovery one of the customary steps in litigation.

This English scheme has worked well in innumerable cases and should be adopted in American practice. To be sure, the number of documents produced in compliance with an American federal order to the same effect as the general scheme of Order 24 might be fewer than the requesting party had hoped; this would result if his interpretation of the bounds of F.R.C.P. 26(b)(1), namely, what is relevant to the subject-matter or reasonably calculated to lead to the discovery of admissible evidence, is broader than his opponent's. If so, the requesting party might take his opponent's deposition under F.R.C.P. 30, 31 or serve interrogatories on him to try to gather evidence to support a motion under F.R.C.P. 37(a) for the production of more documents. But the requesting party might not do so. He might well accept the production made. If so, then interpreting the requirement in F.R.C.P. 34(b) of describing documents with reasonable particularity to be satisfied by a request for all discoverable documents under F.R.C.P. 26(b) (1) (2) (3) would have the advantage of saving the time and expense consumed because the requesting party must at the outset, by interrogatories or depositions, seek information with which to provide a more specific description.

Such an interpretation, however, does not seem permitted by the language of F.R.C.P. 34 and Form 24 of the F.R.C.P.

F.R.C.P. 34(a) allows production of 'any designated documents...which constitute or contain matters within the scope of Rule 26(b)'. Yet F.R.C.P. 34(b) goes on to say, 'The request shall...describe each [document]...and category [of documents] with reasonable particularity.' An interpretation that this part of F.R.C.P. 34(b) is satisfied by the description in question, 'all documents which constitute or contain matters within the scope of F.R.C.P. 26(b) (1) (2) (3)', would mean that it neither adds to nor qualifies F.R.C.P. 34(a) in any way.[20] This interpretation in effect would delete this part of 34(b) rather than apply it. Perhaps language sometimes is so devoid of content that it should be interpreted as meaningless. But 'reasonable particularity' does appear to ring of greater specificity than 'designated documents...which [are]...within the scope of Rule 26(b)'. Surely the drafters of the 1970 amendments to Rule 34 so intended, for they also drafted Form 24 to the F.R.C.P., 'Request for Production of Documents...under Rule 34'; it says, '[L]ist the documents...by category *and* describe each of them'[21] (emphasis added). Hence the request in question is objectionable under Rule 34 as merely designating a category of documents; it fails to describe the category.

Furthermore, while the drafters of the 1970 amendments to Rule 34 did not in their Advisory Committee Note to the Rule disclose the origin of their phrase 'reasonable particularity',[22] one may be rather confident of its origin. The drafters must have consulted in respect to Rule 34 the Report of Proposed Amendments to Rules of Civil Procedure for the District Courts of the United States (1946) by the 1946 Advisory Committee on Rules for Civil Procedure. That Report commented,

An objection has been made that the word 'designated' in Rule 34 has been construed with undue strictness in some district court cases....The Committee, however, believes that no amendment is needed, and that the proper meaning of 'designated' as requiring specificity has already been delineated by the Supreme Court. See *Brown v. United States* (1928) 276 U.S. 134, 143 ('The subpoena...specifies...with *reasonable particularity* the subjects to which the documents called for related.'); *Consolidated Rendering Co. v. Vermont* (1908) 207 U.S. 541...[23] (emphasis added)

Neither of these cases concerned Rule 34. *Brown* concerned a grand-jury subpoena duces tecum; *Consolidated Rendering Co.*

concerned the Vermont counterpart to a grand-jury subpoena duces tecum. They are discussed in Chapter 3, Section B2. Suffice it to say here that neither approved a description of documents as broad as 'all documents which constitute or contain matters within the scope of F.R.C.P. 26(b)(1)(2)(3)'. Both required the description to include factual subjects. It is extremely likely that this learning concerning subpoenas duces tecum was in the minds of those who grafted 'reasonable particularity' to the body of Rule 34 in 1970.

To secure the advantage of saving time and money when disclosure and production of documents are available in one step, as they are in England, Rule 34 should be amended by deleting in the second sentence of F.R.C.P. 34(b) the requirement that the request describe the category of documents[24] and by inserting in lieu thereof that among proper categories to be set forth in the request are 'all documents which constitute or contain matters within the scope of Rule 26(b)(1)(2)(3)'. In the phrase 'any designated documents' in F.R.C.P. 34(a) 'designated' should be deleted to the same end.

The party whose documents are sought would not be treated unfairly by these proposed amendments. A protective order against oppression or undue burden or expense would remain available to him under F.R.C.P. 26(c). All previously available privileges and objections, except to the breadth of the request, would remain intact. If he responded completely, but within his good-faith interpretation of the bounds of relevant issues in the action to a request to produce 'all documents which constitute or contain matters within the scope of F.R.C.P. 26(b)(1)(2)(3)', there is every reason to think that his opposition to the requesting party's successful motion under Rule 37(a) for an order that he produce documents relevant to additional issues would be held substantially justified. Therefore, he would not even be exposed to the sanction of paying the requesting party's expenses incurred in obtaining the order (F.R.C.P. 37(a)(4)).[25] If the requesting party did obtain this order, it undoubtedly would specify the additional issues concerning which documents must be produced. Hence the party ordered to produce additional documents should have no difficulty in doing so. This means that he would not be unfairly exposed to the more severe sanctions in F.R.C.P. 37(b)(2) for failure to comply with a F.R.C.P. 37(a) order. It is true that his narrow interpretation of the bounds of relevance will have resulted in an order, for failure to comply with which he will be subject to the more severe sanctions. But if the requesting party had specified documents relevant to the additional issues, the same narrow interpretation of the bounds of relevance, reflected in his objection to produce these documents as irrelevant, would have resulted in the same order. Hence it would be his interpretation of the bounds of relevance, not the right to request production of all relevant documents conferred by the proposed amendments, which would be responsible for the order against him.

Until Rule 34 is thus amended, American federal courts must be faithful to its requirement that the request describe documents or categories of documents with reasonable particularity. But the rule does not spell out what constitutes reasonable particularity. It leaves it to the courts to supply its content. In doing so they should allow as general descriptions of documents as possible, in order to secure the advantage of economy from requiring production of documents without a previous discovery step resulting merely in disclosure of information concerning the documents. That is, they should hold a category of documents to be described with reasonable particularity when it is described in terms of factual subjects of the case. Some, though by no means all, courts held such a description sufficient before the 1970 amendments to Rule 34. For example, in *United States* v. *United States Alkali Export Ass'n*. 7 F.R.D. 256 (S.D. N.Y. 1946), plaintiff sought to enjoin price and marketing combinations among firms concerning alkalis which it alleged to be in restraint of trade. The court held as sufficiently designated in plaintiff's Rule 34 motion the following category: documents referring or relating to defendants' price and marketing policies as to alkalis.[26] Since the 1970 amendments, *Democratic National Committee* v. *McCord* 356 F. Supp. 1394, 1395, 1396 (D.C. D.C. 1973) held a description to be of reasonable particularity when its broad terms were 'all documents... relating in any way to the Watergate "break-in" or other political espionage operations against the DNC and associated organizations and individuals...'[27] If all courts similarly will apply Rule 34 as amended in 1970, the advantage of making disclosure and production of documents available in a single step will be realized to the extent that the requesting party is capable of specifying relevant factual issues.[28] Unfortunately he may not be able to do so from the pleadings alone.[29] In these instances it will be necessary for him to try to learn of the factual issues by other discovery mechanisms.

When a party must first learn by another discovery mechanism information with which to satisfy Rule 34's requirement that his request describe documents with reasonable particularity, he may minimize the additional time, money, and inconvenience of two steps if the other mechanism is interrogatories. With his interrogatories he would serve a Rule 34 request for production of documents. The request would incorporate by reference the answers to interrogatories as themselves the description of the documents sought. Since the request would not be complete until the answers to interrogatories are served, Rule 34(b)'s '30 days after the service of the request', within which the opponent must serve a written response, would not begin to run until the answers to interrogatories are served. If the anticipated answers to interrogatories turn out to furnish a description of the documents with reasonable particularity, there is no reason that this combination of the two mechanisms should not be held proper.[30] If the party seeking production of documents, however, prefers to pursue disclosures with which to describe them by deposition upon oral examination or written questions under F.R.C.P. 30 or 31, there are substantial obstacles to his combining a Rule 34 request with either. Inasmuch as the request must be served, it must be in writing (see F.R.C.P. 5(a) (b)). Hence the description of documents incorporated by reference into the request probably may not be the opponent's oral answers to written or oral questions, even if the request succeeds in specifying that the description will be, say, the answers to the sixteenth and seventeenth questions asked. Instead the description incorporated by reference into the request would have to be the transcript of the answers to the specified questions. But the answers otherwise may not be transcribed.[31] To have them transcribed for this purpose indubitably will be more expensive and dilatory than preparing a Rule 34 request after the deposition. Even if the answers are to be transcribed in any event, a Rule 34 request usually may be prepared far more speedily.[32]

3. EXTENT OF DISCOVERY

F.R.C.P. 34(a) applies to 'documents ... which are in the possession, custody or control of the party upon whom the request is served'. The English R.S.C. 1965, 0.24, r. 1–(1) has the same applicability except it says 'power' instead of 'control'. This is a distinction without a difference, for 'control' has meant, as has 'power', the right to have or secure possession of documents.[33] Nor is there any other significant difference between the constructions of 'possession, custody, or power-control' made by the American federal and English courts.

As contrasted with documents in one's 'power-control' or 'possession', documents in one's 'custody' seems to mean those of which one has 'mere corporeal holding', that is, no proprietary interest.[34] In 1974 the House of Lords said in effect that documents 'which belonged wholly' to a stranger to the suit, and so were in the party's custody only in this sense, are subject to disclosure and production under R.S.C. 1965, 0.24.[35] But this was dictum since the court said of the actual documents at stake, 'presumably they belong' to the party to the suit.[36]

Similarly, the leading American federal decisions on whether documents in a party's custody in this sense are subject to production may well be dicta.[37] For example, in *Rockett* v. *John J. Casale, Inc.* 7 F.R.D. 575, 576 (S.D. N.Y. 1947), defendant contended that it should not be ordered under F.R.C.P. 34 to produce a written report in its possession on the ground that it belonged to a non-party. The court ordered defendant to produce it. It is not altogether clear, however, that defendant merely had 'corporeal holding' of the report, for the non-party truck driver made out the report of a vehicular collision in the office of defendant, which had leased the truck to the truck driver's employer. It may have been that defendant had required the driver to provide the report. Again, F.R.C.P. 34 was held to apply to the income-tax returns of the defendant's wife in *Mullen* v. *Mullen* 14 F.R.D. 142, 143 (D.C. Alaska 1953), despite his objection 'that they are the returns of a third party'. If the opinion had stated that defendant possessed the returns and if the reason given for the decision had been that they were in his 'custody', the case would have been directly on point. But the court gives but the following nebulous reason: 'not only is the state of the record such as to warrant the inference of possession, custody or control, but there is no denial thereof.' As far as that goes, the rationale of the decision may have been the questionable proposition that a husband controls his wife's income-tax returns in the sense that he has a right to obtain possession of them. In *Martin* v. *Nederlandsche Amerikaansche Stoomvaart Maatchappij* 8 F.R.D. 363 (S.D. N.Y. 1948), the court under F.R.C.P. 34 ordered defendants to produce a written report possessed by their attorney but made for a non-party. The court seemed to explain its decision on the basis that the work-product and attorney-client privileges[38] did not apply; and it cited cases to this effect.[39] Even if the court had thought in terms of the 'possession, custody or control' formula, it probably would have rested its order on the 'control' part, since the non-party for whom the report was made had been defendants' agent apparently at the time and place when plaintiff received personal injuries which were the subject of the case. Finally, in *United States* v. *National Broadcasting Co., Inc.* 65 F.R.D. 415, 420 (C.D. Cal. 1974), appeal dismissed, 421 U.S. 940 (1975), the court seems to imply that plaintiff must make discovery as to documents in its bare 'physical custody' even if wholly under the 'ownership' of former President Nixon. Yet this decision does not necessarily so hold because it adds that the documents were also in plaintiff's 'control' (id., 420, 421). Despite the deficiencies in the case law, the two leading commentators on the F.R.C.P. seem to feel that documents of which a party has custody but in which he has no proprietary interest are subject to production under F.R.C.P. 34.[40]

The position of these commentators and the dicta to the same effect in both the English and American federal decisions are eminently sound. Before 'custody' was expressly added in the English 1965 codification,[41] an objection to this position voiced by Lord Chancellor Cottenham was 'that another party, not present, has an interest in the document which the Court cannot deal with'.[42] This might be a valid objection if production of a document meant that ownership in it, or the right to control it, were being vested in a party or the court instead of the non-party who is entitled to it. But production means no such thing. Under R.S.C. 1965, 0.24, rr. 9, 11, and F.R.C.P. 34(a)(b) production merely means that a party may inspect and copy a document.[43] It remains in the physical possession of the other party. The inspecting party gains but knowledge of its contents and character. Hearsay which a party has picked up from a non-party has always been subject to discovery both in answers to interrogatories and when contained in a party's document.[44] If a party who produces a non-party's document had learned of its contents and character by overhearing the non-party describe them, the party might have to furnish his opponent, by answers to interrogatories, with the very information which his opponent gains by inspecting the document itself. So too, if the party secured the same information by examining the document in the non-party's hands, or otherwise, the party might have to convey this information to his opponent by answering interrogatories.[45] Thus production of a non-party's document need not vary the information about it which a party may secure, but only the form in which he may secure it. That the form of inspection of the document is more likely to be an accurate mode of conveying the information than the form of answers to interrogatories is surely no reason to disallow the former form.

If Lord Chancellor Cottenham's objection reflected a concern against disclosing a non-party's affairs in an action to which they are relevant, it suffices to say that there is no reason that this concern should prevent a non-party's documents from being produced on discovery, when it has never prevented disclosure of his affairs by answers to interrogatories, testimony at trial, or production of a party's own documents, all of which frequently refer to a non-party's affairs. Nor has this concern prevented the non-party's documents from being subpoenaed for presentation at trial (see *United States* v. *National Broadcasting Co., Inc.*, p. 420). Furthermore, any information in a non-party's document which is irrelevant may be sealed up while it is being inspected.[46] Moreover, the inspecting party has a duty not to make public the contents of documents produced, nor to communicate them to strangers to the suit, nor to use them for any purpose collateral to the suit unless the court otherwise orders.[47]

4. PROPOSED REFORM OF DISCOVERY IN AMERICAN COURTS

As has been discussed in Section A2 of this Chapter, the English R.S.C. 1965 have taken the bold course of requiring the parties automatically to disclose and produce all of their documents relating to matters in question in the action, unless they agree otherwise. Although empirical evidence of the frequency of agreements otherwise is unavailable, such agreements are probably rare indeed. A party broached by his opponent to make such an agreement might read this initiative as reflecting his opponent's desire to keep something in his documents secret, especially since it is simple to file a list or affidavit of documents which says that he has none relating to the matters in question. It is a safe assumption, therefore, that documentary discovery takes place in most English cases.

On the other hand, the empirical evidence in American federal cases is that documentary production under F.R.C.P. 34 before the 1970 amendments took place in at most 31 per cent of the cases.[48] The 1970 amendments have facilitated documentary production by eliminating the requirement of showing good cause on motion. Yet they are unlikely significantly to increase the frequency of discovery under F.R.C.P. 34, for before these amendments approximately 63 per cent of the plaintiffs and 84 per cent of the defendants who obtained documentary production did so by informal agreement rather than by motion.[49] These agreements undoubtedly almost always have been made about particular documents whose existence the party seeking them has already known of. There has been no American federal tradition of discovery of all relevant documents, whether by formal mechanism or informal agreement. If the proposal in Section A2 of this Chapter to amend Rule 34 to authorize a request for all discoverable documents is carried out, American federal documentary discovery should take place in more than a third of the cases. By filing one simple request, a party will be entitled to learn of and see all of his opponent's relevant documents. No longer will it be necessary for him to take a preliminary step by interrogatory or deposition to learn of the existence of his opponent's documents. Informal agreements will reflect the formal right; they too will encompass all discoverable documents.

But even though, by eliminating the preliminary step, this proposal should increase the frequency of American federal documentary discovery, it still will fall short of discovery in England, to the extent that parties' self-interest does not stimulate them to overcome their inertia and invest the minimal time and expense necessary to serve a Rule 34 request for all discoverable documents or reach an informal agreement to the same effect. To this extent the litigants and American society as a whole will not achieve the benefits of discovery described in Chapter 1, Section A. Paternalistic concern for the interests of litigants may be incompatible with the adversary nature of the American federal judicial system. Hence if their interests alone were at stake, one might be content with less frequent documentary discovery than in England. But American society has a stake in achieving those benefits of discovery which improve the administration of federal justice, especially by making the outcome of litigation more likely to reflect the true state of the facts by informing a party of a document helpful to him, but in the absence of discovery known only to his opponent. It is an article of faith in an adversary system that a party need not on his own motion bring to the attention of the court a document in his file which would be decisive in favour of his opponent who is unaware of it.[50] But after that party wins in court and tells his friends how he did it, American society is the loser. He and his friends will no longer respect the judicial system as an arbiter who declares the truth. They will have lost confidence in the law. They will see less reason to obey it. The legal structure of society will therefore be less strong.

For discovery to play its role fully in fostering the rule of law in American society, disclosure and production of documents should be made mandatory and automatic in the American federal system, as they are in England.[51] The English experience with this method proves its practicability. Some litigants might complain, however, that the method is an inequitable form of taxation. They would point out that in those cases in which their opponents would not seek to see their documents under Rule 34 as it now is or as it is proposed to be amended in Section A2 of this Chapter, they would be forced by the English method to go to the expense of preparing a list of their documents and making them available for inspection for the well-being of American society. This financial burden, they would say, should be borne by the society as a whole. While that does not seem feasible, their point may be answered by following English practice[52] and providing that by agreement of the opponent a party is relieved of his duty to disclose and produce his discoverable documents. Such a provision would mean that adoption of the English method merely reverses the burden of action under present American federal practice: at present there is no discovery unless the party to benefit from it initiates it; under the proposal there will be discovery unless that party agrees to forgo it. Reversal of the burden of action in litigation has never offended notions of equitable taxation. This reversal, however, should induce a habit of disclosure in litigation. Development of such a habit would smooth down one of the roughest edges in an adversary system of justice.

B. DOCUMENTS UNDER F.R.C.P. 45

1. MECHANICS FOR PRODUCTION

F.R.C.P. 45 provides for conventional subpoenas ad testificandum and duces tecum for hearings or trials (F.R.C.P. 45(a)(b)(c)(e)(f)). It also makes these subpoenas available incident to deposition upon oral examination under F.R.C.P. 30 or deposition upon written questions under F.R.C.P. 31(a) of the person subpoenaed (F.R.C.P. 45(a)(b)(c)(d)(f)). Deposition upon oral examination and deposition upon written questions are American federal discovery devices which have no English counterparts. Depositions upon oral examination proceed like English depositions taken to obtain testimony from a witness who will be unavailable at trial. The principal difference is that the purpose of the American federal deposition under discussion is discovery. A deposition upon written questions is similar to a deposition upon oral examination in that the person from whom discovery is sought answers questions orally, under oath, and his answers are recorded on the spot by a stenographer or electronic recording device (F.R.C.P. 31(b), 30(c)). However, it significantly differs from a deposition upon oral examination in that the legal advisers of parties do not orally put their questions to this person; instead they prepare written questions in advance which an officer authorized to administer oaths or appointed by the court reads to the person examined (F.R.C.P. 31(a)(b), 28(a)). The party initiating the examination serves his written questions on every other party, each of whom may supply written cross-questions. The written cross-questions also are served on every other party before the examination takes place. Similarly written redirect and recross-questions may be prepared and served (F.R.C.P. 31). Depositions upon written questions are rarely used in American federal cases.[53] Undoubtedly their unpopularity is attributable to some of the factors which render interrogatories distinctly less popular and less effective than oral examinations.[54]

At a deposition upon oral examination or deposition upon written questions the production of documents may be secured by service[55] of a Rule 45 subpoena duces tecum on the deponent.

The subpoena may command the person to whom it is directed to produce and permit inspection and copying of designated...documents...which constitute or contain matters within the scope of the

examination permitted by Rule 26(b),[56] but in that event the subpoena will be subject to the provisions of Rule 26(c) and subdivision
(b) of this rule.

The person to whom the subpoena is directed may...serve...writ-
ten objection to inspection or copying of any...of the designated materials. If objection is made, the party serving the subpoena shall not
be entitled to inspect and copy the materials except pursuant to an
order of the court....The party serving the subpoena may, if objection has been made, move upon notice to the deponent for an order at
any time before or during the taking of the deposition. F.R.C.P.
45(d)(1)

F.R.C.P. 26(c), to which this subpoena duces tecum expressly
is subject, empowers the court, upon motion and a showing of
good cause by the person from whom discovery is sought, to
'make any order which justice requires to protect a...person
from annoyance, embarrassment, oppression, or undue burden
or expense...' This discovery subpoena also expressly is subject to F.R.C.P. 45(b) which provides, *inter alia*,

The court upon motion...may (1) quash or modify the subpoena if it
is unreasonable and oppressive or (2) condition denial of the motion
upon advancement by the person in whose behalf the subpoena is
issued of the reasonable cost of producing the...documents...

Thus three overlapping avenues—objection under F.R.C.P.
45(d)(1) and motion under F.R.C.P. 26(c) and 45(b)—are
open for resisting production of documents.[57] Objection under
45(d)(1), which was made available by the 1970 amendments
to the F.R.C.P.,[58] probably will prove to be the most heavily
travelled avenue, for it does not require the resisting person to
initiate a court proceeding. It leaves the decision on whether to
go to court to the party seeking the documents.

Failure to obey a discovery subpoena may be treated as contempt of court (F.R.C.P. 45(f)). A party's outright disobedience of the subpoena is subject to the sanctions of F.R.C.P.
37(b)(2), after 1970,[59] if failure to obey its 'command...to
produce...documents' (F.R.C.P. 45(d)) is held equivalent to
failure 'to obey an order to provide or permit discovery'
(F.R.C.P. 37(b)(2)). This 'command' should be held equivalent to an 'order', since a discovery subpoena is 'issued by the
clerk under the seal of the court' (F.R.C.P. 45(a)). In any event
if, after a subpoenaed party objects to producing documents,
his opponent obtains an order of the court that he do so under

the second paragraph of Rule 45(d) (1), the failure by the subpoenaed party to obey this order appears to fall within the lit-
eral language in Rule 37(b) (2) authorizing application of the
sanctions of that Rule.

As F.R.C.P. 45(d) (1) makes explicit, documents subpoenaed
to a deposition may be inspected and copied there by the subpoenaing party. But must a deposition in the usual sense of
asking questions of the person subpoenaed also take place? It is
well settled that an American federal court subpoena duces
tecum returnable to a grand jury, and not issued pursuant to
F.R.C.P. 45, may properly require production of documents
even though there was no intention to ask questions of the person subpoenaed and none were asked of him.[60] A F.R.C.P.
45(d) (1) documentary-discovery subpoena, however, is expressly 'subject to the provisions of... subdivision (b) of this rule'.
F.R.C.P. 45(b) provides, 'A subpoena may *also* command the
person... to produce... documents...' (emphasis added). 'Also' in 45(b) seems indisputably to incorporate by reference the
provision in 45(a) that 'every subpoena... shall command each
person to whom it is directed to attend and *give testimony* at a
time and place therein specified' (emphasis added).[61] The time
and place to be specified in a documentary-discovery subpoena
must be that at which the deposition of the person subpoenaed
is scheduled, for 45(d) (1) makes 'proof of service of a notice to
take a deposition as provided in Rules 30(b) and 31(a)... a
sufficient authorization for the issuance' of a documentary-
discovery subpoena. While this language leaves room for other
'sufficient' authorizations, Rule 45 contains none. In addition
to depositions in subdivision (d), it authorizes issuance of subpoenas only for hearings or trials in subdivision (e); but they
are not discovery mechanisms. Hence discovery subpoenas may
be issued only if the deposition of the person subpoenaed is
intended to be taken, as evidenced by service of a notice to take
his deposition.[62]

If the requirement of intention to take the deposition is not to
be a mockery, it must be taken. Questions must be asked of the
person whose documents are subpoenaed. F.R.C.P. 45(d) evi-
dently contemplates that this will take place: it is entitled,
'Subpoena for Taking Depositions; Place of Examination'; the
subpoenaing party 'may, if objection [to production of any of
the designated materials] has been made, move upon notice to
the *deponent* for an order... during the *taking of the deposition*'

(F.R.C.P. 45(d)(1) (emphasis added)); and subdivision (d)(2) addresses itself to the place where the 'examination' is to be held. But the questions asked at the deposition need neither be extensive nor range beyond the documents themselves. Witness the sound *obiter dictum* in *Beegle* v. *Thomson* that the questions may be limited to information which would bear on the admissibility in evidence of the documents subpoenaed. To require otherwise would be to demand that the discovering party pursue what he may with reason consider a fruitless inquiry. Better still, requiring a deposition to see documents should be eliminated, as proposed in Section B4 of this Chapter and near the beginning of Section C of Chapter 9.

2. TWO SUCCESSIVE DISCOVERY MECHANISMS

The only requirement for description of documents subpoenaed under F.R.C.P. 45 is that they be 'designated' (F.R.C.P. 45(d)(b)). Does this mean that Rule 45 — like the English R.S.C. 1965, 0.24, rr. 2–(1), 9, but unlike F.R.C.P. 34 and its requirement of 'reasonable particularity' of description[63] — avoids the waste of two steps to secure disclosure and production of documents? This is to ask, are documents properly designated if described in a Rule 45(d) subpoena as 'all documents which constitute or contain matters within the scope of F.R.C.P. 26(b)(1)(2)(3)'?[64]

These questions must be answered in the negative for two reasons. The first is that the courts have considered such descriptions improperly broad. They have repeatedly quashed discovery subpoenas calling, in effect, for all documents relating to the cause of action.[65] The United States Supreme Court itself, in *Brown* v. *United States*, pp. 142–3, distinguished a grand-jury subpoena in an earlier case as unreasonable because *inter alia* 'there was no specification in respect of subject matter'; and a discovery subpoena under F.R.C.P. 45(d)(1) expressly is subject to Rule 45(b), which authorizes the court to quash a subpoena if 'unreasonable'. When a party has known too little about his opponent's documents to be able to describe them in sufficient detail in his subpoena, he has been advised to obtain disclosures about them by interrogatories or depositions under F.R.C.P. 30, 31, or 33 before trying again to secure their production.[66]

The second reason that a Rule 45 discovery subpoena must describe documents with 'reasonable particularity' is that 'the deposition-discovery rules created integrated procedural devices' (*Hickman* v. *Taylor*, p. 505). This notion of integrated discovery devices generally prevented documentary subpoenas under Rule 45 from circumventing the requirement in Rule 34, eliminated by the 1970 amendments, of a showing of good cause as a condition precedent to production of documents;[67] this same notion undoubtedly will prevent documentary subpoenas under Rule 45 from circumventing the requirement in Rule 34, added by the 1970 amendments, of a description with 'reasonable particularity'.

By the same token, the argument made in Section A2 of this Chapter for that construction of 'reasonable particularity' in Rule 34 which allows as general descriptions as possible is strengthened by decisions under Rule 45. Some of them have held a category of documents sufficiently described in a discovery subpoena when described in terms of the factual subjects of the case.[68] For example, in *403–411 East 65th Street Corp.* v. *Ford Motor Co.*, the court refused to quash a discovery subpoena calling for production of all documents relating to the real estate in dispute. It was not persuaded that the subpoena was unreasonably broad for failing to limit the documents to a time-period, for it found the pleadings limited the time-period in issue. Even the two United States Supreme Court decisions on grand-jury subpoenas, which may well be the origin of the 'reasonable particularity' requirement in Rule 34,[69] indicated that a description of documents in terms of the factual subjects of the case would be sufficient. The Supreme Court, in *Consolidated Rendering Co.* v. *Vermont*, p. 554, laid it down that

it can [not] be said that the . . . grand jury never has any right to call for all the books and papers, or correspondence, between certain dates and certain persons named, in regard to a complaint which is pending before such . . . grand jury . . .

In *Brown* v. *United States*, pp. 138–9, the Supreme Court approved a subpoena describing documents in essence as follows: all letters and telegrams between the National Alliance of Furniture Manufacturers, its officers and agents, and its members from 1 January 1922 to 15 June 1925 relating to the manufacture and sale of case goods, and particularly with reference to eighteen categories of subjects. It is noteworthy that the Supreme Court held defective neither the general description of documents nor the description with reference to eighteen particular categories. While both Supreme Court decisions required the descriptions to include limited time-periods, they did so in respect of grand-jury subpoenas, which are served on people who receive no notice of what is involved before the grand jury other than that contained in the subpoena. When a Rule 34 request or Rule 45 subpoena is received by a party, he has notice of what is involved from the pleadings as well.[70] Hence if they show the time-period in issue, as they did in *403–411 East 65th Street Corp.* v. *Ford Motor Co.* just discussed, 'reasonable particularity' should not require that the request or subpoena repeat a statement of this period. As will be seen, a Rule 45 discovery subpoena may be used to secure production of documents from non-parties.[71] It is to them that the reason for requiring the subpoena to provide the time-period in issue of course applies.

3. RELATIONSHIP BETWEEN PERSON AND DOCUMENTS SUBPOENAED

Rule 45 itself is silent as to the requisite relationship between the person and documents subpoenaed. Yet the notion of integrated discovery devices embraced by the United States Supreme Court in *Hickman* v. *Taylor*, p. 505, and discussed in the preceding section, precludes circumventing Rule 34's express requirement that the documents be in the possession, custody, or control of the person from whom they are sought by a Rule 45(d) documentary-discovery subpoena. Accordingly, documents have been held to be outside the applicability of Rule 45 unless within the possession, custody, or control of the person subpoenaed, as that phrase has been interpreted in Rule 34.[72]

As Section A3 of this Chapter shows, American federal cases under Rule 34 have not unequivocally decided whether documents which are in a party's custody, but in which he has no proprietary interest are subject to production. Cases under Rule 45 are no clearer on this question. The closest Rule 45 case on this question is *Alma-Schuhfabrik AG* v. *Rosenthal* 25 F.R.D.. 100, 101 (E.D. N.Y. 1960), where the court stated, 'The question posed is whether defendant Rosenthal ... can be compelled [by a F.R.C.P. 45(d) subpoena] to produce the books of Arby, a third person.' The court noted that the subpoena did not limit the books to those in the defendant's possession and that the record did not show that any of the third person's books were in the defendant's possession. However, in the next sentence it ambiguously called the defendant 'a custodian' of the books, and so *sub silentio* seemed to assume that at least some were in his possession. 'In this situation' the court expressed its belief that, before production is required, the third-person owner should be served with formal notice that his books may be produced. The purpose of this notice is to afford the 'owner . . . an opportunity to be heard in order to protect his rights and interests which may extend far beyond the books . . . themselves'. By citing at this point *United States* v. *Guterma* 24 F.R.D. 134 (S.D. N.Y.), rev'd., 272 F.2d 344 (2nd Cir. 1959), the court indicated that by the owner's 'rights and interests' it had in mind his protections under the United States Constitution against criminal liability involving unreasonable searches and seizures and self-incrimination. Up to this point in the opinion it appears that the court feels that, so long as the owner is afforded an opportunity to assert his criminal constitutional protections against production of the documents,[73] documents in a party's custody are subject to production by a F.R.C.P. 45(d) subpoena even though he has no ownership interest in them. However, the opinion concludes on this point, 'Production of the books . . . can be required by the simple expediency of serving discovery process upon Arby, [the non-party owner].' American federal discovery does provide for production of documents from non-parties, as discussed in Chapter 9. But this conclusion on the point renders the court's view on 'custody' in the 'possession, custody or control' formula an *obiter dictum* at most.

4. PRODUCTION FROM PARTIES UNDER F.R.C.P. 34 IS PREFERABLE

The immediately preceding subsections 1, 2, and 3 show that there are no advantages to proceedings under F.R.C.P. 45 rather than F.R.C.P. 34 for discovery of documents from a party.[74] Yet there are considerable disadvantages to proceedings under Rule 45. As appears from subsection 1, the party seeking production of documents under Rule 45 must ask questions at his opponent's deposition even though he may only wish to see his documents. Also he must take the steps necessary to arrange a deposition — schedule a time and place, arrange and pay for an officer to preside[75] and for a stenographer or electronic recording device,[76] and give notice to all parties[77] — not to mention seeing to it that the subpoena is served on the person of his opponent.[78] On the other hand, a

Rule 34 request is served on his opponent's attorney by post or other convenient method.[79]

Not only do proceedings under Rule 34 avoid these disadvantages, but also they possess a number of advantages. Rule 34(b) gives the party from whom documents are sought 30 days within which to object, whereas Rule 45(d)(1) gives him *10 days* at the most.[80] Yet American federal interrogatories before F.R.C.P. 33 was amended in 1970 gave rise to a disproportionately high rate of objections because the time for making objections — *10 days* — was too short.[81] Rule 34(b) also discourages baseless objections by requiring that the reasons for objection be stated. Moreover, it requires that a motion for an order overruling an objection be made under F.R.C.P. 37(a), which provides for an award of expenses against the party whose objection to production was not substantially justified. Baseless motions for an order overruling an objection likewise are discouraged by a converse award of expenses. Rule 45, on the other hand, contains none of these provisions.

If a party wishes both to inspect his opponent's documents and to take his deposition, he will usually prefer to see the documents before the deposition in enough time to plan questions concerning the documents or to conceive of lines of inquiry suggested by the documents. Even in the rare case in which a party wishes to depose his opponent and inspect his documents simultaneously, Rule 45 is not preferable to Rule 34. When the deposition is to be upon oral examination, 'The notice to a party deponent may be accompanied by a request made in compliance with Rule 34 for the production of documents... at the taking of the deposition. The procedure of Rule 34 shall apply to the request' (F.R.C.P. 30(b)(5)). There is no comparable provision when the deposition is to be upon written questions, for the party initiating it usually does so in order to save the expense of having his lawyer attend the examination. Hence he ordinarily would not wish his opponent's documents made available for inspection at that place. Should he so desire, however, he would still be in a position to use Rule 34 by specifying in his request the time and place of the deposition as the time and place of the inspection. Such a specification surely would satisfy 34(b)'s requirement that it be reasonable, since his opponent would have to attend at that time and place for his deposition in any event.

For all these reasons F.R.C.P. 45(d) should be eliminated as an alternative course to F.R.C.P. 34 for obtaining production of documents from parties. This may be brought about by amending F.R.C.P. 45(d) so that it no longer applies to any 'person' but only to persons who are not parties to the civil action.

Real and Personal Property

A. PROPOSED REFORM OF DISCOVERY

American federal inspection of personal property is available under the same Rules 34 and 45 which govern documentary discovery. With the exception of Chapter 3, Section A4, what has been said about documents in Chapter 3 also applies to personal property.[1] Real property too is subject to inspection under F.R.C.P. 34.[2] Again with the exception of Chapter 3, Section A4, what has been said about documents in Chapter 3, Section A, applies to real property as well.

Chapter 3, Section A4, does not apply fully to the inspection of real and personal property, for neither in England nor in the American federal system are discoverable real and personal property automatically and mandatorily disclosed and made available for inspection. Such a discovery method modelled after the English documentary procedure, described in Chapter 3, Section A2, should be adopted in both countries. The arguments for this method discussed in Chapter 3, Section A4, apply to real and personal property as much as to documents.

Until such a method is adopted by either country, the current American federal practice is preferable to the English practice. English inspection of real and personal property requires a court order (R.S.C. 1965, 0.29, rr. 2–(1)(2)(4)(6), 3–(1)(2)(3)). Comparable inspection is available under F.R.C.P. 34 and 45 extrajudicially[3] in the ways described in Chapter 3, Sections A1 and B1. In addition to saving court time, the absence of the obstacle of obtaining a court order should result in more property inspection in American federal practice than in England.[4]

B. EXAMPLES OF ENLIGHTENED, FLEXIBLE INSPECTION ORDERS

English orders for property inspection over the centuries have been admirably flexible. A review of conditions regulating inspection is instructive. The court has admonished inspecting parties to take 'care to impose as little inconvenience as possible on those on whom the order is made'.[5] The inspecting party has been made liable to indemnify the opponent against damage arising from the inspection.[6] Yet the opponent has been ordered, for example, to 'give all reasonable facilities for access to and in the mine, and for ventilation...',[7] to remove obstructions to inspection which he had erected,[8] to restore facilities necessary for inspection,[9] and not to alter his works until the inspection takes place, 'but not so as to prevent the regular working of...[the opponent's] mines'.[10] The court has also permitted a party to break up his opponent's soil to carry out an inspection when the matter to be inspected had been created in the course of the controversy giving rise to the litigation.[11]

Opponents not infrequently have resisted property inspection with the argument that the party's ulterior motive has been to learn the opponent's trade secret.[12] When the English courts have sensed the flavour of truth in this argument, they have harmonized the legitimate interests of both sides by ordering that the inspection be made by third persons who report their findings to the party's solicitor and that neither these third persons nor the solicitor describe to the party (or anyone else other than the court) the opponent's alleged trade secret.[13]

Lastly, English courts have been enlightened in providing that the opponent observe, and share the fruit of, the inspection. In 1804 the order to inspect a mine had the proviso that the opponent and viewers selected by him be permitted to attend the inspection.[14] By observing the inspection, the opponent is in a position to refute an inaccurate report of it; and the opponent himself may acquire information leading to a just verdict.

C. EXCHANGE OF EXPERTS' REPORTS

In England in 1962 a party sought leave for a handwriting expert to (1) test for authenticity an agreement allegedly signed by a deceased person by infra-red or micro-chemical techniques and (2) inspect other documents than this agreement which bore the signature of the deceased. Wilberforce, J., ordered this inspection on the condition that the expert's resulting report be disclosed to the opponent before trial.[15] This condition wisely minimized the likelihood that the opponent would find it necessary to employ discovery to secure the report or to engage his own handwriting expert.

Similarly, F.R.C.P. 35(b) provides that a party who is

ordered to submit to a physical or mental examination may have a copy of the written report of the examining physician. This American federal Rule in several ways carries even further the salutary notion that the fruits of discovery, like other relevant information, should be known by both sides. First, it grants the examining party who has delivered the report of his expert to the opponent the right to a copy of reports of the same mental or physical condition made by experts on behalf of the opponent, whether before or after the examination which triggers this scheme (F.R.C.P. 35(b)(1)). Second, the Rule tends to assure that there will be written reports to exchange by authorizing the court to exclude the testimony of examining physicians at trial if they have failed to make written reports (ibid.). Third, Rule 35(b)(2) deems the obtaining by the opponent of a report of the examination to be a waiver of 'any privilege' the opponent 'may have ... regarding the testimony of every other person who has examined or may thereafter examine him in respect of the same mental or physical condition'. Finally, this scheme for discovery of experts' findings and opinions is applicable 'to examinations made by [informal] agreement of the parties, unless the agreement expressly provides otherwise' (F.R.C.P. 35(b)(3)).

In order to promote and institutionalize the sharing of relevant expert information, both the English and American federal rules governing inspection of property and documents should be amended by adding provisions like the judgment of Wilberforce, J., and F.R.C.P. 35(b), which should apply whenever an expert makes the inspection.[16]

D. INSPECTION OF METHODS OF OPERATION IN ENGLAND

There may be some question in England as to whether a method of operation is subject to inspection. 1 *Supreme Court Practice 1979*, ¶ 29/2–3/3 says of property inspection, 'This Rule is limited to physical things: inspection of the plaintiff's method of manufacture and packing was refused in an action against carriers (*Tudor Co.* v. *China, etc. Co.* [1930] W.N. 200).' One cannot quarrel with the proposition that the 'Rule is limited to physical things'. Nothing capable of being inspected is not physical. However, one should quarrel with the implication that as a matter of principle a method of manufacture and packing, or any other continual method of operation, is not subject to an order for inspection.

In *Tudor Accumulator Co. Ltd.* v. *China Mutual Steam Navigation Co. Ltd.* [1930] W.N. 200 (CA), it is true, the Court of Appeal reversed an order for inspection of a party's method of manufacturing and packing battery-plates; and one of the reasons Lawrence, L.J., gave for the decision was that 'the method of manufacturing and packing the plates was not "property"...within [R.S.C. 1883,] Order 50, r. 3.'[17] Grier, L.J., seemed to intend to give the same reason when he said, 'The inspection authorized by Order 50, r. 3, was limited to an inspection of some physical thing.'[18] But this case is not a precedent in the strict sense of that word for the proposition that a method of manufacturing and packing is not subject to an order for inspection. This is because Lawrence, L.J., also gave an alternative reason for the decision totally divorced from this proposition; and this alternative reason apparently was the only one advanced by Scrutton, L.J.[19]

Nor, precedent aside, should a method or process of continual operation be held not subject to inspection because it is not 'property' in the sense that it is not a physical thing. It is made up, typically, of three classes of physical things — materials or land, machines and tools, and people — which are organized in a given relationship to each other. That the court may order each of the first two classes to be inspected separately has not been doubted since the early days of equity. That the court has power to order people to be inspected separately appears from the common-law practice of ordering examinations of women on writs *de ventre inspiciendo*.[20] By inspecting all three classes together in a functioning process or method the only information acquired, beyond that acquired when they are inspected separately, is their interrelationship, that is, the way in which they are organized with respect to each other. Yet the way in which the parts of a machine are organized with respect to each other has explicitly been the subject of many orders for inspection of machines in patent cases.[21] And there is nothing different between organizing parts of a machine and organizing machines, materials, and people which justifies inspection of the former but not the latter. The organizations are equally human inventions. Moreover, long ago in equity, not only were machines ordered to be inspected but also people were ordered to operate them for the purpose of the inspection.[22] Hence there is long-standing authority for orders for inspection which require participation by people.

There can be no question in American federal practice that a method of operation is subject to inspection, for F.R.C.P. 34(a)(2) provides,

Any party may serve on any other party a request...to permit entry upon...land or other property...for the purpose of inspection and measuring, surveying, photographing, testing, or sampling the property or any...object or *operation* thereon...[23] (emphasis added)

ADMISSIONS OF DOCUMENTS AND FACTS

Since admissions of documents and facts frequently are used to save time and expense at trial, there is a tendency to view them exclusively as a trial mechanism. However, admissions do perform pre-trial discovery functions.[1] The party seeking an admission learns before trial whether his adversary will admit to a fact or the genuineness of a document.[2] The value of this knowledge in managing litigation grows as the probability of proving the fact or genuineness of the document without the admission declines. For example, a barrier to introducing a document in evidence, such as the need to locate someone to authenticate a signature, might be insuperable without an admission. Moreover, an adversary gains inspection of a document whenever a party serves him with a request to admit its genuineness.[3]

The discovery function inherent in admissions is made explicit by the placing of F.R.C.P. 36, entitled 'Requests for Admission', in Part V of the F.R.C.P., entitled 'Depositions and Discovery', and by the fact that F.R.C.P. 36(a) authorizes 'a written request for the admission ... of the truth of any matters within the scope of Rule 26(b) ...', which defines 'the scope of discovery' (F.R.C.P. 26(b)). But in two respects English admissions practice has lost sight of the discovery function. First, R.S.C. 1965, 0.27, r. 5–(1) limits the seeking of admission of the genuineness of documents to 'within 21 days after the cause or matter is set down for trial...';[4] however, no such limitation is contained in the far more frequently used mandatory documentary-admission procedure of 0.27, r. 4, and in the factual-admission procedure of 0.27, r. 2. Second, for the infrequent case when the mandatory, automatic documentary-admission procedure does not apply, the recommended[5] Form for Notice to admit Documents recites that the requesting party 'proposes to adduce [the documents] in evidence...'[6] This recital overlooks the fact that a party may wish to learn whether a document is genuine in order to decide whether to follow a train of inquiry which may result in acquiring other admissible evidence.[7] Worse still, this recital misconceives the realities of trial preparation and strategy. These realities are that skilful counsel often does not decide to introduce a document into evidence until the actual moment of introduction at trial. Not until then does he have the maximum and optimum information with which to decide what evidence to use. As superfluous hypocrisy,[8] this recital should be omitted.

These flaws are not central to English admissions. The central outline of English admissions is in two parts. These parts distinguish admission of facts from admission of documents. R.S.C. 1965, 0.27, r. 2–(1) authorizes a notice to admit specified facts. The facts are not admitted unless the opponent affirmatively so responds within 7 days or such longer time as the court allows: in effect, the absence of a response is deemed a denial.[9] As has been described in Chapter 3, Section A2, under R.S.C. 1965, 0.24 the parties must serve on each other a list of all discoverable documents within 14 days after the close of pleadings. 0.27, r. 4–(1)(2) deems each party who receives such a mandatory list automatically to make an admission to the documents except if he serves a denial within 21 days after inspecting them or after the time for inspecting them expires.[10]

It seems plain that the admission about documents intended by 0.27, r. 4–(1)(2) is that they are genuine, i.e. that they meet the authentication requirement for being admitted into evidence.[11] In respect of original documents the admission worked by Rule 4–(1)(a) would satisfy the authentication requirement, for it is that the document 'was printed, written, signed or executed as it purports...to have been'. But in respect of copies, the admission stated by Rule 4–(1)(b) to be brought about is only that 'a copy is a true copy'. This would satisfy part of the requirement of the best-evidence rule.[12] However, this admission would not meet the authentication requirement in that it does not negate the possibility that the document is a true copy of a document which is not genuine.[13] Yet for a copy to be admitted into evidence, it must satisfy both the best-evidence rule and the authentication requirement.[14] To satisfy the latter, Rule 4–(1)(b) should be amended to bring about an admission that 'a copy is a true copy of a document which was printed, written, signed or executed as it purports...to have been.'

Unlike the English practice, the American federal admissions

mechanism, F.R.C.P. 36, does not distinguish between documents and facts. It operates alike for both. A party upon whom
a written request for admission of facts or genuineness of
documents is served may within thirty days serve a written
answer or objection. If he serves neither a written answer nor a
written objection, he is treated as though he has admitted the
matters in the request. If he serves a written answer in which
he does not make the admission requested,

> the answer shall specifically deny the matter or set forth in detail the
> reasons why the answering party cannot truthfully admit or deny the
> matter. A denial shall fairly meet the substance of the requested
> admission... An answering party may not give lack of information or
> knowledge as a reason for failure to admit or deny unless he states
> that he has made a reasonable inquiry and that the information
> known or readily obtainable by him is insufficient to enable him to
> admit or deny. F.R.C.P. 36(a)

As in England, he may qualify or limit his answer so that he
makes but a partial admission.[15] If he serves a written objection, he must state his reasons. They may be any of the bases
for resisting discovery by other mechanisms.[16] It is no basis for
objection, however, that 'a matter of which an admission has
been requested presents a genuine issue for trial...' (F.R.C.P.
36(a)); since the 1970 amendments to F.R.C.P. 36, which
reversed some earlier case law to the contrary, even the ulti-
mate facts which will determine the outcome of the case are fair
game for a request to admit.[17] While the English admissions
rules say nothing about objections, it cannot be doubted that
an English court would entertain objections on grounds like
privilege and oppressiveness.

F.R.C.P. 36(a) puts the burden on the party requesting
admissions to move that the court overrule an objection or
determine that an answer is insufficient. The loser on this
motion must pay the winner's expenses, including attorney's
fees entailed by the motion, unless the loser's position was substantially justified (F.R.C.P. 36(a), 37(a)(4)). Unless the
requesting party moves that the court overrule an objection, his
opponent is not treated as having admitted the matter, even if
his objection would have been overruled had the court passed
on it.[18]

Likewise, unless the requesting party moves that the court
determine the sufficiency of an answer, his opponent should not

be treated as having admitted the matter. The sufficiency of an answer usually turns on whether the above requirements for an effective denial have been satisfied. Even if they are not, F.R.C.P. 36(a) does not automatically deem the matter admitted. A 1970 amendment changed this Rule to say that 'the matter is admitted unless, within 30 days, ... the party to whom the request is directed serves ... a written answer ... addressed to the matter ...'; whereas it had previously said that the matter was admitted unless the party served an answer 'denying specifically the matter ... or setting forth in detail why he cannot truthfully admit or deny ...'[19] Hence, before 1970, the Rule literally made a matter admitted unless the answer denied it 'specifically' or set forth 'in detail' why the responding party could neither admit nor deny.[20]

[Giving failure to satisfy the present requirements of an effective denial] the automatic effect of an admission may cause unfair surprise. A responding party who purported to deny or to be unable to admit or deny will for the first time at trial confront the contention that he has made a binding admission.[21]

For this reason the 1970 amendment makes a written answer sufficient to avoid an automatic admission if it is 'addressed to the matter' in question. If the requesting party feels that the answer does not satisfy one of the requirements of an effective denial, and moves that the court determine its sufficiency, the court 'may order either that the matter is admitted or that an amended answer be served' (F.R.C.P. 36(a)).[22] To avoid 'unfair surprise', as intended by this amendment, the motion to determine the sufficiency of the answer must be made well before trial.

The effect of an admission under the Rule is that the 'matter ... is conclusively established unless the court on motion permits withdrawal or amendment of the admission'(F.R.C.P. 36(b)).[23] It is so established 'for the purpose of the pending action only ...'

The court may permit withdrawal or amendment when the presentation of the merits of the action will be subserved thereby and the party who obtained the admission fails to satisfy the court that withdrawal or amendment will prejudice him in maintaining his action or defense on the merits.

The English rule on admission of facts, 1965 R.S.C. 0.27, r. 2–(2), similarly provides that 'the Court may at any time allow a party to amend or withdraw an admission... made by him on such terms as may be just.' Although the English rules on admission of documents, R.S.C. 1965, 0.27, rr. 4, 5, are silent on relieving the responding party from an admission, there is no sound reason for a distinction between facts and documents in this respect. After all, most of the contents and the genuineness of documents may be stated as facts in a notice or request to admit. Hence the English courts should allow amendments or withdrawals of documentary admissions too when 'just', that is, when doing so promotes resolving the action on its merits and does not prejudice a party who has relied justifiably on an admission in his preparation for trial.[24]

Another distinction without a difference between the English documentary- and factual-admissions rules runs in the opposite direction. R.S.C. 1965, 0.27, r. 4–(1) expressly provides that a documentary admission is 'without prejudice to the right of a party to object to the admission in evidence of any document' admitted.[25] On factual admissions R.S.C. 1965, 0.27, r. 2 is silent about objections to admissibility in evidence of facts admitted, although the English Forms both of Notice to Admit Facts and of Admissions of Facts recite, 'saving all just exceptions to the admissibility of such facts in evidence...'[26] F.R.C.P. 36 also is silent on this issue, albeit F.R.C.P. Form 25, Request for Admission under Rule 36, recites that admissions are 'subject to all pertinent objections to admissibility which may be interposed at the trial...'[27] Because an admission of facts or documents is a discovery proceeding and because there is no difference in this respect between documents and facts, English factual and American federal admissions should not be admissible in evidence if they do not comply with laws of evidence.[28] Were it otherwise, the scope of discovery, which both in England and in American federal courts is wider than the bounds of relevance in evidence law,[29] would *pro tanto* unintentionally and unwisely modify the evidence law of relevance.

The American federal sanction for the failure to admit as requested under Rule 36 is that, if the requesting party proves the matter, on his application the court shall order his opponent

to pay him the reasonable expenses incurred in making that proof, including reasonable attorney's fees... unless it finds that (1) the request was held objectionable pursuant to Rule 36(a),[30] or (2) the admission sought was of no substantial importance, or (3) the party failing to admit had reasonable ground to believe that he might prevail on the matter, or (4) there was other good reason for the failure to admit. F.R.C.P. 37(c)[31]

In England R.S.C. 1965, 0.62, r. 3(5) (6) contain the same costs sanction; however, the English exception is expressed not in four categories but as 'unless the court otherwise orders'.

Other American federal sanctions may be applied if, following the requesting party's successful Rule 36(a) motion to determine the sufficiency of an objection or answer, his opponent fails to obey the court order to serve an answer or amended answer of the kind defined in F.R.C.P. 36(a). These sanctions are those available generally for disobedience of discovery orders, such as dismissal, default judgment, and contempt. They are authorized in F.R.C.P. 37(b) (2), which applies 'if a party ... fails to obey an order to provide ... discovery'. It should be held that the court has made such an order if, on the requesting party's Rule 36(a) motion to determine the sufficiency of an objection or answer, it orders the opponent to serve an answer or amended answer.[32] If he fails to do so and fails to serve an objection, and if the court orders a time limitation for compliance, Rule 36(a) may arguably contain the sanction of treating him as having admitted the matter,[33] for it provides,

The matter is admitted unless, within 30 days after service of the request, or within such shorter or longer time as the court may allow, the party to whom the request is directed serves upon the party requesting the admission a written answer or objection addressed to the matter ...

This argument seems unsound, however. The time limitation for compliance with the order is not Rule 36(a)'s 'such shorter or longer time as the court may allow'; 'shorter or longer' refers to '30 days after service of the request'; 'time as the court may allow' is time as allowed by modifying the usual extrajudicial rule permitting thirty days for response after service of the request.

In any event, sanctions for violation of court orders to answer are of relatively little importance, since American federal admissions practice, like the English practice, operates overwhelmingly extrajudicially. Thus costs of proof under F.R.C.P. 37(c) are the chief sanction to encourage admissions. Yet a study of more than 3,000 American federal cases terminating in 1973–5 found that not a single motion for application of this sanction had been made.[34] It surely is an understatement to suggest that 'this sanction has not been applied regularly or vigorously enough to deter evasive refusals to admit.'[35] Even if it were so applied, it would be unlikely to deter most baseless refusals to admit.[36] Costs of proof of particular matters very frequently will be insignificant compared to a party's financial stake in winning a case; and naturally, making admissions requested by his opponent will tend to dim his prospects of winning. Moreover, the more uncertain a party is as to the points he will succeed in proving at trial, the more likely his opponent is to negotiate a favourable compromise settlement.[37] Furthermore, the costs sanction will be less effective in American federal practice than in England because trial by jury of civil cases is still widespread in American federal courts.[38] Since these juries usually return general verdicts, the American federal judge often will not know whether the truth of the facts in question was proved and sometimes will not even know whether the genuineness of documents was proved.[39] Yet the party who made the requests for admission frequently will not request a special verdict as to these facts and documents, since he prefers a general verdict for strategic reasons.[40] The upshot is that the requesting party will fail to obtain costs under F.R.C.P. 37(c).

Probably owing to the ineffectiveness of the costs sanction, American federal requests to admit have not been used very often.[41] Before the 1970 amendments to F.R.C.P. 36 they were used in but 10 per cent of federal cases, a lower percentage than that of any other federal discovery mechanism except depositions upon written interrogatories.[42] After the 1970 amendments to F.R.C.P. 36, requests to admit were not used in 52 per cent of federal cases and constituted but 5.6 per cent of the total use of all discovery mechanisms in the remaining 48 per cent of cases.[43] English factual admissions similarly have been seldom used.[44] Their use cannot be expected to increase appreciably by reversing the present English rule that a failure to respond to a notice to admit is deemed to be a denial.[45] After all, in the American federal factual-admission mechanism failure to respond is deemed to be an admission, and yet it too is seldom used.

English documentary admissions also were seldom used until requests for them were made mandatory and automatic incident to the like disclosure and production of documents under R.S.C. 1965, 0.24, 27.[46] A comparable factual-admissions mechanism is not feasible in the present absence of any pre-trial step when all discoverable non-documentary facts are collected together for another purpose analogous to an Order 24 list of documents. To require all such facts to be assembled and contained in a mandatory request to admit facts would probably prove inordinately expensive and time-consuming if judged solely by the volume of admissions, and corresponding saving of trial time and expense, generated.

This gloomy forecast is dictated by the ineffectiveness of current sanctions for unjustified refusals to admit. More effective sanctions which are proposed below should improve this forecast. Be that as it may, the proposal for mandatory requests for factual admissions should not be judged only by the volume of admissible information.[47] In view of the sketchy nature of pleadings at present, the value of this mutual disclosure should be substantial. Its contribution to helping the fact-finder do justice by notifying all parties of discoverable non-documentary information in advance of trial highly commends this proposal to both English and American federal practice.
ure should be substantial. Its contribution to helping the fact-finder do justice by notifying all parties of discoverable non-documentary information in advance of trial highly commends this proposal to both English and American federal practice.

The Report of the Committee on Personal Injuries Litigation, pp. 74, 79, suggested that an English statement of claim, which is like an American federal complaint, be accompanied by a notice to admit the facts in this pleading. This suggestion falls far short of the proposed discovery mechanism. It does not add significantly to the present law, for both in England and the American federal system, an opponent's pleading in response to a statement of claim and complaint already must admit or deny the allegations.[48] Furthermore, the pleadings at present are sketchy. They are thought to be more workable if they contain but a general notice of claim and defence.[49] In contrast, the proposal being made contemplates that the mandatory request for admissions contain the detailed facts, for which evidence is perhaps the more apt term, which the parties will try to prove at trial.

The more detailed the facts requested, the greater the disclosure and the more costs and time saved by admissions. Hence the proposed mandatory factual request should not be required until by other discovery mechanisms and informal investigation the parties have had a reasonable opportunity to unearth the facts they wish to prove. The time for English mandatory exchange of lists of documents under R.S.C. 1965, 0.24, r. 2–(1), within 14 days after the pleadings are closed, would usually be too soon. A more fitting period usually would be in the range of 75 to 120 days.[50]

To maximize the benefits of mutual disclosure and the saving in costs and time of this proposal, the parties should be encouraged to include in the factual request all their evidence. Ways to do so include providing for extrajudicial amendments to the requests before trial and providing that factual (not real or documentary) evidence is inadmissible if omitted from the requests. However, the latter provision should not be so inflexible as to reincarnate the 'fatal variance' between pleading and proof in the early common-law courts. An example of reasonable flexibility is available by paraphrasing part of F.R.C.P. 15(b) as follows:

If evidence is objected to at the trial on the ground that it is not within the mandatory request for factual admissions and the court determines that this is so, the court nevertheless may admit the evidence and shall do so freely when the presentation of the merits of the action will be served thereby and the objecting party fails to satisfy the court that the admission of such evidence would prejudice him in maintaining his claim or defense upon the merits. The court may grant a continuance to enable the objecting party to meet such evidence.

The desirability of encouraging admissions is reflected in R.S.C. 1965, 0.25, r. 4, requiring that 'at the hearing of the summons for directions[51] ... the court endeavour to secure ... admissions ...', and in F.R.C.P. 16 authorizing the court to convene a pre-trial conference with counsel 'to consider [*inter alia*] ... the possibility of obtaining admissions of fact ... which avoid unnecessary proof ...'[52] Encouraging use of the admissions mechanism rather than the interrogatory or deposition mechanism has a particular advantage in American federal practice. A Rule 36 admission generally conclusively establishes the matter (F.R.C.P. 36(b)). However, an interrogatory or deposition answer generally is not binding and may be contradicted by the answering party at trial.[53]

The proposal being made would modify present English and American federal procedure merely by making mandatory the very request for admissions which it is optional now for any party to make under R.S.C. 1965, 0.27, r. 2, and F.R.C.P. 36. An objection to this proposal on the ground that it is excessively paternalistic may be made, as it may be made to the proposal that English mandatory documentary discovery be adopted in America. This objection and its weakness from the viewpoint of society as a whole is discussed in Chapter 3, Section A4. It is there pointed out that if the proposal is deemed excessively paternalistic, it still need not be rejected and its benefits altogether lost. The concern in the paternalistic objection that private parties not be forced to pay for the common good can be accommodated by providing that the factual-admissions request not be mandatory if both sides so agree.

At all events, the English success with mandatory and automatic requests for documentary admissions recommends this mechanism for the American federal system. The admissions feature should be adopted with the documentary mechanism which is urged in Chapter 3, Section A4. At present American federal practice does not have automatic and mandatory documentary discovery; still, it might easily secure a much greater use of documentary admissions by providing that, whenever a party produces documents in response to a request under F.R.C.P. 34 or a subpoena under F.R.C.P. 45, he thereby requests that his opponent admit their genuineness under F.R.C.P. 36.[54] The Rule 34 request and Rule 45 subpoena often separately list the documents. It is argued in Chapter 3, Sections A2 and B2 that they should not be required to do so. When they do not do so, the parties producing the documents should be required by amendments to Rules 34 and 45 to serve on their opponents a list of the documents they produce. This list or the list in the Rule 34 request and Rule 45 subpoena would satisfy the requirement in F.R.C.P. 36 that 'every matter of which an admission is requested shall be separately set forth'.

In Chapter 4 it is proposed to apply the mandatory and automatic documentary-discovery method to real and personal property; if this is done, requests to admit the authenticity of property and the identity of conditions at the time at issue on real property should likewise be made automatic and mandatory, incident to their disclosure. Even if the earlier proposal is not adopted, such factual admissions should automatically be deemed to be requested by a party who complies with an American federal Rule 34 request or 45 subpoena or English court order to disclose his property.

Even if all of these proposals for automatic requests to admit were adopted, parties would undoubtedly continue baselessly to deny the matters; and requests to admit facts not appearing in documents or from property would remain little used. These conditions would remain as facts of litigating life owing to the ineffectiveness of the costs sanction in deterring baseless refusals to admit. Hence the sanction should be improved. Inasmuch as it would be extremely cumbersome, if not impracticable, to let the requesting party show the truth of the fact before trial so that a sanction might be applied at that time to his opponent, the sanction must continue to be applied after trial. But it should not be limited to costs. More compelling sanctions are contempt and dismissal of a plaintiff's action, or default judgment against a defendant. These sanctions have venerable precedents in discovery in English equity[55] and currently are used in England and America to enforce discovery mechanisms other than admissions.[56] Dismissal and default, which are variants of the equity *pro confesso* sanction, remain meaningful after trial when a failure to admit can be determined to be unjustified. Other variants of *pro confesso*, like ordering designated facts to be taken as established,[57] precluding reliance on designated claims or defences, prohibiting introduction of designated matters in evidence, striking out pleadings, and staying an action until a plaintiff makes admissions,[58] obviously could not be meaningfully applied after trial.

If a defendant who had baselessly denied a request to admit lost on the merits at trial, punishment of him for contempt by fine or imprisonment would be the only appropriate sanction. Hence R.S.C. 1965, 0.27 should be amended to empower the court to treat such a denial as contempt. The English courts apply this sanction, however, only against a party who has violated a court order (cf. R.S.C. 1965, 0.24, r. 16–(2), 0.26, r. 6–(2)). Hence R.S.C. 1965, 0.27 should be amended so that, in addition to his present option to serve a notice to admit, a party may also apply for an order that the matter is admitted unless his opponent within, say, thirty days, on good-faith grounds and after reasonable inquiry, files a denial or a statement that he cannot truthfully admit or deny the matter. The amendment also should permit a party first to serve a notice to admit and then apply for an order to the same effect. The party should be left the option of extrajudicially serving a notice to admit, lest he be discouraged from seeking admissions by the greater expense and delay of obtaining a court order and lest the courts be overburdened with applications for orders. But the party who does obtain an order should receive fewer baseless denials, for the sanction of punishment for contempt will face the party filing such a denial after he has lost on the merits.

If the party filing such a denial after such an order wins on the merits at trial, the English courts might, in addition to, or instead of, contempt, dismiss his case or enter a default judgment against him. They apply these sanctions even if there has been no court order as to documents under R.S.C. 1965, 0.24, r. 16–(1). Amendments to R.S.C. 1965, 0.27 should be made authorizing the court to impose dismissals or defaults on those making baseless denials of extrajudicial requests to admit. Applying the contempt, dismissal, or default sanction from time to time should deter far more unjustifiable denials than the costs sanction has done.

The American federal courts do not now have power to use these heavier sanctions against unjustifiable denials except in the rare case when F.R.C.P. 37(b)(2) applies as a result of an F.R.C.P. 36(a) court order to serve an answer or an amended answer.[59] If there is no constitutional bar against applying the sanction of dismissal or default judgment, F.R.C.P. 37(c) or (d) should be amended to empower the court to apply this sort of sanction to an unjustifiable refusal to admit. But this sanction would be meaningless in cases in which the offending party lost on the merits at trial. In these cases the only effective sanction would be punishment for contempt. The American federal courts, like the English courts, punish as contempt only violations of court orders.[60] Hence F.R.C.P. 36 should likewise be amended so that, in addition to his present option to serve a request to admit, a party may also move for an order that the matter is admitted unless his opponent, within thirty days, on good-faith grounds and after reasonable inquiry, files a denial or statement that he cannot truthfully admit or deny the matter. Violation of such an order would make F.R.C.P. 37(b)(2) applicable. It contains both contempt and dismissal and default. When the requesting party obtains the F.R.C.P. 36

order here proposed, the contempt sanction would be available whether his opponent won or lost on the merits. If his opponent won on the merits, dismissal or default also would be available if not unconstitutional.

There are two tiers to the question of whether the American federal Constitution bars applying dismissal or default sanctions to a party who has baselessly denied a matter he was requested to admit, but who has won on the merits at trial. The first tier is the state of the United States Supreme Court precedents in respect to this sort of sanction for violation of discovery requirements regardless of whether the violator is a defendant or plaintiff. In *Hovey* v. *Elliott* 167 U.S. 409 (1897) a lower court had in effect ordered a default judgment against defendant for violation of its order for the preservation of property, pending the outcome of litigation concerning ownership of that property, an order which had nothing to do with discovery. The Supreme Court held that the default judgment offended the Fifth Amendment to the United States Constitution, which prohibits the federal government from depriving a person of property without due process of law. In two subsequent discovery decisions, *Société Internationale Pour Participations Industrielles et Commerciales, S.A.* v. *Rogers*, pp. 211, 212, and *Hammond Packing Co.* v. *Arkansas*[61] 212 U.S. 322, 347 (1909), the Supreme Court indicated that such sanctions would offend the same provision in the Constitution if visited on a party who had acted in good faith but was unable to comply with a discovery order.[62]

Furthermore, these two decisions read *Hovey*'s interpretation of Constitutional due process as barring the dismissal and default sanctions, not in all instances of violations of discovery requirements, but only when used for 'mere punishment'.[63] They decided that the Constitution does not bar such sanctions when a party's bad-faith failure to give discovery gives rise to a 'permissible presumption'[64] 'of fact'[65] of the 'want of merit'[66] in that party's position.

To apply the dismissal or default sanction against a party who has won at trial on the merits, but has in bad faith denied a matter he was requested to admit unquestionably would not be the expression of a 'permissible presumption of fact', but 'mere punishment' and so unconstitutional. A presumption of want of merit in the party's position would hardly be permissible, and would surely not be one of fact, in the face of his victory at trial which shows that the judge or jury did find merit in his position. To snatch his victory from him, which would be the only meaningful sanction in F.R.C.P. 37(b)(2)(C) at this point in the litigation, would be to make the presumption of want of merit in his position an irrebuttable one, that is, one of law rather than fact, and of penal law at that.[67]

The second tier of exploration of the constitutional question is whether the due-process bar applies to plaintiffs as well as defendants. *Hammond Packing* and *Hovey* concerned sanctions applied to defendants. In *Rogers* the application of a sanction to the plaintiff was at stake. But, as the Supreme Court there took pains to note,

> In *Hovey* v. *Elliott, supra*, it was held that due process was denied a defendant whose answer was struck, thereby leading to a decree *pro confesso* without a hearing ... Certainly substantial constitutional questions are provoked by ... [striking the complaint of a plaintiff who has been unable, despite good faith efforts, to comply with a discovery order]. Their gravity is accented in the present case where petitioner, though cast in the role of *plaintiff*, cannot be deemed to be in the customary role of a party invoking the aid of a court to vindicate rights asserted against another. Rather petitioner's position is more analogous to that of a *defendant*, for it ... protest[s] ... against a seizure ... of assets which were summarily possessed by the Alien Property Custodian without the opportunity for protest ... 357 U.S. at 210–12

In *Hovey*, the Court had emphasized that constitutional due process reflects that 'the fundamental conception of a court of justice is condemnation only after hearing. To say that courts have ... power to deny all right to defend an action ... is ... to convert the court ... into an instrument of ... oppression ...'[68] Not only is the *Hovey* opinion replete with such considerations, which are peculiar to defendants,[69] but also it implies that the due-process bar does not apply to plaintiffs, by repeatedly pointing out that 'in early chancery times'[70] plaintiffs who were in contempt of court in effect had *pro confesso* sanctions applied to them by being denied relief in the nature of a 'favor' sought from the Chancellor.[71] However, its discussion of the early English chancery authorities overlooks the fact that plaintiffs to a bill in equity for discovery sometimes were defendants in actions for relief at equity or law.[72] When equity applied *pro confesso* sanctions to such plaintiffs, they were applied to parties who would today be called defendants.[73] Moreover, *Hovey* itself did imply that plaintiffs who are in contempt of court would not be denied relief to which they had a 'strict right';[74] and it guardedly said on the applicability of the due-process bar to plaintiffs,

Whether in the exercise of its power to punish for a contempt a court would be justified in refusing to permit one in contempt from availing himself of a right granted by statute, where the refusal did not involve the fundamental right of one summoned in a cause to be heard in his defence, and where the one in contempt was an actor invoking the right allowed by statute, is a question not involved in this suit... [O]ur opinion is therefore exclusively confined to the case before us. 167 U.S. at 444.

This question of whether a plaintiff's action based on a strict right allowed by a statute may be dismissed on account of plaintiff's 'contempt' in violating a discovery duty was answered in the affirmative in 1976 by the United States Supreme Court in *National Hockey League* v. *Metropolitan Hockey Club, Inc.* In this case the Supreme Court *per curiam* affirmed the District Court's dismissal pursuant to F.R.C.P. 37(b)(2) of plaintiff's action under the anti-trust statutes on the basis of plaintiff's 'flagrant bad faith'[75] ('contempt' in the language of *Hovey*) in substantially failing to answer interrogatories.

National Hockey League neither mentioned the constitution nor cited *Hovey*. Nevertheless, this Supreme Court decision does seem to mean that the constitutional due-process bar against default judgments as punishment against defendants does not apply to dismissals against plaintiffs.[76] This is because the briefs before the Supreme Court in this case cited *Hovey*, *Hammond Packing*, and *Rogers*[77] and because the *National Hockey League* opinion expressly approved the dismissal sanction as punishment in these words:

[dismissal as one of] the most severe... sanctions... must be available to the District Court in appropriate cases, not merely *to penalize* those whose conduct may be deemed to warrant such a sanction, but to deter those who might be tempted to such conduct in the absence of such a deterrent. 427 U.S. at 643 (emphasis added)[78]

Thus it appears that American federal plaintiffs who in bad faith fail to make an admission and who win on the merits at trial may have their actions dismissed. The use of the dismissal sanction in both the American federal courts and English courts, and the use of the default-judgment sanction in English courts, should have a salutary effect in discouraging bad-faith denials of matters requested to be admitted. But just as in early English equity penalties for contempt were applied exhaustively before a *pro confesso* sanction was applied,[79] so today the sanction of dismissal or default judgment should not too readily be applied to a party who has won on the merits and whose bad-faith denials did not prevent his opponent from proving the matters requested at trial. Since this party's victory is not attributable to his fault, snatching it from him has no particular merit as a form of punishment. But to take away from him, say, a $1,000,000 verdict or to enter default judgment against him for, say, £500,000 has the particular demerit of disproportionate punishment. The amount of fine or length of imprisonment for contempt may be tailored to fit the fault.[80] Except when the effect of the dismissal or default sanction would not be grossly disproportionate to the fault, the contempt sanction should be preferred.

6

Oral Examinations or Depositions

In England oral examination as a method of discovery is available only when answers to interrogatories are insufficient.[1] Even in such cases it is rarely employed.[2] Information now acquired by interrogatories with leave of court from a party in England might be acquired instead, or be supplemented, by deposition upon oral examination. As suggested by an English barrister in 1830, and as now employed in the United States under F.R.C.P. 28–32, it might work in broad outline as follows.[3] Without previous notice of the subjects to be covered, a party would be sworn[4] and would then answer orally questions put orally by the legal adviser of his adversary. The legal adviser of the party under examination might object to questions on the same grounds as he might object to interrogatories. Thereupon the lawyer interrogating usually would go on to other questions. After the close of the examination, if he still considered the information protected by the objection important, he might seek a court order that the questions objected to be answered, just as he might do for question unanswered in interrogatories. When he concluded his examination, the lawyer for the party under examination would have an opportunity to put questions orally to his client to clarify the latter's answers or prevent them from being incomplete or misleading.[5] The client would answer these questions also orally and on the spot. The oral questions, answers, and objections all would be recorded by shorthand or an electronic device. This device may be as simple as a two- or three-way telephone call or as sophisticated as videotape.[6]

In jurisdictions in the United States where both such a scheme of oral examination and interrogatories have been available, lawyers, judges, and legal scholars have had the distinct impression that practitioners on the whole prefer the oral mode.[7] The accuracy of these impressions has been confirmed by the detailed field-study of the actual use of discovery in American federal District Courts which has been described in Chapter 1, Section A1.[8] This study determined that depositions upon oral examination are the central discovery mechanism among those available under the F.R.C.P. in three respects. First, lawyers use oral examination far more frequently than other mechanisms[9]— 49 per cent of the lawyers in the cases studied used oral examinations, while 30 per cent used interrogatories, 31 per cent inspected documents and things, and 10 per cent requested admissions.[10] Second, lawyers use oral examinations alone more often than combinations of discovery mechanisms; and when they do use combinations, combinations including oral examinations are much more common than combinations lacking oral examination.[11] Third, lawyers use oral examination for a greater number and variety of purposes than other discovery mechanisms.[12] The preference for oral examination in American federal courts is not surprising, for the same field-study determined that practitioners in these courts believe oral examination to be more fruitful than interrogatories and inspections of documents and things.[13] This study also revealed that oral examination used alone is more productive in informing the lawyer of new evidence, new witnesses, and new issues than interrogatories used alone,[14] that a combination of discovery mechanisms is productive more often than is but one mechanism, and that oral examination combined with interrogatories and inspections of documents and things, or with inspections alone, seems particularly productive.[15]

Whether oral examination would be more productive than interrogatories have been in a jurisdiction like England, in which oral examination has been virtually unavailable, is a somewhat different question. An affirmative answer is suggested by the American empirical evidence.

The same organization which conducted the field-study of the use of discovery in American federal courts made a comparable empirical study of cases which terminated in the fiscal year 1961 in the state Superior Court in Massachusetts.[16] At that time oral examination was not available in the Massachusetts state-court system.[17] Up to thirty interrogatories, however, were available to each party without leave of court; the court might grant leave for filing more than thirty upon a showing of adequate cause.[18] The Massachusetts study found discovery concentrated in negligence cases and conducted primarily by interrogatories.[19] It made the following comparative assessments of the productivity of Massachusetts state discovery, which did not have oral examination, and federal discovery, which did:

[In Massachusetts state courts] the lawyers registered scanty gains in finding new evidence, seeing new issues, or in learning the names of witnesses... Specifically defendants gained information [in one of these forms] in over a third of the cases and plaintiffs in less than one-fifth.[20] In a majority of state cases, neither side obtained new evidence, saw new issues, or learned new witnesses' names. In the Federal system at least one of these events occurred in well over half the cases...[21] In brief, unlike the use of discovery in the Federal system, the Massachusetts procedures were used extensively, quite routinely and with relatively less frequent discernible benefit to the case.[22] The important [lesson]... the Massachusetts study teaches [is]...: where discovery of the far-reaching Federal type is not clearly available, cases do not reap comparable benefits...[23]

Oral examination patterned after the federal model was introduced into the Massachusetts state-court system in 1967.[24] In 1971 Chief Justice Tauro of the Massachusetts Supreme Judicial Court described it as a 'success' and 'probably the most significant advance in recent Massachusetts legal history'.[25]

The preference for oral examination over interrogatories and the greater productivity of oral examination may be readily explained. Oral examination 'has the advantage over written interrogatories that any "confrontatory" method of procedure has over one that is "epistolary"'.[26] One such advantage arises from the fact that testimony at trials today is oral rather than written. Hence in the course of conducting an oral examination legal advisers may evaluate the impact to be made at trial by the demeanour and personality of a witness.[27] One disadvantage of interrogatories is that 'the language of the answer is not that of the... [party] himself, but is entirely the language of his legal adviser, who is allowed to settle every sentence of it.'[28] Sunderland has well expressed four additional advantages of oral examination as follows:

In the first place,... [interrogatories] give the party to whom they are addressed more time to study their effect, which furnishes a better opportunity to frame protective answers which conceal or evade.[29] In the next place, as a means of forcing a specific, detailed and thorough disclosure from a reluctant party,[30] there is a tendency for the interrogatories to grow in number, complexity and variety of form, so as to call for as many aspects of the proof as possible, with the result that they often become difficult to administer. Cases have been reported where more than two thousand interrogatories were employed...

But there is a third and much more serious weakness in the use of written interrogatories. To draw up a series of questions and present them all at once to be answered, is far less searching than to present questions one at a time, framing each succeeding question on the basis of prior answers given. Answers usually suggest lines of further inquiry, which often lead to the most important disclosures. That is, of course, the chief reason for the effectiveness of oral cross-examination. By submitting a complete list of interrogatories, prepared in advance, the party seeking discovery entirely loses this enormous advantage in eliciting the truth...

It is further to be observed that this method, while hampering the examiner in effectively directing and pursuing his investigation, also offers special aid to the deponent in concealing his case. This results from the circumstance that he is informed in advance exactly how far the inquiry is to go, what facts the interrogator knows about, as evidenced by his questions, and what facts he is ignorant of, as evidenced by his silence.[31]

Owing to some of the advantages of oral examination over interrogatories, 150 years ago in England the Common Law Commission of 1830 recommended that the court be empowered to order a party orally to answer written questions before a court officer and in the presence of the legal advisers of both sides.[32] More than 125 years ago the Common Law Commission of 1853 proposed that the court be empowered to order a party's oral examination before a court officer 'in any... case in which it may be made to appear essential to justice...'[33] But within the last thirty years two comparable committees appear wary of proceedings involving oral examination, although neither considered the oral method as an alternative or supplement to interrogatories. Both the Report of the Committee on Personal Injuries Litigation, pp. 101–2, and the Final Report of the Committee on Supreme Court Practice and Procedure, pp. 73–5, reject what they apparently consider suggestions to use oral examinations in lieu of proceedings on summonses for directions, although in the former Report Master Jacob reserved his position on the point.[34] The chief, if not sole, reason that the two Reports seem wary of the oral method is that they anticipate that it would increase costs since they think barristers would be briefed to conduct it.

If the oral method is used as an alternative or supplement to interrogatories, as is here being proposed, the inquiry should be whether barristers would be briefed more frequently, and/or be paid on a higher scale of fees, than they are when interrogatories are the method. In unusual or complex cases barristers are now customarily briefed to frame both interrogatories and answers to them. In such cases they undoubtedly would be briefed by both sides to conduct oral examinations were they to be made available. In routine or simple cases, barristers are not now customarily briefed to handle interrogatories. In such cases it is likely that usually they would not be briefed to conduct oral examinations. At first the novelty of the procedure might lead cautious ''solicitors to do so; but once initial apprehension were overcome, solicitors generally may be expected to consider themselves as well qualified to handle oral examinations as interrogatories. Surely this would be true of those solicitors now eager to enlarge the scope of their right to audience in court.

In cases in which barristers would be briefed to conduct oral examinations, would their scale of fees be that for chambers work or that for court appearances? Certainly it should not be the latter, since the purpose is discovery and since barristers would not bear the responsibilities inherent in appearances before the court — the only officer who need be present would be a person empowered to put the party being examined under oath.[35] However, since more advocacy generally would be required than for interrogatories, the scale of fees may be expected to be somewhat higher than for paper work in chambers. Thus costs in the form of counsel fees for oral examinations may be expected to exceed costs for interrogatories, but not by nearly so much as the two recent Reports seem to contemplate. The increase, if any, may well be modest indeed.[36] While no statistical study of counsel fees occasioned by interrogatories appears to have been made, the empirical study of American federal discovery, referred to in Chapter 1, Section A1, indicated that the median attorney's fee for an oral examination was $258 and for an opponent's oral examination, $150.[37] The difference in counsel fees for interrogatories and oral examination may turn out to be less than one would expect if oral examinations prove to generate far fewer applications to the court for an order to make further answers than do interrogatories, as has been the American federal experience.[38] In calculating the difference in total costs of interrogatories and oral examination, the expense of transcripts of oral examination must be included for those instances when a party desires to peruse the transcript or file it for use at trial.[39] The expense will decline as electronic recording devices replace stenographers.

Moreover, since the benefits of discovery, noted in Chapter 1, Section A, may reduce the total costs of litigation, oral examination as a superior method of securing these benefits may result in a net reduction in the costs of litigation.[40] In any event, the American federal experience suggests that the total costs of discovery when oral examination is available will not be inordinate. The empirical study just referred to determined that the costs engendered by discovery, in all forms by both sides, constituted but one-third of the total costs in the average case.[41] This study also determined that these costs of discovery did not give rise to widespread protest.[42] In American federal courts both interrogatories and oral examination are available without leave of court. Hence they undoubtedly engender more costs than would be engendered in the English courts, in which interrogatories are available only with leave of court, and oral examination as an alternative or supplement to interrogatories would likewise be available only with leave of court.

At any rate, it might be provided in England that the party who desires to use the oral method pay all of its costs,[43] if one's pre-eminent concern is to prevent costs from rising whatever the resulting benefits to the administration of justice. The terms of reference of the Final Report of the Committee on Supreme Court Practice and Procedure, pp. 4, 20, 21, made saving costs its prime purpose. Such single-minded dedication to saving costs would be required if it were true, as Master of the Rolls Brett thought in 1883,[44] that the legal profession so lacks integrity that it takes steps to swell costs, and so its profits, irrespective of its duty to clients and the court. But Master Diamond has set forth a far more realistic view as follows:

Few litigants intend to fight the action when it is begun — they hope and expect a settlement and do not desire to incur unnecessary costs. A solicitor who does not know which side will pay costs is not usually likely to incur intentionally unnecessary costs, still less is counsel.[45]

Despite repeated efforts to reduce costs,

the bane and burden of costs has existed for generations in the English system and the problem of costs remains as intractable today as it was at the beginning of the 19th century, when the first move began towards reform in legal procedure.[46]

While opportunities to save costs should by no means be neglected, saving costs should not become a fetish impeding improvements in discovery. In other facets of English civil procedure the public in recent years has benefited from 'greater thoroughness of the inquisition'[47] and 'more thorough preparation of the case'.[48] The public will likewise benefit from the improvement in discovery here proposed; it will help to justify 'the claim commonly made by Englishmen to excellence in the administration of justice'.[49]

Medical Examinations

F.R.C.P. 35 confers broad power on the court to order, upon motion and a showing of good cause, a physical or mental examination of a person who is a party, or who is in the custody or under the legal control of a party, and whose mental or physical condition (including blood group) is in controversy in any civil case. The empirical study of American federal discovery earlier referred to concluded that plaintiffs do not use this mechanism frequently,[1] that defendants use it in 41 per cent of the cases, a higher percentage than that of any other American federal discovery mechanism except deposition upon oral examination,[2] and that 89 per cent of the uses are by informal agreement.[3]

In England there is no discovery mechanism comparable to F.R.C.P. 35, which is available for any civil case. Broad discovery by medical examination has been available only in limited instances. English ecclesiastical courts did order examinations of women and men by physicians when divorce or annulment was sought on the ground of sexual incapacity.[4]

Equally delicate examinations of pregnant women were ordered at common law on writs *de ventre inspiciendo*.[5] This writ was used when the applicant required evidence to rebut what he anticipated would be a claim based on an impending fraudulent birth. For example, Lord Chancellor King explained that this writ was 'for the security of the next heir, to guard him against fraudulent or supposititious births'.[6] The typical procedure under the writ was in two stages.[7] First, the Chancellor issued a writ ordering the sheriff to have the woman, whom the applicant had alleged was pretending to be pregnant, viewed and searched by matrons to determine whether she were pregnant and, if so, for how long she had been pregnant; they certified their report on these questions to the Court of Common Pleas. Second, if this report certified that the woman was pregnant, the Common Pleas issued a second writ ordering the sheriff to take and keep her in custody until she delivered the child, to have matrons view her daily, and to have matrons present to witness the birth.

There is no reason to suggest that the Supreme Court of Judicature has not retained the power to order such personal examinations in cases of divorce and annulment and when a party requires evidence to rebut a future claim to be based on what he anticipates will be a feigned birth. In England examinations and tests of the person have also been authorized in limited classes of cases by occasional statutes[8] and brought about in personal-injuries cases by an exercise of the court's inherent power to stay actions. This inherent power may pave the way to making medical discovery available in all kinds of civil cases.

The first reported exercise of the inherent power to stay actions in order to encourage personal examinations was by the Court of Appeal in the 1969 case of *Edmeades* v. *Thames Board Mills, Ltd.* [1969] 2 All E.R. 127. There the plaintiff, who sought damages for personal injuries, voluntarily submitted twice to an examination by a physician of defendant's choice. Afterwards defendant received a medical report from plaintiff of his examination by his own physician who found possible 'aggravation of... osteoarthritis of the left knee'.[9] Plaintiff's statement of claim, which had been served on defendant before his physician had made his second examination, had described its injuries only as follows: 'abrasions of the left shin; swelling of the left foot, ankle and thigh; partial rupture of the quadriceps muscle'.[10] In view of defendant's expectation that plaintiff would seek and secure leave to amend his statement of claim to add aggravation of osteoarthritis of the left knee, defendant requested plaintiff to submit to examination on this injury by one of six medical specialists. Plaintiff refused to do so, but apparently offered to be examined again by the physician who had previously twice examined him for defendant but who was not included in its list of six specialists.

In the light of these facts the Court of Appeal granted defendant's application for a stay of all proceedings in the action until plaintiff should submit to be examined by one of the six doctors on defendant's list. The Court spoke but generally and briefly as to the nature of its power to grant this stay. Lord Denning, M.R., said,

This court has ample jurisdiction to grant a stay whenever it is just and reasonable to do so. It can, therefore, order a stay if the conduct of the plaintiff in refusing a reasonable request is such as to prevent the just determination of the cause. ... I think that the request of the defendants was perfectly reasonable. They were faced with a new allegation which had not been made in the statement of claim, an allegation of osteoarthritis. The defendants ought in all reason to have an opportunity of considering it and being advised on it. They would need it in order to assess the amount to pay into court so as to dispose of the whole matter without it coming to trial.[11] It might be different if the defendants had suggested one particular name to which the plaintiff could reasonably object. ... But when six names are suggested and no reasonable objection is taken to them, I have no doubt that the defendants ought to have the opportunity of having the plaintiff medically examined so that evidence can be given by one of those doctors.[12]

Widgery, L.J., agreed that 'the test ... is whether in the circumstances of the particular case it is reasonable that a stay should be ordered so that justice shall be done between the parties.'[13] Davies, L.J., joined Denning and Widgery in the decision but said nothing concerning the nature of the court's power to stay the action. The sole citation by the judges in support of their power to make this decision was the Report of the Committee on Personal Injuries Litigation, ¶ 312.[14] The pioneering decision in *Edmeades* v. *Thames Board Mills, Ltd.* stands as a beacon marking enlarged discovery by the method of medical examination. The light it casts in this direction is strong, for the plaintiff whose action was stayed pending his submission to an examination hardly had been totally unco-operative in submitting to medical examinations requested by defendant — he had voluntarily done so twice when the physician of defendant's choice 'no doubt [made] ... a general examination'[15] of plaintiff including his left knee. The *ratio decidendi* of *Edmeades*, of course, is limited to staying the action of a plaintiff who seeks damages for personal injuries and refuses a reasonable request for his medical examination concerning those very injuries.

The *Edmeades* doctrine now is well established. The holding in *Edmeades* has been reaffirmed by the Court of Appeal in *Starr* v. *National Coal Board*[16] and *Lane* v. *Willis*.[17] Moreover, an *obiter dictum* by Lord MacDermott in *S.* v. *S.*[18] not only says of *Edmeades* and its progeny that 'the jurisdiction of the High Court to order such an examination[19] cannot ... be questioned in this day and age', but also amplifies the nature of the inherent court power employed in *Edmeades* as follows:

Much of the jurisdiction of the High Court can only be made effective by indirect means — such as a stay of proceedings... This is very much the case in... the... inherent jurisdiction to make interlocutory orders for the purpose of promoting a fair and satisfactory trial... It is a jurisdiction which confers powers, in the exercise of a judicial discretion, to prepare the way by suitable orders or directions for a just and proper trial. ... The rule book naturally tends to lag behind new methods of proof and ascertainment, and the essential purpose of this ancillary jurisdiction means that it cannot be tied to what is old and outmoded. For example, the increasing number of claims which put in issue the bodily condition of a party have in recent years produced [the *Edmeades* doctrine.]

Lord MacDermott thus says the court should use its inherent power to promote a 'fair and satisfactory... [,] just and proper trial'.[20] Lord Denning in *Edmeades* explained that the Court of Appeal was using this inherent power to do what was 'just and reasonable'.[21] The specific content of justice and fairness in the context of enabling a party to gain medical information about his opponent in advance of trial are the benefits of discovery discussed in Chapter 1, Section A.

These benefits do not accrue only within the *ratio decidendi* of *Edmeades*, namely, when (a) the party to be examined is a plaintiff and (b) the plaintiff's action seeks damages for his personal injuries. The benefits promise to be the same in all other instances when a party's physical or mental condition is relevant to any civil case. For example, in a case arising out of a collision with a motor vehicle driven by defendant, plaintiff may reap bountiful benefits from an examination of defendant's eyesight.[22] Hence justice and fairness should motivate the English courts to use their inherent power to bring about medical examinations both of defendants and of plaintiffs in actions for other relief than damages for personal injuries. There are dicta tending to this effect. Sacks, L.J., has implied that a plaintiff should be able to secure a medical examination of a defendant, for he has said that a showing that a party 'is unable properly to prepare his *claim* (or defence) without that examination' justifies court intervention (emphasis added)[23]. Furthermore, Lord MacDermott in *S.* v. *S.* has laid it down in effect both that medical examinations should be brought about in other than personal-injury cases and that defendants are subject to being examined. In *S.* v. *S.* paternity was an issue in actions seeking support or provision for children. In Lord MacDermott's speech he expressed the view that the courts have just as much inherent power to order blood-grouping tests of the mother and putative father as to order the knee examination in *Edmeades*.[24]

Lord MacDermott's expansive view seems to have been shared by the Committee on Personal Injuries Litigation, which was cited in *Edmeades*.[25] The Committee on Supreme Court Practice and Procedure, however, did not favour a broad power to order examinations and tests of all parties in all kinds of civil litigation.[26] This Committee would not even go to the extent of *Edmeades*. It advanced three reasons for its opposition to the discovery mechanism of physical and mental examinations.[27]

Its first reason is concern for the liberty of the subject.[28] This goal of liberty from compulsory medical examinations is a worthy one. However, an equally worthy goal is justice in the form of the benefits of discovery, such as ascertainment of truth at the trial by virtue of medical evidence which would be unavailable if the court did not have power to bring about a party's medical examination.[29] These two goals often will clash when one party resists his opponent's request for a medical examination. The enlightened way to resolve this clash is to weigh these goals not in the abstract but on a scale which reflects the facts and context of the particular case. Liberty from a medical examination will not always tip the scale over justice.[30] Hence English courts should not lack the power to bring about medical examinations when they find it 'reasonable' to do so, that is, when they so balance the clashing goals. The statutory and common-law precedents of medical examinations discussed above indicate that Parliament and the courts have disagreed with the proposition that liberty as an unbending absolute must always prevail over justice.

Concern for liberty of the subject, however, has led, and should continue to lead, courts to take pains to shape orders bringing about medical examinations to the sensibilities and convenience of the party to be examined. For example, if it is unreasonable under all the circumstances for a particular doctor to do the examination, a party may successfully object to that doctor.[31] When a married woman was the subject of a writ *de ventre inspiciendo*, the customary order that the sheriff keep her in custody until she delivered her child was not made if her husband entered a recognizance that she would not leave their home, for a married woman 'ought to cohabit with her husband'.[32] In carrying out this writ Lord Chancellor King requested 'giving reasonable notice [of examination] before hand, so that this may be attended with as little inconvenience as possible to the young lady'.[33] Similar solicitude for the liberty of the subject doubtlessly would continue to be exhibited by those administering a general power to order medical examinations in all civil litigation.

The second reason of the Committee on Supreme Court Practice and Procedure for opposing discovery by medical examinations is that plaintiffs in personal-injuries litigation rarely decline to permit a medical examination requested by defendants. This is true.[34] But it is no solace to the defendant who is handicapped by a rare refusal. Moreover, no similar statistical conclusion has been advanced for defendants in such litigation, the quality of whose eyesight, for example, may be in issue, and for litigants in other types of litigation who may well not share the incentives to be examined voluntarily which motivate claimants for personal injuries.

Its final reason seems to be that 'the comment which could be made at the trial, in the event of his declining to submit to examination, is sufficient to deter...[a litigant] from refusing.' A comparable comment on refusal to allow inspection of property voluntarily was available at common law.[35] Apparently it was not sufficient to deter refusals, for despite its availability, litigants at common law to a significant extent resorted for property inspection to bills for discovery in equity in aid of their legal actions, as noted by the Common Law Commission of 1853.[36]

Surely the threat of adverse comment will not deter refusal if the personal examination or test is indispensable for a party to make out the necessary elements of his claim or defence. Nor will it do so if the party refusing has a plausible explanation for the court which therefore may not infer that he refused for fear of exposing a weakness in his position. Examples of such plausible alternative explanations are the outrage displayed by women accused of feigning pregnancy in applications for writs *de ventre inspiciendo*[37] and the distress professed by widows today at the prospect of being examined to determine their life expectancy when they seek damages for deprivation of future support by a husband killed by the defendant's alleged negligence.[38]

On the other hand, if the threat of adverse comment usually leads to voluntary submission to examinations and if for this or other reasons most litigants are willing to be examined, then the liberty of the subject will rarely suffer by a general power to bring about discovery examinations and tests of the person in all civil litigation. This power will, however, foster justice in the sense of the subject's liberty from false claims and capability to secure relief for just claims.[39]

Whether a general authority to bring about discovery by medical examination is instituted through use of the inherent power of the courts or by rule does not fundamentally matter.[40] But whatever the nature of the authority to bring about medical examinations of parties other than plaintiffs in personal-injuries cases, the sanction for refusing an examination cannot be limited to a stay of plaintiff's action, as it is under the *Edmeades* doctrine. A stay patently is inapplicable to defendants. Moreover, even for plaintiffs a stay will not always be the most effective and appropriate sanction, especially in cases where plaintiffs do not seek to recover for the injuries to be examined.

To enforce discovery by medical examination the English court at its discretion should select the sanction most appropriate to the circumstances of the case at bar. Certainly the available sanctions should include all variants of *pro confesso*: for example, default judgment, dismissal, stay, striking out claims or defences, taking facts to be established, and prohibiting introduction of designated evidence. However, the deep-seated English goal of the liberty, inviolability, and privacy of the subject should prevent employment of the imprisonment aspect of the contempt sanction.[41] This is because the value of liberty which some find involved in freedom from examination by a doctor is closer to the value of freedom from confinement in gaol than it is to the value of being free to fully prosecute, or defend against, a claim. Furthermore, the *pro confesso* sanctions, including dismissal against a plaintiff and default judgment against a defendant, should always be efficacious to do justice without imprisoning a recalcitrant party. The fine aspect of the contempt sanction, however, should be permissible, since a money fine does not intrude into the value of liberty any more than *pro confesso* sanctions like stays which burden the money or property interests of civil litigants.

Restriction of Discovery by 'Own Case' Rule

In England before the Judicature Acts merged law and equity the 'own case' rule was a pervasive restriction on discovery.[1] It limited discovery to information tending to help one's own case, that is, to help the case or defence of the party seeking discovery.[2] Conversely, it prohibited discovery of information tending to help the case or defence of the party from whom it was sought.[3]

A. APPLICATION OF THE RULE IN ENGLAND.

1. 'FACT-EVIDENCE' RULE

Since the Judicature Acts the 'own case' rule has not been applied to admissions[4] and was abrogated for documents by the Civil Evidence Act 1968, S. 16(2). But the 'own case' rule has continued to be applicable to inspection of real and personal property[5] and to interrogatories.[6]

In the same period beginning with the Judicature Acts,[7] and usually in the very same cases,[8] when the 'own case' rule has been recognized as applying to interrogatories, a new 'fact-evidence' rule also has been recognized. This rule prohibits interrogatories which would reveal 'evidence', regardless of whose case or defence is helped by the 'evidence'; it limits allowable interrogatories to those revealing 'facts', regardless of whose case or defence is helped by the 'facts'. The decisions recognizing both the 'own case' and 'fact-evidence' rules have been ambiguous on which the court was applying.[9] A decision would not be ambiguous if the nature of the interrogatory in question were such that it would be allowed under one rule but disallowed under the other. This would be so (a) when the interrogatory calls for evidence which helps the case or defence of the interrogating party and (b) when the interrogatory calls for a fact which helps the case or defence of the interrogated party. Thus the 'fact-evidence' rule, which has been applied only to interrogatories, in different instances may have both a more and a less restrictive effect on discovery than the 'own case' rule.

2. DEFINITION OF 'OWN CASE'

The restrictive effect of the 'own case' rule on all mechanisms of discovery has been relaxed by construing the allegations made by a party seeking discovery, which negative or impeach his opponent's case or defence, to be part of the first party's own case or defence. After initial doubts, this construction became well settled in equity and under common-law statutes[10] and has continued unabated since the Judicature Acts.[11] The construction relaxes the restrictive effect of the rule far more if a party seeking discovery may avail himself of it by generally denying his opponent's case or defence without specifying defects. Usually, since the Judicature Acts, such specification has not been required.[12]

However, in one case the Court of Appeal disallowed interrogatories on the basis *inter alia* that they were 'fishing'.[13] Since another basis for this decision was the 'own case' rule and since the party seeking discovery had not specified a defect in his opponent's case, the decision suggests that denials of discovery as 'fishing' may on scrutiny prove to be applications of the 'own case' rule in which the case of the party seeking discovery is not construed to include his allegations negativing or impeaching his opponent's case unless the party specifies defects in it.[14]

B. PROHIBITION OF DISCOVERY OF WITNESSES IN ENGLAND

Just as, before the Judicature Acts, the 'own case' rule prevented a party from learning by discovery whom his opponent would call as witnesses at trial,[15] so afterwards in England interrogatories have not been proper for this purpose alone, although the identity of people who turn out to be witnesses may be revealed incidentally in an answer to interrogatories which are proper for another purpose.[16] For example, to help plaintiff in a slander action locate witnesses whose testimony would tend to prove publication, an interrogatory was allowed which called for the names of people in whose presence defendant uttered the alleged slander.[17]

C. DISADVANTAGES OF ENGLISH 'OWN CASE' AND 'FACT-EVIDENCE' RULES

The 'own case' rule should be abrogated in England in respect to interrogatories and inspection of property, as it has been in respect to documents by the Civil Evidence Act 1968, s.16(2) Rationales advanced for it are not persuasive.

The rationale advanced in English equity, and the cardinal one advanced since the Judicature Acts, is avoiding perjury and subornation of perjury at trial by a dishonest party desiring to counter evidence favouring his opponent which the party learns of by discovery.[18] Even assuming that litigants are dishonest and that this dishonesty will go undetected, as this rationale does, the 'own case' rule facilitates perjury and subornation of perjury at trial by a party whom the rule excuses from giving information supporting his side of the case and opposing his opponent's. It does so by enabling him to surprise his opponent by presenting false or misleading evidence at trial[19] which his opponent might have exposed as such had he been aware of it long enough before trial to have had time to find and marshal contradictory evidence. This has been recognized as a disadvantage of the 'own case' rule both *a priori* and *a posteriori*.[20] It is not circumvented by adjournments of trials or orders for new trials on the ground of surprise, as Jessel, M.R., has argued.[21] In the English adversary system committed to a climactic, continuous, single trial, neither adjournments nor new trials are lightly ordered. Nor are they likely to be ordered on the ground of surprising evidence, in view of the value-judgment behind the 'own case' rule, namely, 'that the possible mischiefs of surprise at a trial are more than counterbalanced by the danger of perjury'.[22] This is because an adjournment or new trial would afford a party wanting to counter his opponent's evidence against him the very time to frame carefully his own perjury or suborn it from a witness which the 'own case' rule is designed to deny him. For this reason, to the extent that Jessel or other judges ordered adjournments or new trials owing to surprising evidence, *pro tanto* did they abrogate the value-judgment enshrined in the 'own case' rule. Abrogating the rule itself, however, is a far less expensive and dilatory route to the same end.

The most reliable safeguard against potential undetected perjury of both sorts — fabrications to counter damaging evidence and surprising fabrications first presented at trial — would be the repeal of the 'own case' rule.

[F]ull and prompt *mutual* disclosure probably tends to minimize the danger of, and the opprotunity for, fabrication that unilateral disclosure might afford, since the potential fabricator is himself tied down in his version of the occurrence before a material chance for fabrication is offered.[23]

This safeguard now generally prevails for documents under R.S.C. 1965, 0.24, which orders mutual, mandatory disclosure.[24] It would prevail in respect to interrogatories and inspection of property if the 'own case' rule were abrogated so that there could be 'full...disclosure...', if both parties sought leave for it at approximately the same point, and if the court ordered discovery by both virtually simultaneously.

Even if the latter two conditions do not come about, the assumption that without the 'own case' rule parties will commit or suborn undetected perjury in order to counter evidence against them has not materialized in other common-law jurisdictions. On the basis of field investigation in nine American states and two Canadian provinces whose discovery law was not limited by the 'own case' rule, Ragland has reported,

> Practically every lawyer and judge who was interviewed in these states was asked whether a party who is allowed to find out in advance of trial what his adversary's witnesses will testify to, is not encouraged to manufacture evidence to meet that disclosed. The uniform answer was that this had not been the experience.[25]

Nor has such perjury been reported to have been noticeable at the times and in the areas when the 'own case' rule has not inhibited discovery in England.[26] It is by no means unique that such a rule should be primarily propped up by an empirically unjustified premise of perjury.

> In the development of the law of evidence, every reform has been opposed on the same ground, — that it would tend to encourage perjury. It is hard to realize that no longer ago than 1851, Lord Brougham's Act for the first time made parties competent witnesses in civil proceedings in the superior courts. There was great dread of the act, lest the interest of parties should encourage false swearing...But the fear felt by the legal profession was groundless, as events have proved.[27]

Lindley, L.J., thought the 'own case' rule is necessary to avoid endless side-issues at trial, especially in cross-examination.[28] This consideration need give little pause. A modification in the scope of discovery affects neither the relevance and admissibility of evidence at trial nor the power of the trial court to limit cross-examination. If upon abrogation of the rule a party learns of evidence against him and secures admissible, true evidence to impeach or negative it, this will help the court to reach the right result. It is to be lauded rather than lamented.

Fletcher Moulton, L.J., defended the 'own case' rule lest a party learn that his opponent is unaware of a crucial defect in the position of the discovering party, and so be emboldened to persevere in the litigation.[29] It is correct that the 'own case' rule prohibits an interrogatory asking in effect, 'What do you know which hurts my case or defence?' However, the party who learns from the answer to this interrogatory that his opponent is unaware of a crucial defect would not be emboldened to persevere if his opponent subsequently learned of the crucial defect by discovery from him; and his opponent could do so if the 'own case' rule were abrogated. Even if what Fletcher Moulton anticipated were to happen after abrogation of the 'own case' rule, the existence of the rule encourages perseverance in litigation just as much, by preventing a party from learning the strength of his opponent's case (including defects in his own) and that his opponent is aware of it. Under the present law a party may carry the litigation to a lengthy trial, while if, by interrogatories or inspection of property, he could find out about the strength of his opponent's case, he might withdraw altogether,[30] settle on much less favourable terms than he had been demanding,[31] or concede part of the issues so that the trial would be appreciably abbreviated. Wigmore would have thought that this evil worked by the present 'own case' rule is greater than that Fletcher Moulton anticipated would be worked by abrogating the rule, for Wigmore found it a

fact of experience that the parties ... are prone to proceed with a blind faith in the strength of their cause and the truth of its essential propositions of fact, or with the misguided assumption that the facts forming its defects and weaknesses are unknown to the adversaries ...[32]

Two unarticulated, uncommendable rationales may underpin the 'own case' rule. One is the English legal 'instincts of sportsmanship',[33] 'a characteristic instinct of the Anglo-Norman community',[34] 'a racial product'[35] 'indigenous to the soil',[36] which originally in equity overpowered the influence of the English ecclesiastical courts, which knew nothing like the 'own case' rule but provided full pre-trial disclosure of evidence.[37] This instinct seems to linger in today's 'own case' rule, for it regards

the concealment of one's evidential resources and the preservation of the opponent's defenceless ignorance as a fair and irreproachable accompaniment of the game of litigation[38] [; and] one of the cardinal moral assumptions in a contest of skill or chance is that a player need not betray beforehand his strength of resource, and that the opponent cannot complain of being surprised.[39]

Yet

so far as practicable, the system of pre-trial procedure should prevent the trial system from ... continuing to be somewhat of a chance or a game because the parties are left in ignorance of each other's case until the trial, but on the contrary it should be designed to reveal what the case of each party is before the trial to encourage settlements, avoid the attendance of witnesses whose evidence is uncontroversial, and reduce the numbers of unnecessary trials and the length of others.[40]

The second possible uncommendable, unarticulated rationale for the 'own case' rule is the legal profession's interest in not losing fees should the abolition of the rule have this net effect.[41] By expanding discovery it would be likely to increase the costs of preparing interrogatories, hearings on applications for leave to interrogate and inspect property, preparation of answers to interrogatories, and the conduct of inspections of property. On the other hand, the abolition of the rule would be likely to diminish costs by making preparation for trial less expensive[42] and particularly by avoiding or shortening trials, where the bulk of costs accumulates,[43] in the ways which have been mentioned in the present Section. It also might well reduce costs indirectly by eliminating what must now be a major reason parties make little use of several cost-saving methods of presenting their evidence at trial. Now if parties present evidence in their favour by the traditional method of oral testimony, they do not have to disclose it to their adversaries before trial. But before they will be granted leave on a summons for directions to present this evidence more cheaply by, say, affidavit or a copy of a newspaper, they must disclose it to their adversaries. They may well conclude that the saving of cost does not compensate for losing the tactical advantage of surprise at trial. But if, owing to the abolition of the 'own case' rule, they will have already disclosed the evidence to their adversaries in discovery, they will lose no tactical advantage of surprise by employing one of the cost-saving methods of presenting evidence.[44]

None of the rationales asserted for the 'own case' rule are worth its price of denying society the benefits of discovery, which have been sketched in Section A of Chapter 1. The rather turbulent history of assaults against the rule has partly succeeded in realizing these benefits, especially by construing a party's 'own case' to include what negatives or impeaches his opponent's;[45] and for documents by the Civil Evidence Act 1968, s.16(2). Concerning interrogatories and inspection of property, the rule is indeed 'out of harmony with the principles which ought to regulate civil litigation'.[46] As a vestige of the misconception of litigation as a game in which victory goes to the more skilful rather than as a social instrument in which the verdict goes to the more just, the rule gainsays the trend of today's enlightened legal thinking.[47] It is high time it were extirpated from English law.

Removing the 'own case' rule from the law of interrogatories might be opposed with the argument that it prevents a party from learning whom his opponent's legal advisers plan to call as witnesses at trial and what evidence his legal advisers plan to offer at trial. This is true, but only incidental to the rationales of the 'own case' rule discussed above. If it is desirable to withhold from a party the tactical plans or other advice of the other party's legal advisers, let the legal professional privilege perform this function.[48] If it does so, then the reason for the restriction will be more evident than when the restriction is papered over by the 'own case' or 'fact-evidence' rule. Except when one of these rules applies, the identity and location of potential witnesses in the sense of people who may have or lead a party to find admissible evidence has long been a proper subject for interrogatories.[49] The Report of the Committee on Personal Injuries Litigation, p. 104 rejects a proposal for 'an exchange of names and addresses of potential witnesses' without giving any reasons except for a reference to 'a common law atmosphere...' The Final Report of the Committee on Supreme Court Practice and Procedure concluded that generally 'there is no great point and some appreciable risk in a compulsory disclosure of witnesses' names...'[50] It does not spell out the nature of this risk. Perhaps both Reports have in mind witnesses to whom the legal professional privilege should apply. This seems true in the former Report from its reference to 'a common law atmosphere' and its description of '*opposing parties' witness . . .*' While no party has proprietary rights over any potential witness, those a party's legal advisers plan to call at trial are commonly referred to as that party's witnesses. The same seems true in the latter Report, for it reaches its conclusion about witnesses' names in conjunction with considering exchange of witnesses' proofs. In any event, neither Report proposes giving lawyers a special privilege protecting from discovery the identity of people who may have or lead to admissible evidence. Yet, except where the legal professional privilege applies, the identity of such people, who are potential witnesses, should not be privileged from disclosure by interrogatories once the 'own case' and 'fact-evidence' rules are abrogated. This is because they are the only analytically discernible principles which authorities could have relied on in disallowing interrogatories seeking this information.

No rationale for the 'fact-evidence' rule alone as a restriction on interrogatories has been enunciated. If the rationale is to curb inordinately detailed interrogatories, the oppressiveness objection, to say nothing of the court's discretion in granting leave to interrogate, is sufficient for this purpose. The rationales asserted for the 'own case' rule come no closer to justifying denial of the benefits of discovery by the 'fact-evidence' rule than they do by the 'own case' rule itself. The former rule obviously is less desirable than the latter when the former would deny discovery the latter would permit; the 'fact-evidence' rule does this by preventing discovery of an opponent's 'evidence' which helps the interrogating party's case or defence.[51]

The 'fact-evidence' rule should be abrogated for three additional reasons. First, its semantic hollowness, which probably reflects the want of a reasoned policy behind it, makes it difficult to apply. For example, in *Nash* v. *Layton*, an issue was whether plaintiff had been a money-lender. The interrogatories in question asked plaintiff whether during a relevant period he had lent money and renewed loans, and for what security, of what amounts, and at what rates of interest. The three Court of Appeal judges tested these interrogatories by the 'fact-evidence' rule. Fletcher-Moulton, L.J., felt they should be disallowed as seeking 'evidence', not 'facts'.[52] Yet Cozens-Hardy, M.R., and Buckley, L.J., held that they were proper as seeking 'facts', not 'evidence'.[53] Neither characterization can be said to be wrong. If the answers to these interrogatories turned out to be other than wholly negative, they would contain 'facts' which defendant would be expected to offer in 'evidence'. The meaninglessness of a 'fact-evidence' dichotomy[54] also may be seen from the following illustration of it given by Buckley, L.J.:

Suppose for instance the question of fact was whether a man sold sugar. It would be evidence of that fact that A went to his shop and bought sugar, that B went to his shop and bought sugar, and so on. But that would be mere evidence on the dispute whether he sold sugar or not.[55]

But surely what Buckley, L.J., says would be 'evidence' are also 'facts' according to the usual meaning of 'fact'. If by 'fact' Buckley means a matter on which the court gives judgment or must rule in order to give judgment, then the 'fact-evidence' rule, so construed, would render interrogatories exceedingly rarely available.

Second, often it has been ambiguous whether the 'fact-evidence' or 'own case' rule was being used, as pointed out in Section A1 of this Chapter. This ambiguity often reflects obscurity in objections to interrogatories, which in turn reflects the method for objecting to interrogatories since the Judicature Acts. Objections have not been stated in formal writings, as have objections to discovery of documents in lists or affidavits of documents. Instead objections to interrogatories have been stated informally, flexibly, and sometimes merely orally, primarily at hearings on applications for leave to administer interrogatories.[56] The consequence of this obscurity and ambiguity is that it is difficult to predict whether the 'own case' or 'fact-evidence' rule will be applied. Such unpredictability makes it hard to advise clients and encourages avoidable contests and appeals over applications for leave to interrogate. The 'fact-evidence' rule thus entails two undesirable, cumulative levels of uncertainty—whether the 'fact-evidence' or 'own case' rule will be used and how the semantically hollow 'fact-evidence' dichotomy will be applied.

A third reason to abrogate the 'fact-evidence' rule is this. By definition of the 'own case' rule, any discovery it would allow, but which the 'fact-evidence' rule would deny, would either support the case of the party interrogating or negative or impeach the case of his opponent. For the 'fact-evidence' rule to deny discovery of such information is for it to deny a significant antidote against one of the excesses of a game-like adversary

Ralph W. Porter

system. The English adversary system places no obligation on a party voluntarily to inform the court of factual matters supporting his opponent's case or negativing or impeaching his own.[57] He must of course reveal them if his opponent questions him about them in the box at trial. But if his opponent has not learned of these factual matters by discovery or otherwise before trial, his opponent may well not question the other party about them at trial lest the answers redound to the benefit of the other party or even embarrass his opponent in the eyes of the court for having asked such questions. Such questions may be the 'one question too many' which every careful cross-examiner strives to avoid but which he would not hesitate to ask in an interrogatory. Thus by denying discovery of these factual matters, the 'fact-evidence' rule may indirectly but indisputably prevent the court from learning of them, and so from reaching the right result. Even if the adversary system is not discredited in this fashion, it may be similarly sullied if the opponent is led by his ignorance of these factual matters to agree to a compromise settlement which he would have rejected out of hand had he learned of them by interrogatories.

1. FISHING

If the 'own case' rule is not abrogated in respect to interrogatories and inspection of property, as it should be, the courts should be careful to continue to construe it as permitting discovery of matters which negative or impeach an opponent's case or defence and not to require the party seeking such discovery to specify the defects in his opponent's case which he anticipates will be revealed.[58] Otherwise, discovery will be severely limited, and the antidote against the excess of the adversary system which has just been set forth will become unavailable except for matters supporting the case of the party seeking discovery. The courts should be particularly wary of facile objections of 'fishing' which on scrutiny are demands that a party specify defects in his opponent's case before being permitted to have discovery of what impeaches or negatives it.[59]

D. F.R.C.P. 26(b) (1)

In the American federal courts the 'own case' rule has been thoroughly abrogated, for F.R.C.P. 26(b)(1), which applies to all discovery mechanisms,[60] provides,

Parties may obtain discovery regarding any matter, not privileged, which is relevant to the subject matter involved in the pending action, *whether it relates* to the claim or defense of the party seeking discovery or *to the claim or defense of any other party* ... (emphasis added)[61]

1. RESTRICTION ON DISCOVERY OF WITNESSES BY 'OWN CASE' RULE

Under the reign of the 'own case' rule in England, a party has not been permitted to learn by discovery whom his opponent has planned to call as witnesses at trial.[62] Despite F.R.C.P. 26(b)(1), quoted just above, which has toppled this rule from its reign, most American federal courts have reached the same result.[63] While they have not expressed the 'own case' rule or its various rationales as the bases of their decisions, they may well have embraced this rule, at least subliminally. They may no longer do so for expert witnesses, for in 1970, F.R.C.P. 26 was amended to provide,

A party may through interrogatories require any other party to identify each person whom the other party expects to call as an expert witness at trial, to state the subject matter on which the expert is expected to testify, and to state the substance of the facts and opinions to which the expert is expected to testify and a summary of the grounds for each opinion. F.R.C.P. 26(b)(4)(A)(i)[64]

Even though most American federal courts have marched to the drum of the 'own case' rule when discovery of trial witnesses has been sought by discovery, they have left its ranks by ordering this information to be disclosed at pre-trial conferences.[65] Disclosure at such a conference, at which counsel appear before the court and which usually takes place shortly before trial, is not an adequate substitute for disclosure of trial witnesses on discovery, for it is optional. Furthermore, 'in some [federal] districts ... its use is confined to selected cases, and in ... others it has been resorted to perfunctorily if at all'.[66]

The party who may not learn whom his opponent plans to call as witnesses by discovery or at a pre-trial conference is not at a complete loss. In American federal courts, as in England,[67] he may learn by discovery the identity of all potential witnesses for his opponent, since F.R.C.P. 26(b)(1) expressly entitles him to 'obtain discovery ... of ... the identity and location of persons having knowledge of any discoverable matter'.[68] If the discovering party's desire is to interview or depose[69] all potential witnesses against him, it does not commend the American federal judicial system to identify for him the larger group from whom his opponent's witnesses must be drawn, while denying him identification of those in this group whom his opponent plans to use as witnesses. To the extent that he interviews or deposes people whom his opponent does not plan to call as witnesses solely in order to find out what they may testify against him,[70] he goes on a fool's errand. To that extent, his respect for the law will decline. To be sure, he may engage in what turns out to be unnecessary effort even if by discovery he is permitted to learn whom his opponent plans to call as witnesses. His opponent's list of intended witnesses may honestly be very tentative when he provides it in response to discovery. The realities of trial tactics may leave it very tentative up to the moment his opponent at trial decides to say, 'I rest'. Yet this unnecessary effort will never exceed, and usually will be less than, that made when a party does not have a right to learn whom an opponent *plans to call* as witnesses.

F.R.C.P. 26(b)(1) should be amended to make clear that there is such a right to discovery.[71] This amendment should reflect the realities of trial practice by not requiring disclosure of who *will be* his witnesses at trial. Early in a case a party's response that he has not yet planned who his witnesses will be may well be perfectly appropriate. His adversary would be free to ask him again closer to the time of trial (see F.R.C.P. 26(a); cf. F.R.C.P. 33(b), 36(a)). Whenever a party who had answered this inquiry decided he might use an additional witness, he would be under a duty to inform his adversary as F.R.C.P. 26(e)(2) now stands, for it requires seasonable amendment of a prior response if a failure to do so 'is in substance a knowing concealment'. If, a reasonable time before resting at trial, he decided not to use a witness whom he had included in his response, he might not be held obligated to inform his adversary under F.R.C.P. 26(e) as it now stands—disclosing too much probably would not be held 'in substance a knowing concealment' under F.R.C.P. 26(e)(2); and F.R.C.P. 26(e)(1)(A)'s requirement to 'supplement' a response giving 'the identity and location of persons having knowledge of discoverable matters' probably would not be held to cover deleting a member of a narrower group.[72] Yet if the time permits, a party should be obligated to inform his adversary that he no longer plans to use a witness, lest his adversary unnecessarily interview or depose the person, or rely to his prejudice on the expectation that the person will be available to testify for him because his opponent will have him present at the trial. Hence F.R.C.P. 26(e) also should be amended to require a party who has provided his opponent with a list of his intended witnesses at trial to notify his opponent when he decides to drop a person from this list.[73]

2. DISCOVERY OF AMERICAN CONTENTIONS

One of the results of the 'own case' rule in England was, at times, to prevent discovery of an opponent's contentions.[74] While not expressly relying on the 'own case' rule, some, but not all, American federal courts reached the same result before the 1970 amendments to the F.R.C.P.[75] These amendments to F.R.C.P. 33 and 36 have extirpated this remnant of the 'own case' rule.[76]

The 1970 amendment to F.R.C.P. 33 provides,

An interrogatory otherwise proper is not necessarily objectionable merely because an answer to the interrogatory involves an opinion or contention that relates to fact or the application of law to fact[77] but the court may order that such an interrogatory need not be answered until after designated discovery has been completed or until a pre-trial conference or other later time. F.R.C.P. 33(b)

Such an interrogatory, like all other Rule 33 interrogatories, must be answered 'by the party served' 'in writing under oath'.[78] This is undesirable for two reasons. First, the party himself usually does not know what his relevant contentions are. He knows facts. He engages an attorney to formulate his contentions on the basis of the facts he lays before him and learned by the attorney's investigation.[79] Second, an attorney may advise a client that his contentions should be stated inconsistently, alternatively, or hypothetically until the attorney gains additional information by discovery or at trial, as authorized for pleadings by F.R.C.P. 8(e)(2). It denigrates the oath for it to be applied to inconsistent, alternative, or hypothetical contentions, especially since the party customarily signs what his attorney writes without reading or fully understanding it.[80] Hence F.R.C.P. 33(b) should be amended to provide that if a party is represented by an attorney, his attorney should sign the answers to interrogatories involving 'an opinion or contention that relates to...the application of law to fact'. It also should provide that such answers are not to be made under oath. An attorney would feel no more comfortable in taking an oath to inconsistent contentions than would a layman. An attorney's answer should, however, be made subject to the obligations in F.R.C.P. 11, as are pleadings under F.R.C.P. 8(e)(2). These obligations are that the purpose of his answer is not to cause delay, that he has not inserted scandalous or indecent matter in the answer, and that to the best of his knowledge, information, and belief there is good ground to support the answer. The obligations of Rule 11 hardly may be expected to be more readily disregarded than those of the oath, for Rule 11 provides, 'For a willful violation of this rule an attorney may be subjected to appropriate disciplinary action.'

The undesirable requirement in this context of Rule 33 that answers be made by a party under oath is not shared by Rule 36. It also was amended in 1970 to permit requests to admit 'the truth of any matters... that relate to... opinions of fact or of the application of law to fact...' (F.R.C.P. 36(a)). It should be observed that the Rule 36 amendment says only 'opinions', while the Rule 33 amendment says 'opinion or contention'. The omission of the word 'contention' in Rule 36 does not necessarily mean that the admissions mechanism is unavailable for discovery of contentions.[81] Rule 36 expressly authorizes a request to admit 'matters... that relate to... opinions... of the application of law to fact...'; and lawyers refer to such opinions as contentions. Moreover, if under Rule 36 a party admits that at the time of an accident in question A was acting as the servant of B, this admission is, owing to the Rule 36(b) effect of an admission, equivalent to an admission that the party will not contend at the trial that A was not acting as the servant of B at the time of the accident.[82] Yet the former admission is surely one of an opinion about application of law to fact, and so within the explicit language of Rule 36(a) as amended in 1970. Since the request to admit that A was acting as the servant of B is authorized, its equivalent, namely, the request to admit that the party will not contend that A was not acting as the servant of B, should he held authorized as well.

Furthermore, the principal rationales for these amendments to Rules 33 and 36 were essentially the same, and these rationales call for discovery of contentions.[83] The rationale for the Rule 36 amendment is that 'an admission on a matter of opinion may... narrow the issues[84]... [A]dmissions function very much as pleadings do... The broadening of the rule to encompass mixed questions of law and fact reinforces this feature.'[85] Similarly, the rationale for the Rule 33 amendment is that 'requests for opinions or contentions that call for the application of law to fact... can be most useful in narrowing and sharpening the issues.'[86]

This rationale of discovery in terms of narrowing the issues must be understood against the background of the extremely general pleading in the American federal legal system. For example, under the F.R.C.P.

a plaintiff... 'sets forth a claim for relief' when he makes 'a short and plain statement of the claim showing that the pleader is entitled to relief [Rule 8(a)(2)]'....Form 9...attached to the Rules, 'intended to indicate...the simplicity and brevity of statement which the rules contemplate',[87] contains this concise allegation of negligence: 'defendant negligently drove a motor vehicle against plaintiff who was then crossing said highway'.[88]

Since 1948 bills of particulars have been unavailable to add flesh to such bare bones of general pleadings.[89] Hence even before the 1970 amendments to Rules 33 and 36, American federal authorities, unlike their counterparts in England, where particulars are available,[90] have looked to 'discovery...to disclose more precisely the basis of both claim and defense and to define more narrowly the disputed facts and issues'.[91]

This use of discovery of contentions to give parties an option to convert their opponents' general pleadings into detailed positions and thus narrow the issues apparently crystallized in the 1970 amendments to F.R.C.P. 33 and 36, since their purpose was to narrow the issues, as has been seen. But one may not be certain that this has taken place, for the same Advisory Committee which drafted these amendments and which articulated this purpose has taken a contradictory position on Rule 33.

It has said in respect to the contentions amendment to Rule 33,

The general rule governing the use of answers to interrogatories is that under ordinary circumstances they do not limit proof. See, e.g., *McElroy* v. *United Air Lines, Inc.*, 21 F.R.D. 100 (W.D. Mo. 1967); *Pressley* v. *Boehlke*, 33 F.R.D. 316, 317 (W.D. N.C. 1963). Although in exceptional circumstances reliance on an answer may cause such prejudice that the court will hold the answering party bound to his answer, e.g., *Zielinski* v. *Philadelphia Piers, Inc.*, 139 F.Supp. 408 (E.D. Pa. 1956), *the interrogating party will ordinarily not be entitled to rely on the unchanging character of the answers he receives and cannot base prejudice on such reliance*[92] (emphasis added, except to cases)

But if he is not entitled to rely on the unchanging character of the contentions in his opponent's answers to interrogatories, inasmuch as his opponent is free at trial to seek a verdict based on other contentions, then these answers to interrogatories do not narrow the issues. The interrogating party must still prepare to meet other issues. If the interrogatory asks, 'What does plaintiff contend defendant did or failed to do which constitutes negligence', and plaintiff answers, 'Defendant was inattentive to approaching traffic', defendant must still prepare to meet contentions at trial that he was negligent in a host of other ways, such as driving at an excessive rate of speed and failing to keep his brakes in working order. If the Advisory Committee really intended that the interrogating party should not be entitled to rely on contentions stated in an answer as limiting proof at trial, then the only utility of authorizing interrogatories about contentions is to enable a party to learn of possible contentions he may not have imagined which he must prepare to meet in addition to all those he thinks of on his own.

If the purpose of allowing discovery of contentions really is to narrow the issues, as the Advisory Committee has said, then the interrogating party must be held entitled to rely on the fact that at the trial he will not without reasonable notice be confronted with contentions different from those in the answer to interrogatories.[93] The legal system cannot have it both ways. The three cases cited by the Advisory Committee against having it in the way which narrows the issues are not insuperable barriers. Since they were decided before the 1970 amendments, they may be held not to apply to Rule 33 as amended in order to narrow the issues. If the party who answers an interrogatory by giving his contentions decides before trial to raise different contentions, he should notify his adversary by an amended answer. His adversary would then be in a position to pursue discovery concerning the new contentions. If he should fail to notify his adversary, this failure often would violate F.R.C.P. 26(e) as 'in substance a knowing concealment' and so be subject to sanctions.[94]

Moreover, if the purpose of narrowing the issues by discovery is to prevail, the narrowing should not be inordinately rigid. Discovery of contentions 'should have a limiting effect on the scope of proof at the trial just as if the matters involved were stated in the pleadings...'[95] This limiting effect, however, should not be the inflexible one 'of discarded devices which narrowed issues at the cost of substantive justice'.[96] It should be made compatible with securing substantive justice by amending F.R.C.P. 33(b) and 36(a) so that contentions defining issues disclosed in discovery will be subject to a provision like F.R.C.P. 15(b).[97] This Rule now provides,

When issues not raised by the pleadings are tried by express or implied consent of the parties, they shall be treated in all respects as though they had been raised in the pleadings. Such amendment of the pleadings as may be necessary to cause them to conform to the evidence and to raise these issues may be made upon motion of any party at any time, even after judgment; but failure so to amend does not affect the result of the trial of these issues. If evidence is objected to at the trial on the ground that it is not within the issues made by the pleadings, the court may allow the pleadings to be amended and shall do so freely when the presentation of the merits of the action will be subserved thereby and the objecting party fails to satisfy the court that the admission of such evidence would prejudice him in maintaining his action or defense upon the merits. The court may grant a continuance to enable the objecting party to meet such evidence.

The amendment to tie the flexible notion of F.R.C.P. 15(b) to issues revealed by discovery would of course substitute 'discovery' for 'pleadings' in the wording of F.R.C.P. 15(b). To achieve the purpose of narrowing the issues, 'prejudice' in the penultimate sentence of Rule 15(b) must be permitted to be based on reliance on statements of contentions in answers to interrogatories, contrary to the Advisory Committee note to Rule 33(b) quoted above. Even when there would be such prejudice, this penultimate sentence permits the court flexibly to achieve substantive justice — at its discretion the court may allow amendment of the statements of contentions, so that a party who had not stated a contention of claim or defence on the merits before trial will not be foreclosed from taking this position at trial. If the court exercises its discretion to allow the amendment at trial, the last sentence of Rule 15(b) empowers the court to grant a continuance to enable the opponent, who had relied on the expectation that the only contentions he would have to meet at trial would be those disclosed on discovery, to prepare to meet the additional contention by discovery and other means.[98] Thus sound exercise of judicial discretion will mean that a party will have to prepare to face contentions not disclosed by discovery only when it becomes clear that his adversary will advance them. Even in this event he will have been spared the burden of preparing to face all possible additional contentions his adversary might have made. On the other hand, in a case of prejudice resulting from relying on contentions disclosed in discovery, if the court in exercising the discretion conferred by the penultimate sentence of Rule 15(b) decided not to allow an amendment at trial, the opponent will have avoided the expense and delay of preparing to meet any contentions not disclosed by discovery.[99] The penultimate sentence of Rule 15(b) also means of course that the mere fact that a party did not disclose a contention on discovery will not bar him from making the contention at trial, so long as his opponent is not prejudiced by the absence of advance notice of it.

Unless F.R.C.P. 33(b) is construed to entitle the interrogating party to rely on the fact that he will not be confronted at trial to his prejudice by contentions other than those in answers to his interrogatories, parties will be able to secure notice of contentions which effectively narrows the issues only by using F.R.C.P. 36. Under F.R.C.P. 36(b) a party expressly is bound to Rule 36 admissions when 'withdrawal or amendment will prejudice...[his opponent] in maintaining his action or defense on the merits'.[100] Admissions that a party will not make particular contentions, for example, that he will not contend that A was not acting as the servant of B, thus will narrow the issues in a way that his opponent may rely on. As has already been discussed in the present Section, F.R.C.P. 36(a) should be held to render contentions as such proper matters of which to request admissions. Even if it is not so held, the same effect of narrowing the issues may be gained by securing an equivalent admission, for example, that A was acting as the servant of B, as has also been discussed in the present Section. But the imagination of the party seeking to narrow the issues limits the utility of admissions for this purpose.[101] He must imagine what contentions his opponent might make and then frame requests to admit that his opponent will not so contend (or that his opponent admits the contrary, if contentions may not directly be the subject of requests to admit). But by admissions he will not learn of any his opponent's contentions which he himself does not conceive of. Hence he should not use only admissions. He should also by an interrogatory ask his opponent to state his contentions. He would prepare to meet at trial the contentions revealed in answers to his interrogatories and those additional contentions which his opponent denied he would not raise in response to his requests to admit.[102]

On the assumption of this discussion that answers to interrogatories listing contentions may not be relied on as exhaus-
tive, the party still might suffer at trial by a surprising contention not listed in answers to his interrogatories, and, since he
had not thought of it, not the subject of one of his requests to
admit. Nevertheless, the party is better off for thus using
requests to admit by having avoided the need to prepare to
meet the possible contentions of his opponent eliminated by his
requests to admit. Harm to a party from a surprising contention at trial, which he would have defeated had he had time to
prepare to do so, may be prevented in all instances only if his
opponent is limited at trial to the list of contentions in his answers to interrogatories or may assert additional contentions
only within the spirit of the conditions of F.R.C.P. 15(b).

E. DISCOVERY OF INFORMATION IMPEACHING CREDIBILITY

In England R.S.C. 1965, 0.26, r.1(4) expressly directs that
leave not be granted for an interrogatory not at all tending to
bear on a substantive issue but generating an answer 'admissible in oral cross-examination of a witness'.[103] While neither
the rules nor other authorities appear to have addressed this
question in respect to mechanisms of discovery other than
interrogatories, should the question arise, there is nothing
peculiar to other mechanisms of discovery which would require
a different answer.[104] Thus; information whose only effect is to
impeach the credibility of witnesses is not subject to discovery
in England. This rule goes beyond the 'own case' rule by prohibiting discovery of information which impeaches the credibility of witnesses whose testimony will hurt the discovering party.
The American federal law on this question, however, treads the
line of discoverability drawn by the 'own case' rule. It generally
allows discovery of information whose only effect is to help the
party seeking the discovery by impeaching witnesses for his
opponent.[105] But a substantial body of American federal cases
disallows discovery of information whose only effect[106] is to
hurt this party's case by impeaching his own witnesses.[107]

The primary rationale advanced by this body of American
federal cases is the need to avoid perjury and subornation of
perjury at trial by a dishonest party wanting to counter evidence helping his opponent, as it is for the 'own case' rule
itself.[108] A leading statement of this rationale is as follows:

If every witness consistently told the truth, and none cut his cloth to the wind, little possible harm and much good might come from maximum pretrial disclosure. Experience indicates, however, that there are facile witnesses whose interest in 'knowing the truth before trial' is prompted primarily by a desire to find the most plausible way to defeat the truth.[109]

The weakness of this rationale is discussed early in Section C of this Chapter, where it is proposed that the 'own case' rule should be abrogated in all its manifestations. One such manifestation is the denial of discovery of information impeaching one's own witnesses.[110] This vestige of the 'own case' rule should be eliminated.

Discovery from Non-parties

A. GENERAL RULE AGAINST DISCOVERY FROM NON-PARTIES IN ENGLAND

In England both in equity and at common law there was no discovery from non-parties as a general rule.[1] This same general rule has prevailed since the merger of law and equity.[2] The English courts feel they lack power to order discovery from non-parties even though all parties consent to doing so.[3]

1. EXCEPTION FOR MEMBER OR OFFICER OF A CORPORATE PARTY

When a corporation or other body of persons is a party, R.S.C. 1965, 0.26, r.2[4] provides that the court may order any member or officer to answer interrogatories. The representative has not been made a party, though, as he was in equity.[5] While the applicant has been permitted to request a particular representative, the selection has been at the court's discretion.[6] The representative is not entitled to his separate costs, if any, from the interrogating party.[7] While he would have a right to indemnity by his corporation for his proper separate costs, if any, the practice is for the corporation to provide its legal advisers for its representative.

2. EXCEPTION TO DETERMINE WHOM TO SUE

Despite the general rule against discovery from non-parties, in equity a person contemplating an action for substantive relief was permitted to have discovery from a named party of the identity of the person who would be the defendant to the action, even though this named party might well become a non-party in respect to the contemplated action for substantive relief.[8] This exception to the general rule has continued since the Judicature Acts.[9]

3. EXCEPTION OF BANKER'S BOOKS EVIDENCE ACT 1879, S.7

The Banker's Books Evidence Act (42 Vict. c.11) 1879, s.7 empowered the court to order inspection 'of any entries' in a banker's books 'for any of the purposes of' a legal proceeding. When the entries refer to accounts or other affairs of a party, the statute constitutes an exception to the general rule denying discovery from non-parties, because the books are owned by the banker and are not normally in the power, possession, or custody of the party.[10] The letter of the statute seems to constitute an exception to the general rule when the entries refer to a non-party. However, the Court of Appeal has expressed conflicting views on whether it would apply the statute to entries relating to non-parties.[11] Owing to the context of this statute within an Act primarily concerning the introduction of a banker's books in evidence at trial, it has been applied only to entries admissible in evidence at trial as opposed to the broader scope of discovery in general.[12]

4. EXCEPTION FOR REAL PLAINTIFF IN INTEREST

The Court of Appeal in *Willis & Co.* v. *Baddeley* [1892] 2 Q.B. 324 created an exception to the general rule by ordering discovery from a non-party who had the real interest in the suit, but who sued in the name of a nominal party.[13] It did not think it could do so directly under the terms of the R.S.C. 1883 authorizing an order for an affidavit of documents, but it did so indirectly by ordering a stay of the nominal plaintiff's action until the non-party delivered an affidavit of documents such as he would have had to make had he been the named plaintiff.[14] Lord Esher, M.R., explained this order as follows: 'In order to prevent palpable injustice the Court by reason of its inherent jurisdiction will insist that the real plaintiff shall do all he ought to do for the purposes of justice as if his name were on the record.'[15]

5. EXCEPTION FOR DOCUMENTS AND PROPERTY IN PERSONAL—INJURIES CASES

Under the influence of the Report of the Committee on Personal Injuries Litigation,[16] Parliament in the Administration of Justic Act 1970, s.32(1)(2) empowered courts to order non-parties to disclose and produce relevant documents in their possession, custody, or power and to permit inspection of their relevant property including 'any land, chattel, or other corporeal property of any description'.[17] Regrettably, however, it clothed the courts with power to order discovery by these methods from non-parties only in cases 'in which a claim in respect of personal injuries to a person or in respect of a person's death is made...',[18] although discovery from non-parties in other kinds of cases may be as or more desirable. The statute authorized rules to be made to carry out the power it confers.[19] It required that rules be made to ensure that costs incurred by the non-party be awarded to him unless the court otherwise directs.[20]

The rules made to carry out this power to order discovery from non-parties are R.S.C. 1965, 0.24, r. 7A, for documents and 0.29, r. 7A, for property. These rules provide that an originating summons and affidavit must be served on the non-party and all parties.[21] The affidavit must describe the document or property sought to be inspected and show that it is relevant to the personal-injuries case; concerning documents the affidavit also must show that the non-party 'is likely to have or have had them in his possession, custody or power'.[22] Such an order 'may be made conditional on the applicant's giving security for the costs of the person against whom it is made or on such other terms, if any, as the court thinks just...'[23] 0.24, r. 7A(6)(b) provides that a non-party shall not be compelled to produce any documents which he might not be compelled to produce by subpoena duces tecum at the trial. 0.29, r. 7A–(7) does not explicitly vest in the non-party all the bases for resisting discovery available to a party, for it says only that the Court shall not order inspection of property if this 'would result in the disclosure of information relating to a secret process, discovery or invention not in issue in the proceedings...' However, the courts undoubtedly will not construe this Rule as stripping non-parties of the protections of privileges and other legitimate objections to discovery enjoyed by parties.[24]

B. PROPOSED REFORM OF ENGLISH CIVIL DISCOVERY

In England since the merger of law and equity in 1875 no reasons for the general rule against non-party discovery have been asserted in addition to those current before 1875. There were five such reasons, none of which are persuasive. To achieve the benefits of discovery, which are as much available from non-parties as from parties, the general rule should be abrogated.

The first reason advanced against discovery from non-parties was that non-parties are permitted to testify at trial as witnesses.[25] Before 1851 parties had been incompetent to testify at trials at common law. Up to that time a bill for discovery in aid of an action or defence at law was the sole means of obtaining testimony to be introduced at trial from a party.[26] Therefore, until 1851 discovery from a party was far more a desideratum than discovery from a non-party. But once parties were made competent to testify at trial in 1851,[27] the denial of discovery from non-parties could no longer be justified on the ground that they were permitted to testify at trial. To the substantial extent that the general rule against discovery from non-parties was established for this historical reason, the rule has outlived the reason for it.

On the other hand, if availability as a trial witness removes the need for discovery, discovery from parties would have been denied after 1851. That this did not occur shows that the valuable functions of discovery are by no means duplicated by testimony at trial. Nearly 140 years ago Lord Wynford pointed out that discovery improves the presentation of a case at trial by minimizing surprise and permitting informed preparation.[28]

Furthermore, as Lord Eldon put it, 'the production [of documents] and inspection of goods may be better compelled' on discovery than at trial.[29] For instance, the unjustified failure of a non-party to obey a trial subpoena or subpoena duces tecum will not result in a new trial being ordered;[30] and trial may well be completed before punishing a non-party for contempt in disobeying a trial subpoena is effective in inducing obedience.[31] Yet discovery takes place long enough before trial for sanctions against disobeying an order to produce or to answer questions to have the effect of inducing the non-party to do so. In addition, a trial surely is smoother and more economical if not subject to lengthy interruptions to peruse documents and inspect property; and such perusal and inspection promise to be more fruitful if carried out at the relatively leisurely stage of pre-trial discovery.

Other functions of discovery from a non-party which examining him at trial cannot fulfil include disclosing information which indicates 'how to draw and pen ... interrogatories, towards obtaining a better discovery'[32] from a party, which improves the litigants' opportunities to evaluate their cases,[33] and which encourages compromise settlements before trial.[34] Discovery from non-parties which 'would better enable the Plaintiff to supply and conduct his evidence'[35] at trial cannot be rendered unnecessary by the evidence he turns out to elicit at trial.

A second explanation advanced for the general rule against

discovery from non-parties was that discovery responses by a non-party generally are inadmissible at trial as hearsay.[36] This explanation is specious, for the valuable functions of discovery are far greater than obtaining evidence admitted at trial, as has just been discussed. Moreover, parties are required to give discovery responses which are inadmissible at trial, such as hearsay.[37]

A third reason asserted against discovery from non-parties was 'the mischief of enabling one party to discover what will be the testimony of a witness for the other, thereby affording him an opportunity of collecting evidence to encounter and contradict it'.[38] It is hardly 'mischief' to collect evidence to contradict that anticipated from an opponent's witness except if the evidence collected is false. Hence the danger of perjury is being invoked to justify the denial of discovery from non-parties. The same putative danger of perjury is the cardinal justification for the 'own case' rule. The fatal weaknesses in this justification of the 'own case' rule, set forth early in Section C of Chapter 8, apply with equal force to discovery from non-parties.

Another argument against discovery from non-parties assumes parties as unscrupulous as those who would suborn perjury. This argument is that, if there were a right to discovery from non-parties, defendants would delay trial indefinitely by arranging the absence of non-parties and by claiming that discovery from them was indispensable to their defences.[39] This argument is unrealistic not only in assuming that defendants would unscrupulously abduct non-parties or collude with them to obtain their unavailability, but also in assuming that non-parties would co-operate. Furthermore, there is no reason to expect that unscrupulous defendants will abduct non-parties with greater frequency or bravado than they now abduct plaintiffs; after all, the unavailability of the plaintiff generally would be more effective to delay trial.

In addition, even given an unscrupulous defendant and a colluding non-party, any machination to delay trial at the discovery stage usually would be more promising if done at the trial stage. If the defendant persuaded the court at trial of the indispensability of the testimony, documents, or goods of a non-party, who was unavailable despite diligent, timely efforts to subpoena him for trial, and who could not be compelled to give a deposition abroad,[40] the defendant would be more likely to achieve an adjournment than if his showing was that he had been unable to secure discovery from this non-party. Whatever may be said of the benefits of discovery beyond yielding evidence admissible at trial, deprivation of them would not necessarily work more injustice than deprivation of evidence at trial.

Lastly, this argument is concerned that plaintiffs would suffer in the surely few cases in which the far-fetched postulate of illegal conduct by defendants might occur. Yet, through wholly legal conduct by the real plaintiffs in interest, the general rule against discovery from non-parties has the potential to deprive defendants of all the benefits of discovery. This legal conduct is for the real plaintiff in interest to have a nominal party sue in his stead, and thus insulate himself from discovery.[41] As Lord Wynford declared with perhaps pardonable hyperbole, 'If you are to be tied down to an examination merely of persons whose names are upon the record,... in ninety-nine cases out of a hundred, frauds will escape...'[42] Fortunately, this loophole has been plugged by the exception to the general rule requiring discovery from the real plaintiff in interest; this exception is set forth in Section A4 of this Chapter. Since the authority for this exception is shaky, as pointed out in note 13 to this Chapter, it should be strengthened by a rule of court, legislation, or Court of Appeals or House of Lords decisions.

The fifth and final reason asserted for the general rule against non-party discovery has been that the peace and privacy of non-parties should not be disturbed.[43] If discovery from a non-party were sufficiently significant for a party to go to the expense and trouble necessary to secure it, in the absence of a right to such discovery the party would be likely to seek its results as nearly as possible by two other methods, namely, informal interviewing of the non-party and subpoenaing him as a witness at trial. Thus the crucial question is the probable effect on a non-party's privacy and peace of adding a right to discovery from him to the existing rights to interview him informally and to subpoena him to testify at trial.[44]

An effect of adding a right to discovery from a non-party probably would be to render interviews less frequent and less disagreeable to a non-party. They should become somewhat less frequent because lawyers would find it more convenient to use formal discovery in which they would receive an incontrovertible record of a non-party's disclosure and in which they would not have to go out into the field to find and interrogate a non-party; however, a party's lawyer might still prefer to conduct *ex parte* informal interviews rather than employ discovery, (1) in order that his opponent should not learn what the non-party discloses[45] and (2) in order that he should not be denied access to any of the non-party's information which would not be revealed in discovery by virtue of his opponent's possible objection on the basis of the 'own case', 'fact-evidence', or similar rules. Interviews should become less disagreeable to a non-party, since if a non-party does not appear co-operative to a party interviewing him, instead of becoming more aggressive in the interview, the party would have the alternative of formal discovery to turn to.

The effects on a non-party of adding a right to discovery from him to the right to subpoena him to testify at trial might well go in opposite directions. His privacy and peace might be more disturbed inasmuch as in discovery he must disclose what would be inadmissible at trial.[46] But they would be less disturbed if the discovery he gave rendered it unnecessary for him to testify at trial by inducing a compromise settlement before trial, or by resulting in the parties' stipulation on the issue on which he had information, or by demonstrating that his information was inadmissible or unnecessary for trial. Another reason why his privacy and peace would be less disturbed is that the time and place for giving discovery may be arranged to suit the convenience of a non-party far more frequently than the time and place of trial, which involves the schedules of many more people.[47] A third reason is that discovery receives substantially less publicity than trial testimony.

For all these reasons, the net effect of adding a right to discovery to the rights informally to interview a non-party and subpoena him to attend trial might well not be to increase interference with his peace and privacy. If so, the parties should not be denied the benefits of discovery from non-parties on the pretext that it increases interference with the latters' peace and privacy. At worst, the addition of a right to discovery would not increase interference with a non-party's privacy even if it did not diminish that interference at trial and in informal interviews — if a non-party's secrets are disclosed at trial and in an interview, they will become none the more public by being disclosed on discovery as well. It is true, though, that, at worst, interference with a non-party's peace would be increased if he had to respond to discovery in addition to appearing at trial and giving informal interviews. Even this 'worst-case' analysis, however, does not justify the general rule against discovery from non-parties. This is because their interest in peace is not the only interest at stake. At stake too are the interests of the parties in having the many benefits of discovery and the over-riding interest of the legal system (and the society as a whole) in providing informed, just adjudication. The slight degree to which non-parties' peace may be disturbed by discovery certainly is outweighed by these competing interests.

Moreover, it should be borne in mind that if a general power of discovery from non-parties were introduced, non-parties would be given applicable privileges and protections from discovery like those parties enjoy, including protection against oppressive discovery.[48] Moreover, it may be anticipated that non-parties would not be subject to at least one duty of discovery incumbent on parties. This is the duty of searching all their documents and then disclosing the relevant ones. Just as a subpoena duces tecum calling on a non-party merely to produce all his relevant documents at the trial of a named action will not be enforced,[49] so, on discovery, a non-party should not be required to produce or disclose documents so described. This is because he should not be presumed to know the nature of the action and should not be put to the trouble and expense of finding out or engaging a solicitor to do so. Instead, documents should be described by categories he should understand, for example, correspondence between the named plaintiff and named defendant during specified years, as they may be in a subpoena duces tecum.[50] Also, an interrogatory might set out a group of facts and ask him what documents and other information he has concerning it.

The mechanics of discovery from a non-party can and should be tailored to minimize inconvenience to him. For example, he might generally provide documentary discovery by posting to the parties documents they wished to see, under a scheme similar to that which has been conceived for production at trial pursuant to a subpoena duces tecum.[51] He might be given an option to answer interrogatories orally before a shorthand stenographer who would be empowered to put him under oath[52] or by posting his sworn written answers to the parties; whichever he chose, he might be provided a form which would entitle the stenographer and the commissioner for oaths, before whom he elected to appear, to be paid by the party serving the interrogatories.

Convenient means can be devised. Commitment to the end of creating the power of discovery from non-parties is more pressing than consideration of the means. Recent English legal thought and the many exceptions to the general absence of discovery from non-parties augurs well for achieving it.[53]

C. SUGGESTED EXTENSION AND IMPROVEMENT OF AMERICAN
DISCOVERY

The F.R.C.P. provide for production of a non-party's documents and movable property[54] and for taking his deposition upon oral examination or written questions, unlike the general rule in England. His discoverable documents and movable property are subject to inspection, incident to his deposition, by ·
subpoena duces tecum under F.R.C.P. 45(d)(1). The discussion of F.R.C.P. 45 in Chapter 3, Sections B1, 2, and 3 applies to non-parties as well as parties, except that the requirement of a description of documents or things 'with reasonable particularity' is desirable only in respect to non-parties, as pointed out on in Section B2 of Chapter 3. In view of the concern in England for the peace and privacy of non-parties, it should be noted that ·
a non-party may resist production of his documents or movable property by objecting or seeking a protective order in the ways discussed in Section B1 of Chapter 3.

A non-party may be subpoenaed to a deposition upon oral examination, at which all parties have an opportunity to question him (F.R.C.P. 30(a)(c), 45(d)(1)). The examination takes place in the district in which the non-party resides or in which the subpoena is served on him.[55] He may move for a protective order that *inter alia* the examination not be taken (F.R.C.P. 26(c)). Once his examination begins he may move to limit or terminate it (F.R.C.P. 30(d)). He may make objections and claim privileges in the course of the examination (F.R.C.P. 30(c)). The transcript of his testimony is submitted to him so that he may make changes in it, and state his reasons for doing so, before signing it (F.R.C.P. 30(e)). He may purchase a copy of the transcript if he so desires (F.R.C.P. 30(f)(2)). The operation of a deposition upon written questions of a non-party is essentially the same.

Thus the present American federal scheme makes a non-party's deposition indispensable for parties to gain the benefits of seeing his documents and movable property[56] and learning information he can relate. This scheme is sufficient for this purpose. But in many instances the deposition is unnecessary. If a party wishes to learn a limited number of straightforward facts from a non-party, he should not have to go to the expense and trouble to arrange to ask the non-party for these facts at a deposition.[57] Nor should the non-party be required to interrupt his business day to appear before an officer to provide these facts orally. To save expense and time for all concerned and to minimize the burden on a non-party, a form of interrogatories for non-parties should be made available. Rule 45(d)(1) should be amended to give the discovering party an option to have the subpoena to the non-party require him to appear on the appointed day for his deposition only if he does not post to all parties his sworn, written answers to the interrogatories annexed to the subpoena within, say, fourteen days before the day scheduled for his deposition.[58] If he does file answers to these interrogatories and any party wishes to interrogate him further on the matters, such a party might still take his deposition (F.R.C.P. 26(a)).

For the same reasons a form of Rule 34 request to a non-party to produce documents or movable property should be available. If the non-party is literate enough to understand from a Rule 45(d) subpoena which documents or movable property he should produce at his deposition, then he is literate enough to understand from a subpoena which documents or movable property he should produce at an appointed place. Rule 45(d)(1) should be amended so that a subpoena duces tecum may command a non-party to produce documents or movable property for inspection at a reasonable place and time.[59] This form of Rule 34 request must be created through Rule 45, for a subpoena is necessary for there to be a court order for disregard of which a non-party will be in contempt, and so subject to sanctions (see F.R.C.P. 45(f)). Disregard of a Rule 34 request by a non-party would expose him to no sanction. If any party wished to question the non-party about his documents or movable property, that party still might do so by deposition or the optional interrogatories just proposed (F.R.C.P. 26(a)). He should do so more effectively for having had considerable time to think about the document or tangible thing before asking questions concerning it. But the proposed subpoena duces tecum would suffice when the parties wished merely to see the documents or movable property. And it would be less upsetting to the non-party's peace.

Conspicuous by its absence from the F.R.C.P. is inspection of the real property of a non-party.[60] The 1970 amendments to the F.R.C.P. added Rule 34(c), which provides, 'This rule does not preclude an independent action against a person not a party for . . . permission to enter upon land.' The drafters of this rule explained it as follows:

Comments from the bar make clear that in the preparation of cases for trial it is occasionally necessary to enter land . . . in the possession of a person not a party,[61] and that some courts have dismissed independent actions in the nature of bills in equity for such discovery on the ground that Rule 34 is preemptive. While an ideal solution is to provide for discovery against persons not parties in Rule 34, both the jurisdictional and procedural problems are very complex. For the present, this subdivision makes clear that Rule 34 does not preclude independent actions for discovery against persons not parties.[62]

While Rule 34 does not preclude an independent action in the nature of a bill in equity for discovery of a non-party's land, as a general rule no such bill would lie in English equity.[63] Not until Parliament passed the Administration of Justice Act 1970, ss.32, 33, have the English courts felt they have power to order discovery of a non-party's land; and the power conferred by this statute is limited to personal-injuries cases.[64] Nor did the drafters of Rule 34(c) cite any American precedent for an action in the nature of a bill in equity for discovery of a non-party's real property.[65] This commentator is aware of none.

The drafters of Rule 34(c) unfortunately considered the 'jurisdictional and procedural problems' in achieving 'the ideal solution' of providing for discovery of non-parties' real estate so complex that they did not bring it about. It is difficult to see why there is so complex a jurisdictional problem. Inspection of a non-party's real estate does not introduce any problem of jurisdiction over the person of the non-party which is not present when his documents or movable property are inspected or his deposition taken. Yet the latter forms of discovery have taken place under the F.R.C.P. with no inhibition from want of jurisdiction over the person.[66] Nor has the centuries-old common-law practice of subpoenaing non-party witnesses and their documents and movable property to trials foundered for want of jurisdiction over the person. Real estate may be thought to be distinguishable from other objects of discovery in that the involvement of real estate sometimes renders an action 'local' rather than 'transitory' as a notion of subject-matter jurisdiction or venue.[67] But even if a non-party's real estate is not located within the American federal district where the action is pending and even if a proceeding to inspect it is 'local' and must be brought in the different district where the real estate is located, the F.R.C.P. may be amended to provide for this. A well-settled precedent for doing so is the practice of taking depositions of non-parties in districts other than that in which the action is pending — the distric court for the district where the deposition takes place issues the subpoena to the non-party and enforces it (F.R.C.P. 45(d)(1)(f)).

On the other hand, inspection of a non-party's real property does involve a different procedural dimension from the forms of non-party discovery provided in the F.R.C.P. Because these forms operate by service of a Rule 45 subpoena on the non-party, they are enforceable. Disobedience of a subpoena to be examined on deposition or a subpoena duces tecum may be punished as contempt of court (F.R.C.P. 45(f)). But it has never been the function of a subpoena to order a non-party witness — at trial or in discovery — to permit inspection of his real property. Hence a subpoena is not a ready procedural device to render inspection of a non-party's property enforceable. Assuming proper personal and subject-matter jurisdiction, a court order to a non-party to permit inspection of his real estate would be enforceable; its violation by the non-party would be contempt. It might be argued that such an order might issue *ex parte* and without opportunity for the non-party to be heard, inasmuch as this is the well-settled tradition for subpoenas, and inasmuch as a non-party's examination on deposition or exposure of his documents and movable property pursuant to a subpoena might hurt him more than exposure of his real estate. Of course he would have the same opportunity to object or claim privileges after the real estate order was issued as he does after being served with a subpoena or subpoena duces tecum.

If this argument should not prevail, affording the non-party an opportunity to be heard before the court decides whether to order inspection of his real property is no insuperable procedural barrier. The English R.S.C. 1965, 0.29, r.7A does so in personal-injuries cases by service of a summons and affidavit on the non-party. The affidavit describes the real estate sought to be inspected and alleges that it is discoverable. The summons notifies the non-party when the court will pass on the application for the order and that he then may be heard. Similarly the F.R.C.P. may be amended to authorize service of a summons and complaint on the non-party. Third-party practice (F.R.C.P. 14(a)(b)) is an analogous procedure. As the relief sought by the complaint would be only inspection of the 'non-party discovery' defendant's real property, bills in equity for discovery in aid of actions at law, in which the furnishing of the discovery terminated the suit, would be procedural precedents.[68]

The substantive precedents for the power to obtain discovery from a non-party are F.R.C.P. 30, 31, and 45. They have established the principle that parties to litigation have a right to discovery from non-parties. Discovery of a non-party's real property may yield the valuable benefits of discovery. Yet there is no right to this discovery in the F.R.C.P. One might have attributed this deficiency in early English equity to design, for real property then was the predominant repository of wealth. Now that documents and movable property perform this function, this deficiency must be attributed to insufficient attention.

Another deficiency in the F.R.C.P. is the absence of provision for physical or mental examination of a non-party who is not 'in the custody or under the legal control of a party'.[69] Unlike inspection of a non-party's real property, there is no jurisdictional problem in examining a non-party's person which distinguishes such an examination from taking his deposition and inspecting his documents and movable property.

As a purely procedural proposition a non-party who is not in the custody or under the legal control of a party might be subpoenaed to appear at a physician's office to have his person examined, just as he now may be subpoenaed to appear at an office to be examined orally on deposition (F.R.C.P. 45(d)). But even the right to physical and mental examination of parties has never operated extrajudicially under the F.R.C.P. Instead solicitude for 'the privacy of the person' and 'the sensibilities of people or even their prejudices as to privacy'[70] has been reflected in two cautionary limitations of F.R.C.P. 35. The first is that there must be a court order for a physical or mental examination and that the court may make such an order on motion of a party only if notice of the motion has been given to the person to be examined, the mental or physical condition of this person is in controversy in the case, and good cause for the examination has been shown. The second limitation is that the court in its order 'shall specify the time, place, manner, conditions, and scope of the examination and the person or persons by whom it is to be made' (F.R.C.P. 35(a)).[71] The United States Supreme Court has insisted that the district courts 'in every case'[72] make 'a discriminating application of the [two] limitations'.[73] The same solicitude for the sensibilities of non-parties means that it is preferable to use a complaint and summons, such as has just been proposed for the inspection of real property, as the procedure to obtain a physical or mental examination of non-parties rather than a subpoena. Of course the panoply against unjustified examinations in the two limitations in F.R.C.P. 35(a) would be available to non-parties served with such a summons and complaint.

The only practicable sanction for baseless disobedience of an order to submit to a physical or mental examination by a non-party who is not in the custody or under the legal control of a party would be to punish him for contempt. This would not be novel—contempt under F.R.C.P. 45(f) is the sole sanction available against a non-party whose documents, movable property, or oral examination is sought by discovery.

A commentator has suggested, however, that such a sanction might lead the United States Supreme Court to hold that the Rules Enabling Act does not authorize an amendment to the F.R.C.P. providing for examinations of the persons of non-parties.[74] The commentator bases this suggestion on the fact that in *Sibbach* v. *Wilson & Co., Inc.*, in which the Supreme Court held that F.R.C.P. 35 as applied to a plaintiff was authorized by the Rules Enabling Act,[75] it also held that F.R.C.P. 37(b)(2)(iv), as it then read, 'exempts from punishment as for contempt the refusal to obey an order that a party submit to a physical or mental examination'.[76] This suggestion seems far-fetched. The opinion of the Court in *Sibbach* mentioned the contempt sanction in but three places. The first was in the course of briefly sketching the facts of the case, where the opinion made a matter-of-fact reference to the district court's order that the plaintiff be committed for contempt for refusal to obey its order for her physical examination.[77] The second was a single paragraph at the end of the ten-page opinion. The Court added this paragraph after it had discussed at length a number of considerations affecting whether physical examinations of parties had been authorized by the Rules Enabling Act and after it had announced its conclusion that they 'are within the authority granted'.[78] It treated this paragraph as a relatively minor addendum after having disposed of the momentous issue in the case, namely, the statutory authority for F.R.C.P. 35. In this paragraph the Court held that the district court was in error in adjudging plaintiff in contempt and so ordering her committed, since 'section (b)(2)(iv) of Rule 37 [as it then was numbered] exempts from punishment as for contempt the refusal to obey an order that a party submit to a physical or mental examination.'[79] The Court in no way connected this holding to its statutory-authority holding. It found this exemption in Rule 37 'plain', as indeed it was.[80]

The third place in which the Court referred to the contempt sanction was in one sentence in its reasoning leading to its holding of statutory authority. Here it said, 'The suggestion that the rule offends the important right to freedom from invasion of the person ignores the fact that, as we hold, no invasion of freedom from personal restraint attaches to refusal so to comply with its provisions.'[81] The holding here referred to is that in the single paragraph at the end of the opinion. But this reliance on the absence of a contempt sanction was fallacious reasoning by the Court. Because F.R.C.P. 37(b)(2)(i)(ii)(iii), as it then was numbered,[82] provided several variants of *pro confesso* sanctions, including entering a default judgment or dismissing the action, for a party who refused to obey a Rule 35 order to submit to a physical examination,[83] Rule 35 could have had a chilling effect on a party's exercise of his putative 'freedom from invasion of the person' in the sense of freedom to refuse to permit a physician to touch or observe his body. If punishment for contempt in the form of 'personal restraint' or arrest had been an available sanction, it would have had but the same chilling effect. The Court unsoundly equates 'invasion of the person' by a physician with 'personal restraint' by arrest. Freedom from each is freedom from different things. As Mr. Justice Frankfurter wrote in the dissenting opinion,

That disobedience of an order under Rule 35 cannot be visited with punishment as for contempt does not mitigate its intrusion into . . . the privacy of the person. Of course the Rule is compulsive in that the doors of the federal courts otherwise open may be shut to litigants who do not submit to such a physical examination.[84]

Since the sole role played by the absence of the contempt sanction in the Court's line of reasoning to its conclusion that compulsory physical examination of parties is within the mandate of the Rules Enabling Act is a fallacious one, the presence of the contempt sanction in an amendment to the F.R.C.P. providing for physical examination of non-parties *ipso facto* should not bring about a holding that such an amendment is not within the Rules Enabling Act.

Another reason to think that the presence of the contempt sanction will not bring about such a holding is that the Supreme Court in *Schlagenhauf* v. *Holder*, pp. 112–14, held without even allusion to the absence of the contempt sanction that Rule 35 as applied to a defendant is within the mandate of the Rules Enabling Act.[85]

In any event, if amendment of the F.R.C.P. to provide for physical or mental examinations of non-parties were not authorized by the Rules Enabling Act, the same desirable result may be achieved by statute. Such action by Congress would not be unconstitutional. Other forms of discovery from non-parties under the F.R.C.P. have never been held unconstitutional. Thus a constitutonal challenge would be very unlikely to focus on the non-party applicability of such a statute. But if it focused on a putative right to inviolability of the person, there seems no basis to conclude that a party's person is less inviolable than a non-party's. Yet discovery by physical or mental examination of parties has been held constitutional by the Supreme Court.[86]

In view of the sensibilities of people to medical examinations, it is well advised for the present F.R.C.P. 37(b)(2)(D)(E) to exempt parties' disobedience of Rule 35 orders from the contempt sanction. The availability of *pro confesso* sanctions against them under F.R.C.P. 37(b)(2)(A)(B)(C)(E) prevents injustice to their opponents and consequent disrespect for the American federal adversary legal system. The infeasibility of *pro confesso* sanctions against non-parties means that injustice and consequent disrespect for American federal law will ensue unless the contempt sanction is available against them. Surely courts will employ it sparingly against citizens whose physical or mental conditions happen to be in controversy in cases in which they stand neither to gain nor lose. But its availability should remind citizens that they bear responsibilities to help make the legal system just. By enhancing the justice of the system, the security of the legal rights of all is improved. Justices Brewer and Brown sagaciously took this long view in 1891 when they declared, 'It is said that there is a sanctity of the person which may be outraged. We believe that truth and justice are more sacred than any personal consideration...'[87]

Analytic Summary of Discovery Law Reform Proposals

There often is tension between the purposes of discovery law. On the one hand, discovery promotes just adjudication of disputed factual issues by enlarging the quantity of information known to parties and thereby improves the quality, if not also the quantity, of information presented to the court at trial. On the other hand, discovery in some instances advances the interest of economy by facilitating the speedy and inexpensive resolution of litigation. Some of the proposals in this work generally advance the interest of economy; others, the interest of just adjudication; and still others, both interests in their encouragement of greater use of discovery by rendering it more convenient and less burdensome.[1]

The interest of economy is advanced by the proposal in Chapter 3, Section B4 that property- and documentary-discovery subpoenas under F.R.C.P. 45 be eliminated for parties by amending F.R.C.P. 45(d) so that it applies only to non-parties. This interest also is advanced by the proposal in Chapter 4, Section A that English property inspection be made available on request rather than by court order as is now required. This is because it seems that the English courts do not now refuse to make orders appreciably more frequently than they would sustain objections to property inspection were it available by request.

The interest of just adjudication is advanced by a number of proposals which probably, on balance, militate against the interest of economy. One is the recommendation in Chapter 5 of mutual mandatory requests for admission of discoverable matters. Another such proposal is for expanded application of the concept of mandatory, extrajudicial discovery. Chapter 3, Sections A 2 and 4, and Chapter 4, Section A recommend the application of this concept to American federal disclosure and production of documents and to both American federal and English real and personal property production. Chapter 5 recommends application of this concept by deeming American federal and English property inspection to constitute a request to admit the authenticity of the property inspected and by deeming American federal documentary production to constitute a request to admit the genuineness of the documents produced. A third such proposal, urged in Chapter 5, is to encourage parties to admit by authorizing the English and American federal courts to order a party to admit as requested unless he has a good-faith basis for denial and to punish his failure to do so as contempt, or by *pro confesso* sanctions when appropriate and, in the American federal system, not unconstitutional. A fourth such proposal is made for both English and American federal law in Chapter 8, Section E. It is that discovery of information impeaching witnesses should be allowed.

Six such proposals advancing the interest of just adjudication, even if militating against the interest of economy, are made for the English legal system. One, in Chapter 5, is that the R.S.C. 1965, 0. 27, r. 5 be amended so that documentary admissions may be requested earlier than the time a matter is set down for trial. Another, in Chapter 3, Section A2, is to eliminate the exception to mandatory, extrajudicial documentary discovery for defendants in vehicular-accident cases. Chapter 8, Section C recommends the abrogation of the 'own case' and 'fact-evidence' rules in all their manifestations. Chapter 9, Section B proposes that non-parties be subject to discovery as a general rule. Chapter 7 proposes that discovery by the method of physical and mental examinations of the person should be available in all civil litigation. Chapter 6 argues that oral examinations should be available as an alternative or supplement to interrogatories.

A final group of proposals advances both the interests of just adjudication and economy. One is for the English legal system. Chapter 5 recommends that the English courts permit amendment or withdrawal of documentary admissions when doing so promotes resolving the case on its merits and does not prejudice a party who has relied on an admission in his preparation for trial. Another is for both the English and American legal systems. It is that inspection of documents or property by experts should trigger exchange of experts' reports, as spelt out in Chapter 4, Section C.

The remaining proposals in this group, and in this Summary, are for the American federal legal system. Chapter 2, Section B proposes that F.R.C.P. 33(c) be amended so that the option to produce documents rather than answer interrogatories applies to documents of any nature in a party's possession, custody, or control when the burden of ascertaining the answer is not substantially greater for the interrogating party than for his opponent.

If the recommendation of mandatory, extrajudicial production of documents and property, already referred to in this Summary, is not implemented, Chapter 3, Section A2 and Chapter 4, Section A recommend (1) the deletion of the requirement in F.R.C.P. 34 that parties' documents and real and personal property be described 'with reasonable particularity' and (2) an amendment to F.R.C.P. 34 making it proper to request production of all property or documents which constitute or contain discoverable matters. Unless and until this recommendation is put into effect, it is urged in these same places and in Chapter 3, Section B2 that in regard to production by parties the courts hold that general descriptions of documents and property in terms of the factual subjects of cases satisfy the 'reasonable particularity' requirement. It is proposed in Chapter 3, Section A1 that a request for production at a time and place and in a manner convenient to a party be held authorized by F.R.C.P. 34(b) and that this party be held obligated to notify the requesting party reasonably promptly of such a time, place, and manner. Chapter 3, Section A2 recommends that it be held that a request under Rule 34 may incorporate by reference anticipated answers to interrogatories.

Chapter 8, Section D1 argues that F.R.C.P. 26(b)(1) should be amended to provide for discovery of the identity of the witnesses a party plans to call at trial and that F.R.C.P. 26(e) correspondingly should be amended to require a party to notify his opponent when he decides not to call such a witness.

Chapter 8, Section D2 urges that the courts hold that an interrogating party may rely on the fact that his opponent's proof at trial will be limited by the contentions stated in answers to interrogatories unless he receives reasonable notice to the contrary.

Chapter 9 deals with discovery from non-parties. It proposes that the F.R.C.P. be amended so that there is available from non-parties physical and mental examinations, inspection of their real property, answers to a form of interrogatories, and production of documents and personal property at a reasonable time and place without the necessity of a deposition.

Epilogue: Anticipated Opposition To Expanding American Discovery

This Book proposes reforms expanding discovery. They are summarized in Chapter 10. These proposals, like any proposals to expand discovery, are likely to encounter vigorous opposition. Largely unfounded allegations of abuse of American federal discovery persist despite convincing empirical evidence to the contrary. History teaches that we must continue to expect a chorus chanting for less rather than more discovery. This chorus reflects the psychological frustrations of practising litigators.

Most practising lawyers who work with the law of discovery consider themselves trial lawyers; although perhaps not consciously, they find discovery to be the least enjoyable part of litigation. They aspire to the eloquent closing argument or brilliant cross-examination in the spotlight of a public trial. But, instead of basking in the glory of the triumphant court-room gladiator, they find themselves spending large chunks of their professional lives in their offices or in inconspicuous conference rooms doing discovery—poring over documents, conducting depositions, drafting interrogatories. Frustration of the aspiration for court-room glory undoubtedly generates significant, personal (not societal or professional) dissatisfaction. This dissatisfaction in turn gives rise to pleas for the restriction of discovery because it is 'abused'. As the United States Supreme Court recently observed, 'There have been *repeated* expressions of concern about undue and uncontrolled discovery...' (emphasis added).[1]

The most commonly alleged abuse has been that of 'over-discovery',[2] that is, that the use of discovery is so excessive as to cause unnecessary expense and delay and to permit the better-financed litigant to coerce his opponent into an unfair settlement. Before 1970 there were frequent allegations of discovery abuse in American Federal courts.[3] To learn whether they were valid, the Advisory Committee on Civil Rules felt it should rely neither on anecdotal examples in law-review articles and bar-association speeches, nor on reported decisions, which are but the tip of the iceberg of total litigation. Instead, the Advisory Committee requested a nation-wide field-study of cases terminating in 1963, which has been described in Chapter 1, Section A1.[4]

The empirical finding of this sophisticated study was that generally the alleged abuses did not occur. On the contrary, the study concluded that in the majority of cases discovery involved a minimum of effort and conflict, and that over all discovery did not entail excessive expense, time, or effort.[5] Nor was it found that lawyers improperly use discovery for tactical rather than informational purposes.[6] The data collected by this study were persuasive enough for the Advisory Committee to recommend, and the Supreme Court to promulgate, the continuation and expansion of discovery in the form of the 1970 Amendments to the F.R.C.P.[7]

Notwithstanding this persuasive empirical study, the literature on American federal discovery since 1970 has continued to abound with allegations of the same sorts of abuse,[8] and it has continued to be a prevalent 'perception' that discovery therefore requires restriction.[9] The pleas denouncing discovery abuse since the study of 1963 data carry an aura of *déjà vu* to anyone familiar with the same pleas pre-dating this study.

The wave of American allegations of discovery abuse since 1970 has been as devoid of statistically significant supporting data as the earlier wave. Hence one would not have expected the second wave to be taken seriously. However, it happened to coincide with the American legal establishment's well-intentioned efforts to promote law reform in commemoration of an American legal milestone. In 1976, on the seventieth anniversary of the seminal address by Roscoe Pound, 'The Causes of Popular Dissatisfaction with the Administration of Justice', a National Conference on the same subject took place under the joint sponsorship of the American Bar Association, the Conference of Chief Justices, and the Judicial Conference of the United States.[10] Several speakers at the Pound Conference, including the Chief Justice of the United States Supreme Court, pointed to allegations of abuse of civil discovery as a promising field for law reform. Although the speakers had no sizeable, systematically gathered body of data to support these allegations, the allegations nevertheless gained the imprimatur of this prestigious conference.

The Pound Conference of April 1976 set in motion a chain of events which nearly led to unwarranted restrictions being placed on American federal discovery on the basis of unproven allegations of pervasive abuse. In August 1976 the Pound Conference Follow-Up Task Force urged in part that the ABA Section on Litigation draft recommended amendments to the F.R.C.P. to remedy discovery abuse;[11] the ABA Section on Litigation did so in October 1977 under the title, 'Proposed Changes in the Federal Discovery Rules'.[12] The proposed changes were founded solely on 'the experience of... [the] members' of the Section's Special Committee for the Study of Discovery Abuse and on an undescribed poll or questionnaire responded to by some of the members of the Section on Litigation.[13] Of 21 members of the Discovery Abuse Committee, 18 were practising litigators,[14] as are nearly all of the members of the Section itself. Since litigators generally prefer trying cases in public to doing discovery in private, it is not surprising that the Committee concluded that discovery generally is abused[15] and proposed changes in the F.R.C.P. which would restrict its use. The changes would do so in three ways: by modifying the scope of discovery in general from 'any matter... relevant to the subject matter involved in the pending action' to 'any matter... relevant to the issues raised by the claims or defenses of any party';[16] by limiting the number of interrogatories a party may serve to thirty, unless the court should grant leave for more upon a showing of necessity;[17] and by authorizing sanctions upon any party or counsel who 'abuses the discovery process in seeking... discovery'.[18]

These restrictive proposals were presented to the Advisory Committee on Civil Rules, which in March 1978 circulated a Preliminary Draft of Proposed Amendments to the F.R.C.P.[19] This Draft adopted the ABA Discovery Abuse Committee's proposed restrictions, but moderated them in two respects:[20] the scope of discovery would be 'any matter... relevant to the claim or defense... of any... party',[21] rather than 'relevant to the issues raised'; and the Advisory Committee's proposal was that any district court 'may by action of a majority of judges thereof limit the number of interrogatories that may be used ...',[22] rather than limiting the number of interrogatories as of right to thirty in all district courts throughout the country. The Advisory Committee had no objective data to prove the allegations of discovery abuse which spawned the restrictive proposals, but supported the proposals merely by citing the ABA Discovery Abuse Committee's proposals and accompanying report.[23] As has been noted, the subjective and possibly biased data used as a foundation by the ABA Committee were limited to the experience and opinions of some practising litigators.

Neither the ABA Committee in 1977, nor the Advisory Committee's March 1978 Draft referred to the thorough empirical field-study of 1963 cases which had found that abuse of discovery in general did not exist, despite many allegations to the contrary. However, the Pound Conference Follow-Up Task Force in 1976 had called attention to this study, without specifying that it dealt with alleged discovery abuse,[24] and the Task Force had predicted that 'empirical data concerning the nature and extent of the abuse ... may prove helpful.'[25]

The Federal Judicial Center seems to have acted on this cue by conducting a systematic empirical study of over 3,000 American federal cases in different parts of the country which terminated between 1973 and 1975.[26] Like the study of 1963 cases, the later empirical study found that general abuse of discovery does not exist, for it concluded,

[T]he figures on discovery events per case are remarkably small considering the widespread perception that federal civil discovery has gotten out of hand and become a 'rich man's tool' ... [T]he figures ... suggest that relatively little needless discovery is conducted in the typical case.[27]

The data do suggest ... that discovery abuse, to the extent it exists, does not permeate the vast majority of Federal filings. In half the filings, there is no discovery—abusive or otherwise. In the remaining half of the filings, abuse—to the extent it exists—must be found in the *quality* of the discovery requests, not in the *quantity*, since fewer than 5 percent of the filings involved more than ten requests.[28] [In regard to quality,] it is possible for a single request to be abusive, as it is possible for sixty-two requests to be appropriate, relevant and facilitative in the just disposition of a particular case.[29]

This second empirical demonstration that American federal discovery is not generally abused was published in detail a few months after the Advisory Committee's 1978 Draft of Proposed Amendments to the F.R.C.P.[30] In the face of this storm of overwhelming objective data, the edifice of proposals to restrict discovery built by the ABA Discovery Abuse Committee on a foundation of sand—practising lawyers' opinions—collapsed. The Advisory Committee in February 1979 withdrew its 1978 proposals to modify the scope of discovery, to allow individual district courts to establish a maximum number of interrogatories as of right, and to authorize sanctions for seeking discovery abusively.[31] Citing the empirical study by the Federal Judicial Center, the Advisory Committee explained its change of position as follows: 'The Committee believes that abuse of discovery, while very serious in certain cases, is not so general as to require such basic changes in the rules that govern discovery in all cases.'[32] Thus when confronted for the second time by anecdotal complaints of discovery abuse on the one hand and by empirical, systematic evidence to the contrary on the other, the Advisory Committee refused to restrict discovery in 1979, just as it did in proposing the 1970 Amendments to the F.R.C.P.[33]

Likewise, the United States Supreme Court has not been misguided by over-generalized allegations of discovery abuse since 1970, just as it was not misled by the same allegations made before it expanded discovery by promulgating the 1970 Amendments to the F.R.C.P.[34] The Amendments promulgated by the Supreme Court on 29 April 1980, which went into effect on 1 August 1980, for all intents and purposes are the same as the Advisory Committee's 1979 draft; they do not impose significant new restraints on discovery.[35]

If the Supreme Court had been inclined to restrict discovery in general on account of widespread abuse, *Herbert* v. *Lando* was an ideal case for doing so. When deciding *Herbert* in April 1979, the Court was acutely aware of the continuing allegations of abuse and the imprimatur they had received from the 1976 Pound Conference and its progeny.[36] Moreover, *Herbert* was a case in which there had been a large quantity of discovery,[37] unlike the typical American federal case.[38] Hence the 'over-discovery' kinds of abuse which have been most commonly alleged were more probable in *Herbert* than in the average case.[39]

Nevertheless, in the *Herbert* majority opinion the Supreme Court, far from encouraging restrictions on discovery in general, reaffirmed its 1947 and 1964 declarations 'that the... discovery rules are to be accorded a broad and liberal treatment to effect their purpose of adequately informing the litigants in civil trials'.[40] At the same time the majority opinion pointed out that there 'are ample powers of the district judge to prevent abuse', such as F.R.C.P. 26(b)(1) defining the scope of discovery, and

F.R.C.P. 26(c) authorizing protective orders 'which justice requires to protect a party or person [from whom discovery is sought] from annoyance, embarassment, oppression, or undue burden or expense...'; and the majority opinion urged the lower federal courts not to hesitate to firmly apply such powers 'to exercise appropriate control over...discovery...'[41]

Thus while the Supreme Court reaffirmed that discovery in general is salutary, it tacitly agreed with the quotations just cited from the Federal Judicial Center study and the 1979 Advisory Committee that discovery may be abused in any particular 'case'. The remedy for occasional abuse is vigorous but discriminating application of the court's supervisory powers over discovery in F.R.C.P. 26(b)(1), 26(c), 26(f) (added in the 1980 Amendments), 30(d), 45(b), 45(d), and 37, rather than the wholesale restriction of discovery.[42]

Occasional abuse in the quality of discovery aside, the irrepressible stream of complaints of discovery abuse may reflect an exceptional phenomenon beyond the frustration of trial lawyers at finding themselves discovery scriveners. This phenomenon is the relatively rare 'complex' or 'protracted' case involving huge stakes, multitudinous parties or documents, and complicated issues. The complex case entails correspondingly complex problems of managing the litigation, of which discovery problems frequently are no small part.[43] For example, problems arise as to which party will inspect which documents first, and where; in what order depositions will be taken; on what subjects, by whom, of whom, and where. Although a case of any subject-matter may turn out to be complex in this sense, the description often applies to anti-trust, patent, stockholders' derivative, and class actions.[44] The large, complex case frequently involves a larger quantity of discovery than the average case[45]; hence it also involves more opportunity for abuse of discovery. Most of the anecdotal examples of discovery abuse in the literature come from complex litigation.[46]

Whether or not any particular complex case turns out to involve discovery abuse, its unusual management problems alone justify continuing judicial supervision. Supervision facilitates use of the powers in F.R.C.P. 26(b)(1), 26(c), 30(d), 45(b), 45(d), and 37 to curb any abuse of discovery — parties often have to be before the court and thus their inertia against invoking these powers tends to be overcome.[47]

A procedural framework for continuing judicial supervision

of complex cases was already in place prior to the promulgation of the 1980 Amendments to the F.R.C.P.: the Manual for Complex Litigation, which recommends close court supervision by means of a series of pre-trial conferences.[48] Concerning discovery, it recommends *inter alia* establishment of a central document depository,[49] allowing discovery only by leave of court,[50] and retaining court control of the subjects, order, and timing of discovery as well as its date of completion.[51] It should be noted that even if there were no Manual for complex litigation, all of these controls over discovery could have been brought about prior to the promulgation of the 1980 Amendments to the F.R.C.P. by protective orders under F.R.C.P. 26(c).

Nevertheless, for the exceptional complex case the Manual provided a facilitating framework for what the Supreme Court in the *Herbert* case called 'ample powers' under the F.R.C.P. to prevent discovery abuse. By introducing in the new Rule 26(f) the option of a discovery conference, the 1980 Amendments have added a similar framework to facilitate applications of F.R.C.P. 26(b)(1), 26(c), 30(d), 45(b), 45(d), and 37[52] in cases where the Manual is not used.[53]

In summary, this examination of the incessant allegations of abuse of American federal discovery has established two propositions. First, there has not been pervasive, general abuse of discovery in the quantitative sense of over-use. Second, there are adequate powers in general under the F.R.C.P. to check any attempted abuse in (a) the quantity or quality of discovery used or (b) resistance to discovery.

The abuse bugagoo has failed to hoodwink the Advisory Committee and the Supreme Court into amending the F.R.C.P. to restrict discovery. Similarly, it should not be allowed to prevent adoption of the proposals for expanding discovery set forth in this book. The baby should not be thrown out with the bath water; to leave the baby unwashed to avoid the problem of disposing of the bath water would be equally fatuous.

Indeed, the proposals for expanding discovery are called for by a conclusion which has consistently emerged from statistically significant empirical examinations into allegations that discovery is abused — namely, that the quantity of discovery in most cases is small.[54] Of course, little present use of discovery does not alone justify the proposals for expanded discovery. They are justified because discovery promotes justice by providing parties with augmented information, which brings about fairer trials and settlements.[55] This benefit from discovery has not entirely been lost sight of during the latest maelstrom of exaggerated allegations of abuse.[56] To achieve a just society, it must not be lost sight of, whatever the personal dissatisfactions of lawyers who find themselves pushing discovery papers rather than trying cases.

Notes
Chapter 1

[1] Cf. A. Scott and R. Kent, *Cases and Other Materials on Civil Procedure*, p. 626 (Boston, 1967); J. Weinstein, E. Gleit, J. Kay, 'Procedures for Obtaining Information Before Trial', 35 *Texas L. R.* 481 (1957).

[2] *Sutherland (Duke)* v. *British Dominions Land Settlement Corp., Ltd.* [1926] 1 Ch. 746, 753, 757; *Saunders* v. *Jones* 7 Ch. D. 435, 446, (1877); I. H. Jacob, 'The Rules of the Supreme Court (Revision), 1962', *The Legal Executive* 263, 266 November 1963; 26 *Sol. Jour.* 69 (1881); Common Law Commission, 1853, *Second Report*, Parl. Papers, 1852–3, Vol. XL, pp. 36–7; James Wigram, *Points in the Law of Discovery*, pp. 100–1 (London, 2nd edn., 1840); cf. *Heatley* v. *Newton* 19 Ch. D. 326, 388 (1881) (CA); Committee on Personal Injuries Litigation, *Report*, pp. 41, 56, 59 (1968; Cmnd. 3691); id. (Reservations by Master I.H. Jacob), pp. 154–5; but see Maurice Rosenberg, *The Pretrial Conference and Effective Justice*, p. 121 (Columbia University Press, 1964).

[3] *Berry* v. *Haynes* 41 F.R.D. 243, 244 (D.C. Fla. 1966); *Coxe* v. *Putney* 26 F.R.D. 562 (E.D. Pa. 1961); *Broadway & Ninety-Sixth St. Realty Co.* v. *Loew's, Inc.* 21 F.R.D. 347, 353 (S.D. N.Y. 1958); cf. *Zolla* v. *Grand Rapids Store Equipment Corp.* 46 F.2d 319, 320 (S.D. N.Y. 1931) (commenting on English discovery).

[4] *Portugal* v. *Glyn* 7 Cl. & Fin. 466, 500 (1840); Committee on Personal Injuries Litigation (Reservations by Master I.H. Jacob), pp. 154–5; I.H. Jacob, 'The Rules of the Supreme Court (Revision), 1962', p. 266.

[5] *Hickman* v. *Taylor* 329 U.S. 495, 507 (1947); *Anzaldo* v. *Croca* 478 F.2d 446, 450 (8th Cir. 1973); *Greyhound Lines, Inc.* v. *Miller* 402 F.2d 134, 143 (8th Cir. 1968); *O'Donnell* v. *Breuninger* 9 F.R.D. 245, 247 (D.C. D.C. 1949); *Pierce* v. *Pierce* 5 F.R.D. 125 (D.C. D.C. 1946); *G.F. Heublein & Bro.* v. *Bushmill Wine & Prods. Co.* 2 F.R.D. 190, 192 (M.D. Pa. 1941); *Coca Cola Co.* v. *Dixie-Cola Labs., Inc.* 30 F. Supp. 275 (D.C. Md. 1940); *Teller* v. *Montgomery Ward & Co.* 27 F. Supp. 938, 941 (E.D. Pa. 1939).

[6] *Berry* v. *Haynes*, p. 244; *Broadway & Ninety-Sixth St. Realty Co.* v. *Loew's, Inc.*, p. 352; *Tobe Deutschmann Corp.* v. *United Aircraft Prods.* 15 F.R.D. 363, 364 (S.D. N.Y. 1953); *Sutherland (Duke)* v. *British Dominions Land Settlement Corp., Ltd.*, p. 757; *Potts* v. *Adair* 3 Swans. 265, n. (1793); Wigram, p. 2.

[7] *Leach* v. *Greif Bros. Cooperage Corp.* 2 F.R.D. 444 (S.D. Miss. 1942); *Sutherland (Duke)* v. *British Dominions Land Settlement Corp., Ltd.*, p. 757; Common Law Commission, 1853, p. 36; Wigram, pp. 2, 103.

[8] *G.F. Heublein & Bro.* v. *Bushmill Wine & Prods. Co.*; cf. *Zolla* v. *Grand Rapids Store Equipment Corp.*, p. 320 (commenting on English discovery).

[9] D. Karlen, *Judicial Administration: The American Experience*, pp. 34, 66 (New York, 1970).

[10] See *Hickman* v. *Taylor*, p. 500.

[11] See Chapter 8, Section C.

[12] See W.A. Glaser, *Pretrial Discovery and the Adversary System*, Chapter 4 (New York, 1968).

[13] See 28 U.S.C. s.331.

[14] Glaser, p. 44.

[15] These 'arise over … commercial disagreements between individuals or corporations …': id., p. 45, n. 16.

[16] Id., p. 45.

[17] Id., p. 47.

[18] For other imperfections, statistical and otherwise, in the study, see id., pp. 45–50 and 114, n. 21.

[19] Id., p. 49; see also the description of this empirical study in M. Rosenberg, 'Changes Ahead in Federal Pretrial Discovery', 45 F.R.D. 479, 482–3 (1969).

[20] Glaser, p. 107.

[21] Ibid.

[22] Id., pp. 107–9.

[23] Id., pp. 114, 115.

[24] Accord, id., pp. 103, 105, 115.

[25] Rosenberg, 'Changes Ahead in Federal Pretrial Discovery', p. 488; accord, Advisory Committee on Rules of Civil Procedure, 'Proposed Amendments (and Notes thereto) to the Federal Rules of Civil Procedure Relating to Discovery (1970)', 48 F.R.D. 487, 489–90.

[26] Rosenberg, 'Changes Ahead in Federal Pretrial Discovery', pp. 488–9; cf. Glaser, pp. 114, 234; but see A. Doskow, 'Procedural Aspects of Discovery', 45 F.R.D. 498, 504 (1968).

[27] See id, p. 114, including n. 21, 115; Rosenberg, 'Changes Ahead in Federal Pretrial Discovery', pp. 488–9.

[28] Advisory Committee on Rules of Civil Procedure, p. 490; Glaser, p. 114, especially n. 2.

[29] Glaser, p. 42.

[30] Rosenberg, 'Changes Ahead in Federal Pretrial Discovery', pp. 488–9; see Doskow, p. 504 (noting that 95 per cent of the lawyers interviewed by the study believe discovery promotes settlement).

[31] Glaser, pp. 115, 234.

[32] See id., pp. 115, 234.

[33] Rosenberg, 'Changes Ahead in Federal Pretrial Discovery', p. 488.

[34] 48 F.R.D. at 489–90.

[35] American federal discovery largely has eliminated the 'own case' rule. See Chapter 8, Section D.

[36] See Chapter 9, Section C.

[37] Glaser, p. 234.

[38] See Chapter 8, Section D2.

[39] Ibid.

[40] Implementation of the proposal in Chapter 5 for mandatory requests for factual admissions also would indirectly bring about disclosure of contentions and narrowing of the issues.

[41] Glaser, pp. 105, 115–16; but see id., p. 109.

[42] Rosenberg, 'Changes Ahead in Federal Pretrial Discovery', p. 488; accord, Doskow, p. 504.

[43] P.R. Connolly, E.A. Holleman, M.J. Kuhlman, *Judicial Controls and the Civil Litigative Process: Discovery*, Chapter II (District Court Study Series of Federal Judicial Center, Washington, D.C., 1978); see Glaser, pp. 192, 197, 201, 234.

[44] See id., pp. 201, 192, 197; Connolly, p. 35; Chapter 11 below. The costs of oral examination are discussed in Chapter 6. The discussion there draws on this empirical study of American federal discovery and the empirical study by the same organization of Massachusetts discovery in arguing that the oral-examination form of discovery should be available in England.

[45] Advisory Committee on Rules of Civil Procedure, pp. 489–90; see Doskow, pp. 504–5.

[46] *Knapp* v. *Harvey* [1911] 2 K.B. 725.

[47] See S. Williston, *Life and Law*, p. 271 (Boston, 1940).

[48] Address by Justice William J. Brennan, Jr., Round Table on Administration of Justice, San Juan, Puerto Rico, Feb. 5, 1962, quoted in Tauro, 'Improving the Quality of Justice in Massachusetts', 49 *Mass. Law Quarterly* 7, 19 (1964).

[49] *United States* v. *Proctor & Gamble Co.* 356 U.S. 677, 682 (1958) (Douglas, J.).

[50] See F.R.C.P. 1.

[51] See Doskow, pp. 504–5.

[52] Glaser, p. 219; see W.H. Becker, 'A Modern, Efficient Use of the Bar and Other Parajudicial Personnel in Pretrial of Ordinary Civil Actions', 53 F.R.D. 159, 161 (1971).

[53] *United States* v. *Sisson* 297 F. Supp. 902, 911 (D.C. Mass. 1969), appeal dismissed, 399 U.S. 267 (1970).

[54] *Boddie* v. *Connecticut* 401 U.S. 371, 374 (1971).

[55] One successful American federal effort minimizes the time used for discovery. The common components of total discovery time are the time-limits for providing discovery responses, tardiness in meeting those limits, and the periods between pleading and initial discovery request and between subsequent discovery requests. Cf. Connolly, Holleman and Kuhlman, pp. 18, 52. This total time consumed by discovery has been significantly shortened, without inhibiting the use of discovery, when courts at an early point in litigation have established cut-off dates by which discovery is to be completed: id., pp. 52, 54, 57, 59–66. American federal courts may impose such cut-off dates by local rules pursuant to F.R.C.P. 83: id., p. 17. The authority to do so is more explicit under F.R.C.P. 26(f), which was added as a 1980 amendment and which provides for discovery conferences where a schedule for discovery may be fixed.—U.S.—, 64 L. Ed. 2d xli–xlii (1980); Committee on Rules of Practice and Procedure of the Judicial Conference of the United States, 'Revised Preliminary Draft of Proposed Amendments to the F.R.C.P., February 1979', 80 F.R.D. 323, 330–1.

[56] Oral examination may secure the information available by interrogatories, but the converse frequently is not so. This is owing to the unique advantages of oral examination, discussed on both *a priori* and *a posteriori* levels in Chapter 6.

[57] *Portugal* v. *Glyn; Tooth* v. *Dean and Chapter of Canterbury* 3 Sim. 49, 63 (1829); *Griffin* v. *Archer* 2 Anstr. 478 (1794); *Newman* v. *Godfrey* 2 Bro. C. C. 332, 333–4 (dictum).

[58] See Chapter 7.

[59] Glaser, pp. 169–70.

[60] For example, interrogatories generally have not been allowed to obtain an admission of fact not fundamental to the case, and so not significant to the evaluation of his case by the party applying for leave to serve interrogatories, when the applicant has been in a position to prove the fact at trial by a witness who would be called to testify even if the admission had been made. See 1 *Supreme Court Practice 1979*, pp. 444–5 (London, 1978).

Furthermore, leave has not usually been granted until after all parties have pleaded, for the pleadings may make the interrogatories unnecessary or help the court judge their relevance. Cf. id., p. 451.

It should be noted, however, that when appeals have been taken from decisions on the allowance of interrogatories, the Court of Appeals at times has been inconsistent in its decisions on leave for largely indistinguishable interrogatories. Compare *Spiers & Pond, Ltd.* v. *'John Bull', Ltd.* 85 L.J.K.B. 992 (1916) (CA) with *Franklin* v. *Daily Mirror Newspapers, Ltd.* 149 L.T. 433 (1933) (CA) and *Heaton* v. *Goldrey* (1910) 1 K.B. 754 (CA). Such appellate decisions encourage both expensive and dilatory hearings on applications for leave and equally expensive and dilatory appeals from decisions on them.

[61] However, there are American federal district courts which have local rules requiring court orders in order to ask more than a specified number of interrogatories. See D. Segal, *Survey of Literature on Discovery from 1970 to the Present*, p. 49 (Federal Judicial Center, Washington, D.C., 1978).

[62] Cf. *Sibbach* v. *Wilson & Co., Inc.* 312 U.S. 1, 18 (1941) (dissenting opinion).

[63] See *Hickman* v. *Taylor*, pp. 510–11; Rosenberg, 'Changes Ahead in Federal Pretrial Discovery', p. 481; F. Freund, 'Work Product', 45 F.R.D. 493, 498.

[64] See Rosenberg, 'Changes Ahead in Federal Pretrial Discovery', pp. 484–6.

[65] *Hickman* v. *Taylor*, p. 511.

[66] See ibid.; Freund, p. 498.

Chapter 2

[1] A 1946 Amendment to F.R.C.P. 33 eliminated the requirement of leave of court to serve more than one set of interrogatories. Cf. 4A W. Moore and J. Lucas, *Moore's Federal Practice*, ¶ 33.01[3][4] (2nd edn., 1978). Concerning a thus far abortive attempt to resurrect a restriction on American federal interrogatories, see Chapter 11.

[2] Advisory Committee on Rules of Civil Procedure, p. 521.

[3] Glaser, pp. 147, 149–53; Advisory Committee on Rules of Civil Procedure, p. 522.

[4] Ibid.

[5] Id., pp. 522, 523, 539, 540.

[6] Glaser, p. 157.

[7] In the United States, unlike in England, costs do not usually include attorney's fees. See Karlen, p. 63.

[8] R.S.C. 1965, 0.26, r. 4.

[9] Cf. J. C. Day, *Common Law Procedure Acts*, p. 308 (London, 1872).

[10] See Glaser, pp. 189–91.

[11] This burden will usually be heavier in the American federal courts than in England; while leave may be sought when the parties are before the court on an English mandatory summons for directions (which brings the parties before a master, in any event, at an early stage of the litigation on other interlocutory matters, R.S.C. 1965, 0.25, r. 1–(1)), discovery in American federal courts usually has been completed by the time the parties are before the court at a pre-trial conference shortly before trial. See Scott and Kent, p. 664; F. James, Jr., *Civil Procedure*, p. 224 (Boston, 1965); cf. 'Report of Lord Chancellor's Legal Procedure Committee', 25 *Sol. Jour.* 1911, 912 (1881).

[12] Committee on Personal Injuries Litigation (Reservations by Master I. H. Jacob), p. 154. Master Jacob wisely urges 'a more liberal application of the principle[s] relating to interrogatories...' To this end, he proposes that R.S.C. 1965, 0.26, r. 1–(3) 'be amended to empower the Court to order interrogatories to be administered, not only where they are "necessary", but also where they are "desirable"'. It is submitted that this end may and should be achieved even without such an amendment by broadly construing the condition of this rule, 'necessary...for disposing fairly of the cause...', as satisfied when any of the benefits of discovery set forth above may result from interrogatories.

[13] See the instructive flexible co-ordination of discovery mechanisms in *Smith* v. *Great Western Ry. Co.* 6 El. & Bl. 405 (1856).

[14] Advisory Committee on Rules of Civil Procedure, pp. 524–5.

[15] Ibid.; *Thomason* v. *Leiter* 52 F.R.D. 290 (N.D. Ala. 1971); cf. *Atlanta Fixture & Sales Co., Inc.* v. *Bituminous Fire & Marine Ins. Co.* 51 F.R.D. 311 (N.D. Ga. 1970) (*sub silentio*).

[16] Defendant may be relieved of this burden, however, by moving for a protective order under F.R.C.P. 26(c). See Advisory Committee on Rules of Civil Procedure, p. 525.

[17] Interrogatories about the dates and colours of documents should be held proper, F.R.C.P. 34 notwithstanding. See, e.g., *Lee* v. *Electric Products Co.* 37 F.R.D. 42, 45 (N.D. Ohio 1963); *United States* v. *Becton, Dickinson & Co.* 30 F.R.D. 132, 133 (D.C. N.J. 1962).

[18] *Abel Investment Co.* v. *U.S.* 53 F.R.D. 485 (D.C. Neb. 1972); *Ross* v. *Longchamps, Inc.* 336 F. Supp. 434 (E.D. Mo. 1971).

Chapter 3

[1] The amendments also wisely expanded the definition of 'documents' to include 'phono-records, and other data compilations from which information can be obtained, translated, if necessary, by the respondent through detection devices into reasonably usable form...' (F.R.C.P. 34(a)).

[2] Advisory Committee on Rules of Civil Procedure, pp. 525–7.

[3] F.R.C.P. 34(b) says 'set forth' rather than 'list'. But Form 24, as amended in 1970 — which is 'sufficient' (F.R.C.P. 84) — shows that 'set forth' is intended to mean 'list' (id., pp. 544–5).

[4] See 8 Wright and Miller, s.2213, p. 640.

[5] See 4A *Moore's Federal Practice*, ¶34.05[3], pp. 37–9.

[6] Glaser, p. 55.

[7] 8 Wright and Miller, s.2212, p. 636.

[8] Advisory Committee on Rules of Civil Procedure, p. 526.

[9] See id., pp. 525, 544–5; F.R.C.P. 84.

[10] e.g. *Monarch Liquor Corp.* v. *Schenley Distillers Corp.* 2 F.R.D. 51, 52 (N.D. N.Y. 1941); Advisory Committee on Rules of Civil Procedure, pp. 492–7, 508–13, 516–17. The 1970 amendments changed the name of deposition upon written interrogatories to deposition upon written questions (id., pp. 516, 517).

[11] e.g. *Alltmont* v. *United States* 177 F.2d 971, 977 (3rd Cir. 1949); *Kirkland* v. *Morton Salt Co.* 46 F.R.D. 28, 30–1 (N.D. Ga. 1968); *Smith* v. *Central Linen Service Co.* 39 F.R.D. 15, 16–17 (D.C. Md. 1966); *Foundry Equip. Co.* v. *Carl-Mayer Corp.* 11 F.R.D. 108, 109 (N.D. Ohio 1950). Decidedly minority authority was to the contrary: e.g. *Terrell* v. *Standard Oil Co. of N.J.* 5 F.R.D. 146 (E.D. Pa. 1945).

[12] Of course, once a party obtains production, he obtains disclosure as well.

[13] See, e.g., *Monarch Liquor Corp.* v. *Schenley Distillers Corp.* for the negative answer before the 1970 amendments.

[14] These are documents 'relevant to the subject matter involved in the pending action' or 'reasonably calculated to lead to the discovery of admissible evidence' (F.R.C.P. 26(b)(1)).

[15] As to the form of this list, see *Supreme Court Practice 1979*, ¶24/5/1; A.S. Diamond, 'Changes in High Court Procedure', *Notes of a Lecture Given at the Law Society's Hall on December 5, 1963*, p. 10 (The Solicitor's Law Stationery Society, Ltd., Oyez House, Breams Bldg., London, E.C. 4).

[16] See 38 *Sol. Jour.* 74 (1894).

[17] S. Rosenbaum, 'Studies in English Civil Procedure, II', 63 *Univ. of Penn. Law Rev.* 182, 387 (1915).

[18] 1 *Supreme Court Practice 1979*, ¶24/2/5; A. S. Diamond, 'The Summons for Directions', 75 *B.Q.R.* 43, 47 (1959); Committee on Supreme Court Practice and Procedure, *Final Report*, p. 22.

[19] *Rochdale Canal Co.* v. *King* 15 Beav. 11 (1852); E. Bray, *Principles of Discovery*, p. 156 (London, 1885); C. Barber, 'Statement on the Practice and Procedure of the Court of Chancery in England', Parl. Papers, Vol. XV, 1863, pp. 59, 63; but see C. Langdell, 'Discovery under the Judicature Acts, 1873, 1875, Part III', 12 *Harv. L. Rev.* 151, 173 (1898).

In equity's very early days as well, disclosure and production of documents occurred after the single step of filing the bill, for documents were set out in the answer *in haec verba* or according to their purport and effect. See Wigram, pp. 199–200; Bray, *Principles of Discovery*, p. 155.

[20] There is no substantial difference between the description in terms of F.R.C.P. 26(b)(1)(2)(3) and that of F.R.C.P. 34(a) which speaks of F.R.C.P. 26(b), for the other subdivisions of Rule 26(b) do not authorize discovery by request under Rule 34.

[21] Advisory Committee on Rules of Civil Procedure, pp. 544–5. Perhaps their intention also is suggested by their change in the name of Rule 34 from 'Discovery and Production of Documents...' to 'Production of Documents...' (id., p. 525).

[22] Id., p. 527.

[23] 5 F.R.D. 433, 463.

[24] The language to be deleted is, 'and describe each item and category with reasonable particularity'.

[25] Cf. *United States* v. *American Optical Co.* 2 F.R.D. 534, 536 (S.D. N.Y. 1942).

[26] *United States* v. *United States Alkali Export Ass'n.*, p. 260; contra, e.g., *United States* v. *American Optical Co.*, p. 536.

[27] This decision is not precisely on point because it is based on F.R.C.P. 45 as to subpoenas rather than on F.R.C.P. 34; however, as shown in Chapter 3, Section B2, F.R.C.P. 34 and 45 are read as an integrated documentary-discovery mechanism.

[28] Segal reports that Robert Meserve has advanced an unpublished proposal for a change in Rule 34 to the Second Circuit Judicial Conference (D. Segal, pp. 54–5, App. B–3). As described by Segal, however, the Meserve proposal does not amount to an outright change in Rule 34. It only amounts to what some courts already are doing, namely, (a) interpreting a Rule 34 description of documents in terms of 'subject matters on which...[a party] desires documents' to satisfy the Rule's requirement that documents be described with reasonable particularity and (b) interpreting the offices and files of the responding party to satisfy the Rule's requirement of a reasonable place for making the inspection. Segal's description says that the Meserve proposal addresses 'a complex and extended request for production...' (Segal, p. 54). Thus, the proposal may be peculiar to the rare complex case and would require co-ordination with the Manual for Complex Litigation, which is described towards the end of Chapter 11. Inscrutably, Segal's description also says that the Meserve proposal addresses the 'time...wasted in litigating the issue of the scope of a given request and the issue of whether the documents submitted fulfill that request' (Segal, p. 54). One fails to see how the Meserve proposal avoids such litigation. The responding party may still object that a 'subject matter' designated by the requesting party is outside the scope of discovery. Likewise, the requesting party may still object that the documents located in the files described by the responding party are not all of those covered by the designated 'subject matter'.

[29] See, e.g., *Conley* v. *Gibson* 355 U.S. 41, 47–8 (1957).

[30] Cf. 4A *Moore's Federal Practice*, ¶33.22, pp. 33–127, 33–128.

[31] F.R.C.P. 30(c), 31(b).

[32] See F.R.C.P. 30(e), 31(b).

[33] e.g. *United Sheeplined Clothing Co., Inc.* v. *Nat'l. Broadcasting Co., Inc.* 11 F.R. Serv. 2d 34.13, Case 8 (S.D. N.Y. 1968); *Holland Am. Merchants Corp.* v. Rogers 23 F.R.D. 267 (S.D. N.Y. 1959); *Bifferato* v. *States Marine Corp. of Delaware* 11 F.R.D. 44, 46 (S.D. N.Y. 1951); Wigram, pp. 2, 199, 208–9, 210; cf. Langdell, Part II, 11 *Harv. L. Rev.* 205, 211; Bray, *Principles of Discovery*, p. 270.

[34] See 1 *Supreme Court Practice 1979*, ¶24/2/3.

[35] *Alfred Crompton Amusement Machines Ltd.* v. *Customs & Excise Commissioners* [1974] A.C. 405, 429.

[36] Ibid.

[37] Cf. *Goldlaw, Inc.* v. *Shubert* 25 F.R.D. 276, 277 (S.D. N.Y. 1960) (semble).

Société Internationale Pour Participations Industrielles et Commerciales v. *Rogers* 357 U.S. 197, 204–6 (1958) is not on this question. The United States Supreme Court there held *inter alia* that documents in which plaintiff had a proprietary interest—that is, documents belonging to a firm which was 'substantially identical' to plaintiff (see id., pp. 200, 204—were subject to production under F.R.C.P. 34 even though production would expose plaintiff, a Swiss citizen, to Swiss criminal sanctions.

[38] The English call these privileges the legal professional privilege.

[39] 8 F.R.D. 363–4.

[40] 4A *Moore's Federal Practice*, ¶34.17, pp. 34–101; 8 Wright and Miller, s.2210, pp. 623–4.

[41] See 1 *Supreme Court Practice 1979*, ¶24/2/3.

The predecessor codification was known as R.S.C. 1883. The formula in it was 'possession or power', (see id., ¶¶24/2/3, 24/2/4). The addition of 'custody' plainly was not intended to require production of documents previously but no longer in a party's possession, power, or custody. Yet R.S.C.1965, 0.24, r. 9 says that 'a party...must allow the other party to inspect the documents referred to in the list' of documents disclosed. Since this list must include documents previously but no longer in a party's possession, power, or custody (R.S.C. 1965, 0.24, r. 2–(1)), Rule 9 should be construed as though it reads, 'A party…must allow the other party to inspect the documents referred to in the list and then in the party's possession, power or custody.' This construction is necessary lest a party be required to do the impossible. See *Taylor* v. *Rundell* Cr. & Ph. 104, 111 (1841); *Murray* v. *Walter* Cr. & Ph. 114, 124 (1839).

That this construction undoubtedly was intended by the draftsmen appears from R.S.C. 1965, 0.24, r. 11(2). This Rule correctly empowers the court to order production of 'any documents *in* the possession, custody or power of' a party based, according to 0.24, r. 11(3), on the opponent's affidavit 'stating the belief of the deponent that they *are* in the possession, custody or power of that other party…' (emphasis added).

⁴² *Taylor* v. *Rundell*, p. 111.

⁴³ See *In re Saxton* [1962] 1 W.L.R. 859, 861.

⁴⁴ *Hewitt* v. *Piggott* 5 Car. & P. 75, 77 (1831); see Chapter 9 of this book and Bray, *Principles of Discovery*, p. 135.

⁴⁵ *Lethbridge* v. *Cronk* 23 W.R. 703 (1875); *Rishton* v. *Grissel* 14 W.R. 789 (1866); cf. *Alfred Crompton Amusement Machines, Ltd.* v. *Customs & Excise Commissioners*, p. 429; common form of affidavit of documents in *Imperial Land Co.* v. *Masterman* 29 L.T. 559 (1873); 1 *Supreme Court Practice 1979*, ¶¶24/2/3, 24/2/4; R.S.C. 1883, 0.31, rr. 13A, 13B, 19A-(3); 2 *Annual Practice 1963*, App. B, Form No. 8, ¶ 5; Bray, *Principles of Discovery*, p. 135.

⁴⁶ Cf. *Marshall* v. *Goulston Discount (Northern) Ltd.* [1967] 1 Ch. 72, 77(CA); see *Nash* v. *Layton* [1911] 2 Ch. 71, 84, 85 (CA).

⁴⁷ Bray, *Principles of Discovery*, pp. 238–9.

⁴⁸ Glaser, p. 53. The frequency is likely to be less since the 31 per cent figure includes inspections of land and things.

⁴⁹ Id., p. 55.

⁵⁰ See S. Williston, p. 271.

⁵¹ Doing so also has the advantage of minimizing perjury by mutual disclosure. See Chapter 8, Section C.

⁵² 1965 R.S.C., 0.24, r. 1–(2).

⁵³ Glaser, p. 53; 8 Wright and Miller, s.2132, p. 444.

⁵⁴ Id., pp. 442, 444; 4A *Moore's Federal Practice*, ¶31.02, pp. 31-7–31–8; see Chapter 6.

⁵⁵ F.R.C.P. 45(c); *Harrison* v. *Prather* 404 F.2d 267, 273 (5th Cir. 1968); *Gillam* v. *A. Shyman, Inc.* 22 F.R.D. 475, 479 (D.C. Alaska 1958).

⁵⁶ This is the same scope of documentary discovery available under F.R.C.P. 34(a). See Advisory Committee on Rules of Civil Procedure, p. 543.

⁵⁷ Cf. F.R.C.P. 37(a)(2), paragraph 2.

⁵⁸ Advisory Committee on Rules of Civil Procedure, p. 543.

⁵⁹ Id., p. 536; but see id., p. 540.

⁶⁰ *Essgee Co.* v. *United States* 262 U.S. 151, 157 (1923); *Wilson* v. *United States* 221 U.S. 361, 372–5 (1911).

⁶¹ Cf. 9 Wright and Miller, *Federal Practice and Procedure* s.2455, p. 427 (1971).

⁶² *McLean* v. *Prudential Steamship Co., Inc.* 36 F.R.D. 421 (E.D. Va. 1965); *Newmark* v. *Abul* 106 F. Supp. 758, 759 (S.D. N.Y. 1952); *Beegle* v. *Thomson* 2 F.R.D. 82 (N.D. Ill. 1941).

⁶³ Recall Chapter 3, Section A2 above.

⁶⁴ F.R.C.P. 26(b)(4) does not authorize discovery by subpoena unless preceded by another procedural step, viz., a motion and order (F.R.C.P. 26(b)(4)(A)(ii)), or a showing of exceptional circumstances to the court (F.R.C.P. 26(b)(4)(B)).

⁶⁵ e.g. *Seuthe* v. *Renwal Products, Inc.* 38 F.R.D. 323 (S.D. N.Y. 1965) (semble); *403–411 East 65th Street Corp.* v. *Ford Motor Co.* 27 F. Supp. 37 (S.D. N.Y. 1939); cf. *Sientki* v. *Haffner* 145 F. Supp. 435 (S.D. N.Y. 1956).

⁶⁶ Cf., e.g., *Sientki* v. *Haffner*.

⁶⁷ e.g., *Wirtz* v. *Local 169, Hod Carriers' Union* 37 F.R.D. 349, 351 (D.C. Nev. 1965); *Korman* v. *Shull* 184 F. Supp. 928 (W.D. Mich.), app. dismissed, 310 F.2d 373 (6th Cir. 1960).

[68] Cf. *Demeulenaere* v. *Rockwell Mfg. Co.* 13 F.R.D. 134 (S.D. N.Y. 1952); *In re Chapnick* 6 F.R. Serv. 45b, 413, Case 1 (S.D. N.Y. 1942).

[69] Recall Section A2 of this Chapter.

[70] This distinction from a grand-jury subpoena itself suggests that it was unwise to graft a 'reasonable particularity' requirement of such subpoenas to the body of Rule 34, if indeed such was the origin of this Rule 34 requirement added in 1970.

[71] See Chapter 9.

[72] e.g. *Bough* v. *Lee* 29 F. Supp. 498 (S.D. N.Y. 1939); see *Schwimmer* v. *United States* 232 F.2d 855, 859, 860 (8th Cir.), cert. denied, 352 U.S. 833 (1956); *In re Riviera* 79 F. Supp. 510 (S.D. N.Y. 1948); *In re Grand Jury Subpoena Duces Tecum* 72 F. Supp. 1013 (S.D. N.Y. 1947).

[73] The vacuousness of the concept of putative 'rights and interests' of a non-party preventing inspection of his documents in the 'custody' of a party has been pointed out in Section A3 of this Chapter. There remains little or no substance to this position even though his rights are specified to be constitutional privileges against self-incrimination and search and seizure in the rare instance in which the non-party anticipates criminal prosecution. The extent to which the self-incrimination and search and seizure privileges enable a non-party to withhold his documents from subpoena by criminal authorities while they remain in his own possession is very narrow indeed. See *Andresen* v. *Maryland* 427 U.S. 463 (1976); *Fisher* v. *United States* 425 U.S. 391 (1976); cf. P. Devlin, *The Criminal Prosecution in England*, pp. 62–4 (New Haven, 1958). When a non-party allows a party to have incriminatory information in the form of a document, the non-party generally does not have a privilege which will enable the party to withhold the document from criminal authorities. See *Couch* v. *United States* 409 U.S. 322 (1973); J. Israel & W. LaFave, *Criminal Procedure in a Nutshell*, p. 97 (2nd edn., 1975). Therefore, a non-party by and large has no constitutional privilege against a party allowing inspection of the former's documents, just as a non-party generally has no privilege preventing a party from disclosing information derived from the non-party in the party's answers to interrogatories or questions at a deposition.

[74] F.R.C.P. 34 is unavailable for discovery from non-parties, while F.R.C.P. 45 is available. See Chapter 9.

[75] F.R.C.P. 28, 30(c), 31(a)(b).

[76] F.R.C.P. 30(c), 31(b).

[77] F.R.C.P. 30(b)(1), 31(a).

[78] F.R.C.P. 45(c); *Harrison* v. *Prather*: *Gillam* v. *A. Shyman, Inc.*

[79] F.R.C.P. 34(a), 6(a)(b).

[80] Instead of objecting merely by so stating in writing under 45(d)(1), he might take the more onerous course of moving to quash the subpoena under 45(b). Since this motion must be made 'promptly and in any event at . . . the time specified in the subpoena for compliance', he is unlikely to be permitted to make this motion as long as 30 days after he is served with the subpoena.

[81] Advisory Committee on Rules of Civil Procedure, p. 522.

Chapter 4

[1] See, e.g., *Seuthe* v. *Renwal Products, Inc.*, p. 325.

[2] Of course, F.R.C.P. 45 does not empower real property to be subpoenaed to be produced in the room where a deposition will be taken.

[3] Advisory Committee on Rules of Civil Procedure, pp. 526–7.

[4] See id., p. 527.

[5] *Kynaston* v. *East India Co.* 3 Sw. 248, 265 (1819), aff'd., 3 Bligh 153 (1821); W. Kerr, *Treatise on the Law of Discovery*, p. 283 (London, 1870).

[6] *Bennett* v. *Griffiths* 3 El. & El. 467, 475 (1861); Kerr, p. 283; cf. *Bennitt* v. *Whitehouse* 28 Beav. 119, 123 (1860).

[7] *Bennett* v. *Griffiths*, p. 475; *Bennitt* v. *Whitehouse*, p. 123.

[8] *Bennett* v. *Griffiths; Walker* v. *Fletcher* 3 Bligh 172, 178 (1804); *Earl of Lonsdale* v. *Curwen* 3 Bligh 168 (1799).

[9] *Walker* v. *Fletcher*, p. 178; *Earl of Lonsdale* v. *Curwen.*

[10] *Walker* v. *Fletcher*, p. 178.

[11] Compare *Lumb* v. *Beaumont* 27 Ch. D. 356 (1884) with *Ennor* v. *Barwell* 1 De G.F. & J. 529 (1860).

[12] See *Piggott* v. *Anglo-American Telegraph Co.* 19 L.T. 46 (1869); *Whaley* v. *Brancker* 10 Jur. (NS) 535 (1864); *Bennitt* v. *Whitehouse*, pp. 120–1.

[13] Bray, *Principles of Discovery*, pp. 581–2; see *Flower* v. *Lloyd* [1876] W.N. 169, 230; *Davenport* v. *Jepson* 1 N.R. 307 (1862).

[14] *Walker* v. *Fletcher*, p. 178.

[15] *In re Saxton.*

[16] A corresponding amendment should be made to F.R.C.P. 26(b)(4)(B) adding Rules 34 and 45 to 35(b).

[17] [1930] W.N. 200, 201.

[18] Ibid.

[19] Ibid. The alternative reason was that the inspection was remote, oppressive, or irrelevant (ibid.).

[20] *In Re Brown* 4 Bro. C.C. 91, 96, 98 (1792); *Ex Parte Bellet* 1 Cox 297, 299 (1786); *Ex parte Aiscough* 2 P. Wms. 591, 593 (1730); *Theaker's Case* Cro. Jac. 686 (1625); *Willoughby's Case* Cro. Eliz. 566 (1597); Wigmore, Vol. 8, p. 177 (McNaughton rev., 1961).

[21] 1 *Supreme Court Practice 1979*, in its very asserting that a method of operation may not be inspected (¶ 29/2–3/3), concedes, 'In patent actions, inspection of a manufacturing process can be ordered, see 0.103, r.26(2)(f) . . .' This is correct for patent actions. See *Dow Chemical Co.* v. *Monsanto Chemicals Ltd.*, [1969] F.S.R. 504; *British Xylonite Ltd.* v. *Fibrenyle Ltd.* [1959] R.P.C. 252. But neither the language in Order 103 compared with Order 29, nor any peculiarity of patent actions justifies denying the same discovery in other actions.

[22] *Davenport* v. *Jepson; Morgan* v. *Seaward*, 1 Webs. Pat. Cas. 167, 169 (1835); *Brown* v. *Moore* 3 Bligh 178 (1816).

[23] See, e.g., *Gordon, Wolf, Cowen Co., Inc.* v. *Independent Halvah & Candies, Inc.* 17 Fed. Rules Serv. 34.621, Case 1.

Chapter 5

[1] In England interrogatories were used in lieu of admissions for a period. Broadly speaking, the two mechanisms are interchangeable. See *Hoffman* v. *Postill* L.R. 4 Ch. App. Cas. 673, 674 (1869); *Marshall* v. *Feeney* 2 J. & H. 313, 318 (1861); R. Millar, 'The Mechanism of Fact-Discovery', 32 *Northwestern Law Rev.* 261, 445 (1937); 'Report of Lord Chancellor's Legal Procedure Committee', p. 912; Common Law Commission, 1853, *Second Report*, Parl. Papers, 1852–3, Vol. XL, p. 36; compare *Rew* v. *Hutchins* 10 C.B. (NS) 829, 837 (1861) with *Bird* v. *Malzy* 1 C.B. (NS) 308, 312–13 (1856).

[2] Cf. Millar, p. 443.

[3] But see *Rutter* v. *Chapman* 8 M. & W. 388, 1 Dowl, (NS) 118, 11 L. J. Ex. 178 (1841)

[4] This defect may easily be remedied by using the phrase in 0.27, r. 2, 'Not later than 21 days', rather than 'within 21 days'.

[5] I. Jacob, 'The Rules of the Supreme Court (Revision) 1965', Lecture before the Institute of Legal Executives, Maltravers House, Arundel Street, Strand, London, W.C. 2, p. 3 (available at University of London Institute of Advanced Legal Studies, 25 Russell Square, London, W.C. 2).

[6] Form No. PF 62, 2 *Supreme Court Practice 1979*, p. 75.

[7] Cf. *O'Rourke* v. *Darbishire* [1920] A.C. 581, 616, 624, 630.

[8] Cf J. Bentham, *Rationale of Judicial Evidence, Works*, Vol. VI, p. 308 (Bowring edn Edinburgh, 1843).

[9] See R.S.C. 1965, 0.62, r. 3–(5); Form No. PF 60, 2 *Supreme Court Practice 1979*, p. 74.

[10] For the exceptional instances when mandatory, automatic documentary discovery does not take place, 0.27, r. 5–(1)(2)(3) establishes a procedure for admission of documents like that for facts in 0.27, r. 2–(1). A salient difference, however, is that the documents are deemed admitted except if a denial is served.

[11] The 'authenticity' of documents is expressly referred to in these Rules and in the cognate Rule 5–(1)(2)(3) of Order 27.

[12] Cf. R. Cross, *Evidence*, pp. 497–502 (2nd. edn., 1963).

[13] Cf. id., pp. 497–8.

[14] J. Buzzard, R. Amlot, S. Mitchell, *Phipson on Evidence*, ¶1704, p. 751 (11th edn., 1970) cf. Cross, p. 502.

[15] F.R.C.P. 36(a); see Form No. PF 61, 2 *Supreme Court Practice 1979*, p. 75; cf. Common Law Commission, 1830, Parl. Papers 1830, Vol. XI, p. 69.

[16] See Advisory Committee on Rules of Civil Procedure, pp. 530–1, 533; *Shawmut, Inc.* v. *American Viscose Corp.* 12 F.R.D. 488 (D.C. Mass. 1952); cf. *United States* v. *Kelsey-Hayes Wheel Co.* 15 F.R.D. 461, 464–5 (E.D. Mich. 1954); *Walsh* v. *Conn. Mutl. Life Ins. Co.* 26 F. Supp. 566, 572 (E.D. N.Y. 1939).

[17] Advisory Committee on Rules of Civil Procedure, pp. 531, 532. Were this not so, the admissions mechanism would be far less effective in narrowing the issues in a case. See id., pp. 531–2.

[18] F.R.C.P. 36(a), ¶2, sentence 2; see *United States* v. *Taylor* 100 F. Supp. 1016 (W.D. La. 1951).

[19] Advisory Committee on Rules of Civil Procedure, p. 530.

[20] See id., p. 534.

[21] Ibid.

[22] e.g. *Alexander* v. *Rizzo* 52 F.R.D. 235, 236 (E.D. Pa. 1971).

[23] F.R.C.P. 26(e) may at times obligate the responding party to move for withdrawal or amendment. The requirement in F.R.C.P. 36(b) of permission of the court to do so is an exception to the general rule of F.R.C.P. 26(e) which calls for unilateral corrections of discovery responses. See 8 Wright and Miller, s.2264, p. 746.

[24] See Advisory Committee on Rules of Civil Procedure, p. 534.

[25] R.S.C. 1965, 0.27, r. 5 is silent on the admissibility in evidence of an admitted document. But since it is *in pari materia* with 0.27, r. 4, the latter rule's preservation of objections to admissibility should apply to the former rule as well. See 1 *Supreme Court Practice 1979*, ¶27/4/1; Form No. PF 62, 2 *Supreme Court Practice 1979*, pp. 75–6.

[26] Id., pp. 74–5.

[27] See F.R.C.P. 84.

[28] Accord, *Goldman* v. *Mooney* 24 F.R.D. 279 (W.D. Pa. 1959).

[29] See F.R.C.P. 26(b)(1); and the authorities collected in n. 37 of Chapter 9.

[30] It has been seen that the responding party whose objection is not passed on by the court is not treated as having admitted the matter even though his objection would have been overruled. Still he is subject to this sanction unless one of the subsequent three categories in F.R.C.P. 37(c) applies.

[31] F.R.C.P. 37(c) should be amended to authorize such an order not only against the party, but also against the attorney advising him, or both of them, as is now provided in connection with sanctions under F.R.C.P. 37(a)(4), (b)(2), (d).

[32] 8 Wright and Miller, s.2265, p. 748; but see Advisory Committee on Rules of Civil Procedure, p. 540.

[33] This sanction in effect is available under F.R.C.P. 37(b)(2)(A) as well.

[34] Connolly, pp. 2, 24.

[35] Glaser, p. 211.

[36] I. Jacob, 'The English System of Civil Proceedings', 1 *Common Market Law Review* 294, 303 (1963–4).

[37] Ibid.

[38] Karlen, pp. 34, 66.

[39] See Field, Kaplan, & Clermont, p. 556.

[40] See id., pp. 556–7.

[41] Connolly, pp. 28, 30; Glaser, p. 211.

[42] Id., p. 53.

[43] Connolly, pp. 28, 30.

[44] Committee on Personal Injuries Litigation, p.74.

[45] This reform may be opposed on the ground that costs will increase because a notice of denial will be required and these notices will be far more frequent than notices of admissions under the present practice. This position is unsound. By capitalizing on inertia, if for no other reason, deeming silence to be an admission should augment the frequency of factual admissions, which undoubtedly will save costs of proof; these saved costs should neutralize, if not outweigh, the net increase in costs from an increased number of notices of denial in response to requests for factual admissions. Moreover, the costs of preparing notices of denial do not promise to be heavy. Most denials spring either from baseless requests for admission or the baseness of the respondent, who denies solely in order to help defeat his opponent at trial and to prop up his negotiating position. Denials for these reasons do not call for expensively tailored notices of partial, qualified non-admission, but rather for inexpensively prepared notices of refusal to admit.

[46] *Clarke* v. *Clarke* [1899] W.N. 130; Royal Commission on the Despatch of Business at Common Law, *Report*, pp. 81–3 (1936; Cmnd. 5065); Hanworth Committee on the Business of the Courts, *Interim Report*, p. 9 (1933; Cmnd. 4265); Rosenbaum, p. 387, n. 279.

[47] See F.R.C.P. 26(b)(1); and the authorities collected in n. 37 of Chapter 9. Another by-product may be earlier compromise settlements, as there is reason to believe that lawyers put off assessing a case's settlement value until they must do considerable work on it. See A. Levin & E. Wooley, *Dispatch and Delay*, pp. 50, 66 (University of Pennsylvania Law School Institute of Legal Research, 1961).

[48] Committee on Personal Injuries Litigation, p. 153 (Reservations by Master I.H. Jacob); F.R.C.P. 8(b)(d).

[49] Cf. F. James, Jr., & G. Hazard, *Civil Procedure*, pp. 84–5, 86 (2nd. edn., 1977).

[50] The rule fixing the length of this period should of course provide that it may be enlarged, when more time is necessary to prepare for trial, either by agreement of the parties or court order.

[51] The English Summons for Directions is mandatory. It is a proceeding designed to enable the court to direct the future course of the action and deal with interlocutory motions. See R.S.C. 1965, O.24. In some respects, the proceedings are similar to American federal pre-trial proceedings under F.R.C.P. 16.

[52] See ¶5 in 'a typical form of pre-trial order' reproduced in *McCargo* v. *Hedrick* 545 F.2d 393, 400 (4th Cir. 1976).

Note that the present proposal for encouraging admissions has the advantage over the Summons for Directions and Pre-Trial Conference that it need not consume judicial time but operates extrajudicially.

The rare American federal 'complex' or 'protracted' case is described in Chapter 11. In such a case it is already recommended that the final pre-trial briefs perform the same functions as the present proposal for mandatory factual requests for admission. See 'Manual for Complex Litigation', 1 *Moore's Federal Practice — Part 2*, s.3.30 (2nd. edn., 1979); cf. M. Pollack, 'Pretrial Procedures More Effectively Handled', 65 F.R.D. 475, 480–2 (1974); 'Pretrial Conferences', 50 F.R.D. 451, 463–4 (1970). It should be noted that all of the proposals in this Book would not necessarily apply to the rare complex case, inasmuch as it is recommended in such a case that the court control discovery on an *ad hoc* basis (see Chapter 11). It also should be noted that all of the proposals in this Book for mandatory discovery would be subject to a court order to the contrary upon a party's motion, as is English mandatory documentary discovery.

[53] *Freed* v. *Erie Lackawanna Railway* 445 F.2d 619 (6th Cir. 1971), cert. denied, 404 U.S. 1017 (1972); Advisory Committee on Rules of Civil Procedure, p. 524.

[54] Cf. R.S.C. 1965, 0.27, r. 4–(1)(2); 1 *Supreme Court Practice 1979*, ¶27/4/1.

[55] *East India Co.* v. *Kynaston* 3 Bligh 153, 163, 164 (1821); Bray, *Principles of Discovery*, pp. 192, 577; Langdell, Part III, 12 *Harv. L. Rev.* 157; 1 E. Daniell, *Chancery Practice*, p. 420 (5th edn., 1871); Parl. Papers 1852, Vol. XXI, p. 7; G. Spence, *The Equitable Jurisdiction of the Courts of Chancery*, pp. 370–1 (London, 1845); C. Barton, *Historical Treatise of a Suit in Equity*, pp. 74–5, 87, 93, 96, 139 (London, 1796); see Contempt of Court Act, s.15, r. 12 (1830); *Aveling* v. *Martin* 17 Jur. (P.I.) 271 (1853); *Potts* v. *Whitmore* 8 Beav. 317 (1845); *Maitland* v. *Rodgers* 14 Sim. 92 (1844); Bray, *Principles of Discovery*, p. 585; cf. *Farrer* v. *Hutchinson* 3 Y. & C. 692, 698–700, 704, 9 L. J. Ex. Eq. 10, 12, 13 (1839, 1840); *Balfour* v. *Farquharson* 1 Sim. & St. 72, aff'd., *sub nom. Farquharson* v. *Balfour* Turn. & R. 184, 186–7 (1822).

[56] R.S.C. 1965, 0.24, r. 16–(1)(2), 0.26, r. 6–(1)(2). (The English authority to 'order that the defence be struck out and judgment be entered accordingly' is tantamount to authority to order a default judgment against a defendant, or plaintiff in the status of the usual defendant. See F.R.C.P. 37(b)(1)(2)(C)(D)(E); cf. R.S.C. 1965, 0.25, r. 6–(3)).

[57] Langdell, Part III, p. 157; Bray, *Principles of Discovery*, p. 619; 1 Daniell, p. 421; F.R.C.P. 37(b)(2)(A).

[58] *Republic of Liberia* v. *Roye* 1 App. C. 139, 143 (1876); F.R.C.P. 37(b)(2)(B)(C).

[59] F.R.C.P. 37(c) pre-empts the court's inherent power to punish contempts. See *Société Internationale Pour Participations Industrielles et Commerciales, S.A.* v. *Rogers*, pp. 206–8. This is made especially clear by the absence from F.R.C.P. 37(c) of the power in F.R.C.P. 37(b)(2)(D) to use such sanctions 'as are just'.

[60] Compare F.R.C.P. 37(b) with F.R.C.P. 37(d); accord, 8 Wright & Miller, s.2291, p. 813; but see *Chagas* v. *United States* 369 F.2d 643 (5th Cir. 1966).

[61] In *Hammond Packing* the order violated was authorized by a statute providing for depositions of witnesses who were unavailable to testify or produce documents at trial. Such proceedings often incidentally yield discovery. The party which initiated the deposition there did so *inter alia* to obtain discovery. See 212 U.S. at 337.

In *Hammond Packing* the due-process clause of the Fourteenth Amendment was involved rather than that of the Fifth Amendment which had applied in *Hovey*. But they were held equivalent for the purpose of testing the constitutionality of *pro confesso* sanctions (id., p. 349).

[62] Accord, *National Hockey League* v. *Metropolitan Hockey Club, Inc.* 427 U.S. 639, 640 (1976) (Constitution not mentioned).

[63] 357 U.S. at 210; 212 U.S. at 350, 352.

[64] 357 U.S. at 210.

[65] 212 U.S. at 351.

[66] Id., p. 351; cf. id., p. 354.

[67] See *Mitchell* v. *Watson* 361 P.2d 744 (Wash. 1961); *Feingold* v. *Walworth Bros.* 144 N.E. 675 (N.Y. 1924).

[68] 167 U.S. at 413–14.

[69] Id. at 413–17. *Hovey* asserts that in early English equity *pro confesso* sanctions would not be applied to defendants. Contra *East India Co.* v. *Kynaston*, pp. 162–3.

[70] 167 U.S. at 413.

[71] Id., pp. 423–4, 435, 436.

[72] See *Jones* v. *Jones* 3 Mar. 161, 172 (1817); 9 W. Holdsworth, *A History of English Law*, p. 404 (1926); 1 J. Pomeroy, *Equity Jurisprudence*, p. 265 (4th edn., 1918); Langdell, Part II, p. 216; Kerr, p. 4; 1 Spence, p. 677; Wigram, pp. 114–17, 308–9; T. Hare, *Discovery of Evidence*, pp. vii–viii (1st edn., 1836); cf. *Hart* v. *Montefiore* 30 Beav. 280 (1861); *Wynn* v. *Humberston* 27 Beav. 421, 424 (1858); *Atty.-Gen.* v. *Clapham* 10 Hare App. II 69 (1853); *The Princess of Wales* v. *The Earl of Liverpool* 1 Swan. 114, 126 (1818).

[73] Since the merger of law and equity by the 1938 F.R.C.P. and the English Supreme Court of Judicature Acts 1873 and 1875, defendants in both countries in cases which

would have been in equity or at law before merger have not had to become plaintiffs in equity to obtain discovery. As defendants in the single, merged action they have been able to obtain discovery under F.R.C.P. 26–37 and R.S.C. 1965, 0.24, 26, 27, and 29. The Court of Chancery Procedure Act 1852, s.19 had even earlier enabled defendants in equity *qua* defendants to obtain discovery. Before 1852, however, defendants in equity had to become plaintiffs to a cross-bill to obtain discovery. See the authorities in the preceding footnote.

74 167 U.S. at 436.

75 427 U.S. at 640, 643.

76 Likewise, plaintiffs in general do not have a Constitutional due-process right of access to the courts. See *Ortwein* v. *Schwab* 410 U.S. 656 (1973); *United States* v. *Kras* 409 U.S. 434 (1973). The only exception appears to be when the objective sought by a plaintiff requires access to a court as 'the exclusive precondition to the adjustment of a fundamental human relationship' (*Boddie* v. *Connecticut*, p. 383; cf. id., pp. 379–80). Thus far only a plaintiff seeking a divorce has been held by the United States Supreme Court to fall within this exception (ibid.; cf. *Huffman* v. *Boersen*, 406 U.S. 337 (1972) (annulment, custody, and paternity)). Plaintiffs seeking a discharge of debts in bankruptcy, and court review of the decision of an administrative agency reducing welfare payments, have been held to fall outside this exception because (a) the objectives of these plaintiffs — improved relationships with creditors and more money, as opposed to a divorce — may be obtained by other means than court adjudication and (b) economic interests are not fundamental in the Constitutional sense, as is the human, associational interest in marriage. See *Ortwein* v. *Schwab*, pp. 658, 659; *United States* v. *Kras*, pp. 441–6.

77 Petitioner's Brief for Certiorari at 2, 16, 17, 19, 20, *National Hockey League* v. *Metropolitan Hockey Club, Inc.* 427 U.S. 639 (1976); Respondent's Brief in Opposition to Certiorari at 1, 2, 4, 17, 19, 20, id. The Supreme Court rendered its Opinion without additional briefing.

78 When the purpose of the sanction is penal, it may be argued that it may not be applied until the accused party is afforded criminal process, such as proof of guilt beyond a reasonable doubt. The same argument may be made in the present context about contempt rather than dismissal or default, for the purpose is not to force a party to admit after trial what his adversary already has proved but to punish him for failing to admit before trial and thereby deter others.

These arguments for criminal process may well fail. See Note, 'The Emerging Deterrence Orientation in the Imposition of Discovery Sanctions', 91 *Harv. L. Rev.* 1032, 1052–4 (1978). But should they prevail, criminal process will merely lessen the speed and certainty with which the sanction will be applied. And the application of stronger sanctions than costs still will deter parties from baselessly failing to make admissions.

79 *East India Co.* v. *Kynaston*, p. 163; 1 Daniell, p. 420; Barton, p. 87.

80 They should be so tailored since the offending party is unable to cure his contempt — his admission of the matters earlier denied would not put his opponent in any better position than he already is in by having proved the matters at trial.

Chapter 6

1 R.S.C. 1965, 0.26, r. 5.

2 1 *Supreme Court Practice 1979*, ¶26/5/3.

3 Common Law Commission, 1830, Parl. Papers 1830, Vol. XI, Appendix, pp. 38–9 (suggestion of James Manning, Esq.); see for a detailed description of the American federal discovery deposition, 8 Wright & Miller, ss.2081–2157; 4 W. Moore & J. Lucas, Chapter 28; 4A, Chapters 29–32.

4 After putting the party on oath, the person administering the oath need not remain at the oral examination. See 'Preliminary Draft of Proposed Amendments to F.R.C.P.',

77 F.R.D. 629; but see Committee on Rules of Practice and Procedure of the Judicial Conference of the United States, p. 333.

⁵ Another non-discovery purpose of this lawyer's questions might be to preserve the testimony so that it is available for trial should the deposed party be dead or otherwise unavailable to testify in person. Preservation of testimony is usually an incidental effect of oral examination.

⁶ See F.R.C.P. 30(b)(7) added in 1980; cf. Committee on Rules of Practice and Procedure of the Judicial Conference of the United States, pp. 334–5, 337.

⁷ See Tauro, 'The State of the Judiciary', 56 *Mass. Law Quarterly* 207, 208–9 (1971); 'Improving the Quality of Justice', 49 *Mass. Law Quarterly* 7, 20, 23–35 (1964); C. Wright, H. Wegner, L. Richardson, Jr., 'Practicing Attorney's View of the Utility of Discovery', 12 F.R.D. 97, 99 (1952); Comment, 'Tactical Use and Abuse of Depositions Under the Federal Rules', 59 *Yale L. J.* 117, 121 (1949); Sunderland, 'Scope and Method of Discovery Before Trial', 42 *Yale L. J.* 863, 874 (1933); cf. M. Pollack, 'Discovery—Its Abuse and Correction', 80 F.R.D. 219, 224 (1978); but see *Rogers* v. *Tri-State Materials Corp.* 51 F.R.D. 234, 241 (N.D. W.Va. 1970); C. A. Wright, *Law of Federal Courts*, s.86, p. 424 (3rd. edn., 1976).

⁸ Cf. Glaser, pp. 44–9.

⁹ Id., pp. 52–3, 79–82.

¹⁰ Id., p. 53. Another field-study of more than 3,000 American federal cases terminating in 1973–5 made virtually the same finding: of all the discovery mechanisms employed, 43.1 per cent were oral examinations, 35.4 per cent were interrogatories, 15 per cent were inspections of documents and things, 5.6 per cent were requests for admission, 0.7 per cent were medical examinations, and 0.2 per cent were depositions upon written questions (Connolly, pp. 2, 28, 30). 'In the cases with higher discovery volume, however, oral depositions were an increasingly more popular device' (id., p. 33).

¹¹ Glaser, pp. 76–8.

¹² Id., pp. 63, 79–82.

¹³ Id., p. 63.

¹⁴ Id., p. 88. This generalization is based on Glaser's Table 14 which shows that (1) 44 per cent of plaintiffs and 64 per cent of defendants learned of new evidence by using oral examination (called depositions by Glaser) alone as compared to 47 per cent of plaintiffs and 45 per cent of defendants who used interrogatories alone, (2) that 39 per cent of plaintiffs and 39 per cent of defendants learned of new witnesses by using oral examination alone as compared to 30 per cent of plaintiffs and 31 per cent of defendants who used interrogatories alone, (3) that 23 per cent of plaintiffs and 24 per cent of defendants learned of new issues by using oral examination alone as compared to 20 per cent of plaintiffs and 3 per cent of defendants who used interrogatories alone, and (4) that 21 per cent of plaintiffs and 30 per cent of defendants learned of both new evidence and new witnesses by using oral examination as compared to 23 per cent of plaintiffs and 21 per cent of defendants who used interrogatories alone.

¹⁵ Id., pp. 87–8.

¹⁶ *Project for Effective Justice, Columbia University, Field Survey of Federal Pretrial Discovery*, V-1-10 (1965) (Unpublished Report to the American Federal Advisory Committee on Rules of Civil Procedure).

¹⁷ Oral examination as a discovery mechanism was unavailable. It was available, however, to perpetuate testimony and to present at trial testimony of witnesses who were, or might prove to be, unavailable for trial, or who lived more than 30 miles from the place of trial. See Mass. Gen. Laws. ch. 233, s.24–63 (a 1975 amendment to s.24 made this statute inapplicable in proceedings governed by the 1974 Massachusetts Rules of Civil Procedure, which closely follow the F.R.C.P.).

¹⁸ Mass. Gen. Laws. ch. 231, s. 61–7 (a 1975 amendment to s.61. made this statute inapplicable in proceedings governed by the 1974 Massachusetts Rules of Civil Procedure; Rule 33 on interrogatories is in general like F.R.C.P. 33, except a court order is required for more than 30 interrogatories).

¹⁹ *Project for Effective Justice*, pp. V-5-6.

[20] Id., p. V-5.

[21] Id., p. V-7; cf. Glaser, p. 84, Table 12.

[22] *Project for Effective Justice* p. V-7.

[23] Id., p. V-10.

[24] Rules of the Supreme Judicial Court of Massachusetts 3:15 ss.1–5, 8, 9. In 1974 Massachusetts Rules of Civil Procedure 28–32, which are virtually identical to the oral examination provisions in F.R.C.P. 28–32, also were put into effect.

[25] Tauro, 'The State of the Judiciary', pp. 208–9; see Glaser, p. 225.

[26] F. James, Jr., 'Discovery', 38 *Yale L. J.* 746, 774 (1929); Sunderland, 'Scope and Method of Discovery Before Trial', p. 875.

Oral examination would be more effective in securing information from non-parties too, should English discovery be extended to them, as proposed in Chapter 9.

[27] See Glaser, pp. 52–3.

[28] Common Law Commission, 1830, Parl. Papers 1830, Vol. XI, p. 20; see Committee on Supreme Court Practice and Procedure, *Final Report*, p. 100; Parl. Papers 1852, Vol. XXI, Chancery Commission of 1850, pp. 21–2.

[29] Accord, Common Law Commission, 1830, Parl. Papers 1830, Vol.XI, Appendix, p. 39 (noted in suggestion of James Manning, Esq.).

[30] See 81 *Sol. Jour.* 109 (1937).

[31] Sunderland, 'Scope and Method of Discovery Before Trial', pp. 875–6. Sunderland has gone on incisively to point out the especial desirability of the oral method should the scope of English discovery interrogation be enlarged by abrogating the English 'own case' and 'fact-evidence' rules in respect to interrogatories, as is recommended in Chapter 8, Section C: 'In view of these limitations upon the effectiveness of written interrogatories, it is evident that they are not well adapted for the purpose of a general examination. It is only when the facts sought are few, formal and isolated, that this method can be satisfactorily employed. So long as the discovery is restricted to the case of the examiner, and he is not permitted to inquire into the case of his adversary, the facts sought by discovery will usually be few, formal and isolated, and written interrogatories will perhaps serve reasonably well. For a small task a feeble instrument may suffice. But if discovery is to involve a thorough inquiry into the vital and highly controversial phases of the case, resort must be had to an oral examination. It is apparent that the two aspects of the problem of discovery, namely, its scope and its methods, are intimately connected. One depends to a considerable degree upon the other, and both should be dealt with together.

Massachusetts undertook to broaden the scope of discovery while retaining the ancient interrogatory method, with a resulting discrepancy between the authorized extent of the investigation and the capacity of the machinery for doing the work. New York retained the narrow limits of equity, but introduced the new method of oral examination, as a result of which the effectiveness of the method constantly outruns the limits placed upon its use, causing an enormous amount of technical litigation over the application of the rules' (id., p. 876).

[32] Parl. Papers, 1830, Vol. XI, pp. 21–3, 71–2.

[33] Parl. Papers, 1852–3, Vol. XI, pp. 36–7.

[34] Committee on Personal Injuries Litigation (Reservations by Master I.H. Jacob), p. 154.

[35] Most conveniently, this would be the shorthand stenographer or person supervising the electronic recording device.

[36] See Glaser, p. 170; Wright, Wegner, and Richardson, pp. 101–4.

[37] Glaser, p. 169. These fees were for attorneys for defendants. Contingent-fee contracts between plaintiffs and their attorneys unduly distort the fees for plaintiffs' attorneys. See Karlen, pp. 63–4; Glaser, pp. 167, 169–70; Tauro, 'Oral Discovery and the Plaintiff's Tort Bar', 16 *The Legalite* 216 (1965).

[38] Cf. Glaser, pp. 149–54.

[39] In the District Courts of the United States this median expense in 1962–3 for plaintiffs was $112 and for defendants $100 (id., p. 169); see 'Preliminary Draft of

Proposed Amendments to F.R.C.P.', pp. 5–6; Tauro, 'Oral Discovery and the Plaintiff's Tort Bar', p. 218; Wright, Wegner, and Richardson, p. 101.

[40] Cf. I. Jacob and G. Wheatcroft, *Courts and Methods of Administering Justice, Third Commonwealth and Empire Law Conference, Sydney, 1965*, p. 15 (available at University of London Institute of Advanced Legal Studies, 25 Russell Square, London, W.C. 2); Wright, Wegner, and Richardson, pp. 102, 103.

[41] Glaser, p. 179. Reported court opinions and academic discussions of discovery may suggest that discovery accounts for a higher proportion of costs because they usually disproportionately reflect cases in which immense amounts of money are at stake. Cf. id., pp. 185–6.

[42] Id., pp. 179–81; see Tauro, 'Oral Discovery and the Plaintiff's Tort Bar', p. 216; Wright, Wegner, and Richardson, pp. 103–4.

[43] Cf. Jacob and Wheatcroft, p. 15.

[44] *Aste* v. *Stumore* 13 Q.B.D. 326, 328, 329 (1883).

[45] Diamond, 'The Summons for Directions', p. 48; but see id., p. 48, n. 13.

[46] Jacob, 'The English System of Civil Proceedings', p. 313.

[47] Diamond, 'The Summons for Directions', p. 46.

[48] Id., p. 48.

[49] Committee on Supreme Court Practice and Procedure, p. 5.

Chapter 7

[1] See *Schlagenhauf* v. *Holder* 379 U.S. 104, 113 (1964); Glaser, p. 55.

[2] Id., p. 53.

[3] Id., p. 55. The study gave no indication of what the frequency of mental and physical examinations by informal agreement would be were compulsory discovery in this form not available. Undoubtedly it would be lower, but it is impossible to say by how much.

[4] E.g. *S.* v. *S* [1970] 3 All E.R. 107, 114; *Briggs* v. *Morgan* 2 Hag. Con. 324 (1820); see *LeBarron* v. *LeBarron* 35 Vermont 365, 368 (1862).

[5] See the authorities collected in Chapter 4, note 20.

[6] *Ex parte Aiscough*, p. 593.

[7] Cf. *Theaker's Case*; *Willoughby's Case*.

[8] See *Baugh* v. *Delta Water Fittings, Ltd.* [1971] 3 All E.R. 258, 261 (collecting statutes); *Friend* v. *London, Chatham & Dover Ry.* L.R. 2 Ex. D. 437 (1877); Committee on Personal Injuries Litigation, p. 89; Millar, *Civil Procedure of the Trial Court in Historical Perspective*, p. 227; G. Ragland, Jr., *Discovery Before Trial*, p. 193 (Chicago, 1932).

[9] *Edmeades* v. *Thames Board Mills, Ltd.*, p. 130.

[10] Id., pp. 128, 129.

[11] Lord Denning has reformulated this notion as follows: '[The defendant] should be able to check the plaintiff's condition and his injuries so as to be able to assess the damages properly' (*Clarke* v. *Martlew* [1972] 3 All E.R. 764, 766). Sachs, L.J., has similarly expressed the criterion for determining when there should be a medical examination as when 'the preparation of the case for the defence requires an examination' (*Lane* v. *Willis* [1972] 1 All E.R. 430, 436, 437).

[12] *Edmeades* v. *Thames Board Mills, Ltd.*, p. 129.

[13] Id., p. 130.

[14] Id., p. 129.

[15] Ibid.

[16] [1977] 1 All E.R. 243, 247, 249, 254, 256.

[17] [1972] 1 All E.R., pp. 433, 434, 435, 436, 438; accord, *Murphy* v. *Ford Motor Co. Ltd.* [1970], an unreported decision referred to in *Starr* v. *National Coal Board*, pp. 248, 253.

[18] [1970] 3 All E.R., p. 114 (House of Lords).

[19] Under *Edmeades* the court does not literally 'order' a medical examination of a plaintiff, but stays the action if plaintiff unreasonably refuses defendant's request.

[20] Ibid.

[21] *Edmeades* v. *Thames Board Mills, Ltd.*, p. 129.

[22] See *Schlagenhauf* v. *Holder.*

[23] *Lane* v. *Willis*, p. 436.

[24] *S.* v. *S.*, p. 114. F.R.C.P. 35(a) likewise defines physical conditions subject to discovery as 'including...blood group...'.

[25] Committee on Personal Injuries Litigation, pp. 89–91, 102. Of course this Committee limited its consideration to personal-injuries cases.

[26] A decisive sanction like a stay for refusal to be examined in effect renders the examination as compulsory as if it were ordered directly. See *Starr* v. *National Coal Board*, p. 255.

[27] Committee on Supreme Court Practice and Procedure, p. 116.

[28] Accord, *S.* v. *S.*, p. 111 (consider n. 41 of this Chapter with this dictum by Lord Reid); *Pickett* v. *Bristol Aeroplane Co. Ltd.*, an unreported decision by two judges referred to in *Starr* v. *National Coal Board*, pp. 247, 252.

[29] *S.* v. *S.*, pp. 119, 123, 124.

[30] *Starr* v. *National Coal Board*, p. 250; cf. id., pp. 249, 254, 255.

[31] Committee on Personal Injuries Litigation, pp. 90, 102; *Edmeades* v. *Thames Board Mills, Ltd.*, p. 129; compare *Starr* v. *National Coal Board*, pp. 250–1, 254, 265; *Murphy* v. *Ford Motor Co. Ltd.*

[32] *Theaker's Case*; cf. *Ex parte Aiscough*, p. 594.

[33] Id., p. 593.

[34] Id., p. 89; A.S. Diamond, *The New Summons for Directions*, p. 10 (The Law Society, Notes of a Lecture) (London, 1954).

[35] *Turquand* v. *Guardians* 8 Dowling 201 (1840).

[36] Parl. Papers, 1852–3, Vol. XL, p. 37.

[37] E.g. *Ex parte Aiscough*, p. 593.

[38] See Committee on Personal Injuries Litigation, pp. 90–1, 216–18. In such a case a single judge expressed his view that *Edmeades* was 'wrongly decided' (*Baugh* v. *Delta Water Fittings Ltd.*, pp. 262–3). This view was disapproved by all three Court of Appeal judges participating in *Lane* v. *Willis*, pp. 434, 436, 437. Two of these judges went on in dictum to say that the *Edmeades* doctrine applies to examinations of widows to determine their life expectancy, although the request for such an examination may be held unreasonable unless defendant shows some reason to think that the widow's life expectancy is less than average (id., pp. 434, 435, 438; cf. Committee on Personal Injuries Litigation, p. 90).

[39] Cf. *S.* v. *S.*, pp. 119, 123, 124.

[40] Recall that in this context Lord MacDermott noted that 'the rule book naturally tends to lag behind new methods of proof and ascertainment...' (id., p. 114). Should a rule concerning medical examinations be promulgated, it should codify the trend to treat discovery by medical examination as setting in motion mutual exchange of reports by medical experts. See *Clarke* v. *Martlew*, pp. 766, 767; *Lane* v. *Willis*, p. 437; F.R.C.P. 35(b). The rule also may encourage waiver of privilege against disclosing such reports. Cf. *Causten* v. *Mann Egerton Ltd.* [1974] 1 All E.R. 453; F.R.C.P. 35(b)(2).

[41] F.R.C.P. 37(b)(2)(D); *Sibbach* v. *Wilson & Co.*, p. 16; *Edmeades* v. *Thames Board Mills, Ltd.*, p. 130. The *Edmeades* doctrine and the proposal in this Chapter that medical examinations should be allowed in all civil litigation respect the liberty of the subject to the extent of not compelling examinations against a party's will, although a party who refuses examination is subject to sanctions. Parliament has reached a similar compromise. Compare s.21–(1) with s.23 in the Family Law Reform Act 1969.

Chapter 8

[1] e.g. *Commissioners of Sewers of City of London* v. *Glasse* L. R. Eq. 302, 304 (1873); *Preston* v. *Carr* 1 Y. & J. 175, 179–80 (1826); *Tomlinson* v. *Lymer* 2 Sim. 489 (1829); *Firkins* v. *Lowe* 13 Pri. 193 (1824); *Tyler* v. *Drayton* 2 Sim. & St. 309 (1825); *Ivy* v. *Kekewick* 2 Ves. Jun. 679 (1795); *Buden* v. *Dore* 2 Ves. Sen. 445 (1752); *Davers* v. *Davers* 2 P. Wms. 410 (1727); Bray, *Principles of Discovery*, pp. 444–5, 468, 498–9; Wigram, pp. 259–61, 293; cf. The Evidence Act 1851, s.6; *Minet* v. *Morgan* L.R. 8 Ch. App. Cas. 361, 364, 21 W.R. 467, 468 (1873); *Princess of Wales* v. *The Earl of Liverpool; Shaftesbury* v. *Arrowsmith* 4 Ves. 66 (1798); but see *Atty.-Gen.* v. *Corp. of London* 2 Mac. & G. 244, 2 H. & Tw. 1, 19 L. J. Ch. 314 (1849); *contra Lowndes* v. *Davies* 6 Sim. 468, 472–3 (1834) (dictum); *Bettison* v. *Farringdon* 3 P. Wms. 363, 364 (1735); *Earl of Suffolk* v. *Howard* 2 P. Wms. 177, 178 (1723).

[2] The rule applied comprehensively to a party's case or defence, although it often was expressed in terms of a party's 'title'. See *Jenkins* v. *Bushby* 35 L. J. Ch. 400, 401 (1866); *Atty.-Gen* v. *Thompson* 8 Hare 106 (1849).

[3] The 'own case' rule did not apply to information helping plaintiff as well as defendant. See *Coster* v. *Baring* 2 C.L.R. 811, 813 (1854); *Smith* v. *Duke of Beaufort* 1 Hare 507, 520, aff'd., 1 Phil. Ch. R. 208, 220 (1843); *Combe* v. *Corp. of London* 15 L.J. Ch. 80, 83 (1845); *Stainton* v. *Chadwick* 3 Mac. & G. 575, 585 (1851); *Storey* v. *Lord George Lennox* 1 Keen 341, 357, 6 L. J. Ch. (NS) 99, 106, aff'd., 1 My. & Cr. 525 (1836); *Burrell* v. *Nicholson* 1 Myl. & K. 680 (1833); *Atty.-Gen.* v. *Lambe* 11 Beav. 213, 17 L. J. Ch. 154 (1848); *Earp* v. *Lloyd* 3 K. & J. 548 (1857); *Lind* v. *Isle of Wight Ferry Co.* 8 W.R. 540 (1860); Wigram, pp. 4, 70–1, 244, 260–2; C. Pollock, *Power of Courts of Common Law to Compel Production of Documents for Inspection*, pp. 21–2 (London, 1851); Kerr, pp. 249–50; cf. *Brown* v. *Wales* L.R. 15 Eq. 142, 146–7 (1872). But see *Hungerford* v. *Goring* 2 Vern. 38 (1687). Nor did it apply 'where by reason of death one of the parties...has no...[source of informational] to meet the...[case or defence] of the other...' (*Hills* v. *Wates* 43 L.J.C.P. 380, 381, 382 (1874)).

[4] This may be a salutary instance in which the discovery function of admissions has been lost sight of in England. Other instances were discussed at the beginning of Chapter 5.

[5] This rule applied to property inspection in equity. See *Batley* v. *Kynock* L.R. 19 Eq. 90, 92 (1870); *Barlow* v. *Bailey* 1870 W.N. 136; *Piggott* v. *Anglo-American Telephone Co.; Ennor* v. *Barwell; Lewis* v. *Marsh* 8 Hare 97, 98 (1849); *Crofts* v. *Peach* 1 Webs. Pat. Cas. 268, 269 (1837); but see 6 Wigmore, *Evidence*, s.1862, p. 632 (rev. Chadbourn, 1976). And equity discovery principles remain applicable in the Supreme Court of Judicature in the absence of a provision in R.S.C. 1965 to the contrary. See, e.g., *Lyell* v. *Kennedy* (No. 1) 8 A.C. 217, 223, 224 (1883); *Kearsley* v. *Philips* 10 Q.B.D. 465, 466 (1883) (CA); *Atty.-Gen* v. *Gaskill* 20 Ch. D. 519, 526, 530 (1882) (CA); 1 *Supreme Court Practice 1979* ¶ 24/1/1; see also Bray, *Principles of Discovery*, pp. 5, 6, 9, 152.

[6] e.g. *The Shropshire* 38 T.L.R. 667 (1922) (CA); *Dalgleish* v. *Lowther* [1899] 2 Q.B. 590, 591, 593 (CA); *Hennessy* v. *Wright* (No. 2), 24 Q.B.D. 445, 4 T.L.R. 662 (1888) (CA); *Marriott* v. *Chamberlain* 17 Q.B.D. 154 (1886) (CA); *Benbow* v. *Low* 16 Ch. D. 93, 100 (1880); *Ashley* v. *Taylor* 37 L.T. 522 (1877), see 38 L.T. 44 (1878); *Eade* v. *Jacobs* 47 L.J. Ex. 74, 76, L.R. 3 Ex.D. 335, 37 L.T. 621, 26 W.R. 159 (1877) (CA) (exception to 'own case' rule when interrogating party is a representative of the deceased); see *Hall* v. *Truman, Hanbury & Co.* 29 Ch.D. 307, 320 (1885); *Bidder* v. *Bridges* 29 Ch.D. 29, 37 (1884), rev'd. on unclear grounds, 29 Ch.D. 46 (1885) (CA); *Johns* v. *James* 13 Ch.D. 370 (1879) (objection of party); *Kettlewell* v. *Dyson* 18 L.T. 285 (1868); *Daw* v. *Eley*, 2 H. & M. 725, 729–30 (1865); *Stoate* v. *Rew* 11 W.R. 595, 14 C.B. (NS) 209 (1863); *Ingilby* v. *Shafto* 33 Beav. 31 (1863); *Adams* v. *Lloyd* 3 H. & N. 351 (1858); *Moor* v. *Roberts* 2 C.B. (NS) 671 (1857); *Edwards* v. *Wakefield* 6 E. & B. 462 (1856).

[7] *Nash* v. *Layton.*

[8] *Dalgleish* v. *Lowther*, pp. 591, 593; *Marriott* v. *Chamberlain*, pp. 158, 159, 161, 163;

Benbow v. *Low*, p. 100; *Eade* v. *Jacobs* 47 L.J. Ex. 76, L.R. 3 Ex.D. 337, 37 L.T. 621, 26 W.R. 160.

[9] These decisions are collected in the preceding footnote.

[10] e.g. *Commissioners of Sewers of City of London* v. *Glasse*, p. 304; *Boyd* v. *Petrie* 20 L.T. 934, 935, 17 W.R. 903, 904 (1869); *Derby Commercial Bank* v. *Lumsden* L.R. 5 C.P. 107 (1870); *Goodman* v. *Hobroyd* 15 C.B. (NS) 839 (1864); *Bayley* v. *Griffiths* 1 H. & C. 429 (1862); *Scott* v. *Walker* 2 El. & Bl. 555, 561, 563 (1853); Bray, *Principles of Discovery*, p. 511; Kerr, p. 267; see *Combe* v. *Corp. of London*, p. 84; *Smith* v. *Duke of Beaufort; Knight* v. *Marquess of Waterford* 2 Y. & C. 23, 31–2 (1835) (dictum); *Bellwood* v. *Wetherell* 1 Y. & C. 211, 219 (1835); *Duke of Bedford* v. *Macnamara* 1 Price 208, 215 (1814); see Langdell, Part III, p. 166; cf. *Jenkins* v. *Bushby; Combe* v. *Corp. of London; Atty.-Gen.* v. *Corp. of London*, 2 H. & Tw. 1, 10, 16–7, 2 Mac. & G. 244, 260, 261, 19 L. J. Ch. 314, 316, 318; *Combe* v. *City of London*, 4 Y. & C. Ex. 139 (1840); *Stroud* v. *Dracon* 1 Ves. Sen. 37 (1747); Bray, pp. 498–9; Pollock, p. 22; Wigram, pp. 57–8, 261–2; *contra Bolton* v. *Corp. of Liverpool* 3 Sim. 467 (1831), aff'd., 1 Mg. & K. 88 (1833); Hare, p. 197.

[11] *Lyell* v. *Kennedy* (No. 1), p. 227; *Griebart* v. *Morris* [1920] 1 K.B. 659, 664, 665; *Dawson* v. *Dover and County Chronicle, Ltd.* 108 L.T. 481, 485 (1913) (CA); *Plymouth Mutual Cooperative and Industrial Society*, Ltd. v. *Traders' Publishing Assoc., Ltd.* [1906] 1 K.B. 403, 417 (CA); *Atty.-Gen.* v. *Newcastle-Upon-Tyne Corp.* (No. 1) [1897] 2 Q.B. 384, 390, 391, 394 (CA); 1 *Annual Practice 1962*, p. 695; Bray, *Digest*, p. 17; cf. *Brookes* v. *Prescott* [1948] 2 K.B. 133.

[12] 1 *Annual Practice 1962*, p. 695; cf. *Atty.-Gen.* v. *Newcastle-Upon-Tyne Corp.* (No. 1); but see *Bidder* v. *Bridges*, pp. 35–6.

[13] *Hennessy* v. *Wright* (No. 2) 24 Q.B.D. 445, n., 448, n., 449, n., 4 T.L.R. 662, 664.

[14] There is another reason too to suspect that 'fishing' is a disguise for the 'own case' rule. Properly used, 'fishing' is a pejorative description of discovery by a potential plaintiff who is exploring to find a profitable claim (Wigram, p. 12). 'Fishing', therefore, does not fit discovery by a defendant. Hence when plaintiffs object to discovery sought by defendants as 'fishing', it is likely that the 'own case' rule really is the ground for the objection.

[15] e.g. *Preston* v. *Carr*, pp. 179–80; *Daw* v. *Eley*, p. 730; *Potter* v. *Metropolitan District Ry. Co.* 28 L.T. 231 (1873) (semble).

[16] *Griebart* v. *Morris*, p. 666 (dictum); *Knapp* v. *Harvey*, pp. 729–30, 732; *Marriott* v. *Chamberlain*, pp. 161, 163, 165–6. This has been true too when the 'fact-evidence' rule has perhaps superseded the 'own case' rule (e.g. *Eade* v. *Jacobs* L.R. 3 Ex. D. 337, 44 L. J. Ex. 76, 26 W.R. 160).

[17] *Dalgleish* v. *Lowther*; cf. Bray, *Digest*, pp. 3–4.

[18] *In re Strachan* [1895] 1 Ch. 439, 445 (CA); 1 *Annual Practice 1963*, p. 698; Bray, *Digest*, p. 17; *Benbow* v. *Low*, p. 95; Wigram, pp. 265–6, 4; *Bligh* v. *Benson* 7 Price 205, 207 (1819).

[19] Of course, a surprising presentation of true evidence or evidence leading to a true inference is not to be deplored, for it does not tend to generate the wrong verdict. Cf. 6 Wigmore, s.1845, pp. 486–7.

[20] See Wigram, pp. 265–6; Ragland, p. 124.

[21] *Benbow* v. *Low*, p. 96.

[22] Wigram, p. 265.

[23] James, Jr., *Civil Procedure* (Boston, 1965), s.6.2, p. 183; accord, *Martin* v. *Long Island Railroad Co.* 63 F.R.D. 53, 54 (E.D. N.Y. 1974); see *In re Strachan*, pp. 447–8.

[24] See Chapter 3, Section A2.

[25] Ragland, p. 124.

[26] See *Eade* v. *Jacobs; Owen* v. *Nickson* 3 El. & El. 602, 608 (1861); *Earl of Suffolk* v. *Howard; Bettison* v. *Farringdon*; Bray, *Principles of Discovery*, pp. 265–6.

[27] E. R. Sunderland, 'An Appraisal of English Procedure', 24 *Mich. L. R.* 109, 116 (1925).

[28] *In re Strachan*, p. 445.

[29] *Knapp* v. *Harvey*, pp. 730–1.

[30] *In re Strachan*, p. 445; see *Egremont Burial Board* v. *Egremont Iron Ore Co.* 14 Ch.D. 158, 159, 161 (1880).

[31] Cf. Committee on Personal Injuries Litigation, p. 42; id. (Reservations by Master I. H. Jacob), p. 154; 6 Wigmore, s.1845, p. 491.

[32] Ibid.

[33] Id., pp. 488–9.

[34] Id., p. 490.

[35] Id. s.1846, p. 493.

[36] Ibid.

[37] See id., p. 493; Langdell, Part I, pp. 144–6; J. Dawson, *A History of Lay Judges*, pp. 153–4 (Cambridge, Mass., 1960).

[38] 6 Wigmore, s.1845, p. 490.

[39] Id., p. 489.

[40] Jacob and Wheatcroft, p. 13.

[41] See 6 Wigmore, s.1845, pp. 491–2.

[42] *Benbow* v. *Low*, p. 100; Sunderland, 'An Appraisal of English Procedure', p. 116.

[43] Jacob & Wheatcroft, p. 13; Diamond, 'The Summons for Directions', p. 46.

[44] See Committee on Supreme Court Practice and Procedure, p. 28.

[45] See Section A2 of this Chapter.

[46] Law Reform Committee, *Sixteenth Report, Privilege in Civil Proceedings*, p. 13 (1967; Cmnd. 3472).

[47] See Committee on Personal Injuries Litigation, pp. 57, 113, 81–2; id. (Reservations by Master I.H. Jacob), p. 154; Committee on Supreme Court Practice and Procedure, pp. 97–8, 117; Jacob and Wheatcroft, p. 14; but see Committee on Personal Injuries Litigation, p. 104.

[48] This privilege in America is called the work-product or trial-preparation privilege.

[49] Recall Section B of this Chapter.

[50] Committee on Supreme Court Practice and Procedure, p. 100.

[51] For example, the interrogatories in question in *Nash* v. *Layton* would be readily allowed if tested by the 'own case' rule. Yet in applying the 'fact-evidence' rule to these interrogatories, Fletcher-Moulton, L.J., would have disallowed them as seeking 'evidence', not 'facts' (id., pp. 80–1).

[52] Ibid.

[53] Id., pp. 76, 83.

[54] Accord, *Bidder* v. *Bridges*, p. 37.

[55] *Nash* v. *Layton*, p. 83.

[56] But see *Knapp* v. *Harvey*, p. 730.

[57] See, e.g., Fletcher Moulton, L.J., id., pp. 730–1 on 'awkward facts'.

[58] Recall Section A2 of this Chapter.

[59] Ibid.

[60] Advisory Committee on Rules of Civil Procedure, pp. 490–1, 497.

[61] Accord, e.g., *Webster Motor Car Co.* v. *Packard Motor Car Co.* 16 F.R.D. 350 (1954); *Shrader* v. *Reed* 11 F.R.D. 367 (D.C. Neb. 1951).

[62] Recall Section B of this Chapter.

[63] e.g. *Brennan* v. *Engineered Products, Inc.* 506 F.2d 299, 303, n. 2 (8th Cir. 1974) (collecting authorities); *St. Paul Fire & Marine Ins. Co.* v. *King* 45 F.R.D. 521 (W.D. Okla. 1968); *Richards* v. *Maine Central R.R.* 21 F.R.D. 595 (D.C. Me. 1957); contra, e.g., *United States* v. *216 Bottles* 36 F.R.D. 695 (E.D. N.Y. 1965).

[64] This rule expressly bars a work-product objection. It authorizes the court to order further discovery in the same vein by other mechanisms; when it does so, it usually will require the discovering party to pay the expert's fees (F.R.C.P. 26(b)(4)(A)(ii),(c)).

[65] e.g. *Wirtz* v. *Hooper-Holmes Bureau, Inc.* 327 F.2d 939, 942 (5th Cir. 1964); see F.R.C.P. 16; cf. *Brennan* v. *Engineered Products, Inc.*, p. 304.

[66] Field, Kaplan, & Clermont, p. 74.

[67] Recall Section B of this Chapter.

[68] *Brennan* v. *Engineered Products, Inc.,* p. 303, n. 2. This group must include all potential witnesses, for 'discoverable matter' is that 'relevant to the subject matter involved in the...action' or 'reasonably calculated to lead to the discovery of admissible evidence' (F.R.C.P. 26(b)(1)).

[69] See Section C of Chapter 9, which points out that American federal non-parties are subject to discovery by deposition.

[70] While he may learn from them more than he is looking for, this will not always be the case.

[71] The right to discovery of the identity of the persons an opponent plans to call as witnesses at trial of course would not extend to the identities of those enjoying privileges, such as the 'informer's privilege' enjoyed by the government in civil actions enforcing the Fair Labor Standards Act (F.R.C.P. 26(b)(1); see *Brennan* v. *Engineered Products, Inc.,* p. 302).

[72] Cf. Advisory Committee on Rules of Civil Procedure, p. 508.

[73] Amendment to F.R.C.P. 26(e) also should tie it to the sanctions in F.R.C.P. 37, in order to close the present gap between the two rules pointed out in 8 Wright and Miller, s.2050; cf. Advisory Committee on Rules of Civil Procedure, p. 508.

[74] See *The Shropshire; Ingilby* v. *Shafto,* pp. 39, 40, 41, 42; *Stoate* v. *Rew; Moor* v. *Roberts,* 679; *Edwards* v. *Wakefield,* pp. 467–8; Wigram, pp. 285–6; *contra Knapp* v. *Harvey; Cayley* v. *Sandycroft Brick, Tile & Colliery Co.* 33 W.R. 577 (1885); *Lyon* v. *Tweddle* 13 Ch.D. 375 (1879); *Johns* v. *James; Ashley* v. *Taylor; Saunders* v. *Jones; Kettlewell* v. *Dyson; Flitcroft* v. *Fletcher* 11 Exch. 543, 544 (1856); *Atty.-Gen* v. *Corp. of London* 2 Mac. & G. 256–7, 258, 259, 261–2, 262–3, 265–6, 2 H. & Tw. 12, 13–4, 15, 18, 19, 22–3, 19 L. J. Ch. 317, 318, 319, 320: 1 *Annual Practice 1962,* p. 694.

[75] Compare, e.g., *Katz Exclusive Millinery, Inc.* v. *Reichman* 14 F.R.D. 37 (W.D. Mo. 1953); *Close* v. *Sanderson & Porter* 13 F.R.D. 123 (W.D. Pa. 1952) with, e.g., *Sierocinski* v. *E.I. DuPont de Nemours & Co.* 103 F.2d 843 (3rd. Cir. 1939) (dictum); *United Sheeplined Clothing Co., Inc.,* p. 895.

[76] See *Scovill Mfg. Co.* v. *Sunbeam Corp.* 357 F. Supp. 943, 948 (D. Del. 1973). Those American federal courts which permitted contentions to be discovered on depositions may still do so after the 1970 amendments. Cf. *Moore's Federal Practice,* ¶26.56[3], pp. 26–168–26–169.

[77] '[U]nder the new language interrogatories may not extend to issues of "pure law"', i.e., legal issues unrelated to the facts of the case' (Advisory Committee on Rules of Civil Procedure, p. 524).

[78] F.R.C.P. 33(a).

[79] This division of function between client and attorney probably explains why the 1970 amendments made contentions discoverable by interrogatories and requests to admit, the responses to which an attorney formulates for his client, but not by deposition at which the client himself responds orally. Another possible explanation is that a party may not be in a position to state his contentions until he has conducted considerable discovery of his own; and responses to interrogatories and requests to admit conveniently may be deferred from an early to a later point in litigation, while a deposition may not be. See F.R.C.P. 33(b), 36(a); 4 *Moore's Federal Practice,* ¶26.56[3], pp. 26–168–26–169.

Whether the work-product privilege applies to contentions under F.R.C.P. 33(b) and 36(a) is unclear. See Advisory Committee on Rules of Civil Procedure, p. 502; compare 8 Wright & Miller, s.2026, p. 232 with 4 *Moore's Federal Practice,* s.26.64[1], pp. 26–413–14, s.26.64[4], pp. 26–451–4.

[80] *Hartsfield* v. *Gulf Oil Corp.* 29 F.R.D. 163, 165 (E.D. Penn. 1962); see *Rogers* v. *Tri-State Materials Corp.,* p. 246; cf. *Leumi Financial Corp.* v. *Hartford Accident & Indemnity Co.* 295 F. Supp. 539, 543 (S.D. N.Y. 1969).

[81] Cf. 8 Wright & Miller, s.2255, p. 713.

[82] See 4A *Moore's Federal Practice,* ¶36.04[4], pp. 36–40–36–41.

[83] A subsidiary rationale is the difficulty of drawing sharp lines between facts and opinions (Advisory Committee on Rules of Civil Procedure, pp. 524, 532; see *Dusek* v.

United Air Lines 9 F.R.D. 326 (N.D. Ohio 1949); cf. C. McCormick, *Law of Evidence*, ss.11, 12 (St. Paul, Minn., 1954)).

⁸⁴ Advisory Committee on Rules of Civil Procedure, p. 532.

⁸⁵ Id., p. 533.

⁸⁶ Id., p. 524; see *Leumi Financial Corp.* v. *Hartford Accident & Indemnity Co.*, p. 542; *Montecatini Edison* v. *Rexall Drug & Chemcial Co.* 288 F. Supp. 486, 490 (D. Del. 1968); cf. J. Ebersole, 'Discovery Problems. Is Help on the Way?', 66 *American Bar Association Journal* 50, 53 (1980).

⁸⁷ This form now is 'sufficient under the rules...' (F.R.C.P. 84). See Field, Kaplan, & Clermont, p. 34, n. f.

⁸⁸ *Sierocinski* v. *E.I. DuPont de Nemours & Co.*, pp. 843–4; accord, *Conley* v. *Gibson*, p. 47.

⁸⁹ See *Report of Proposed Amendments to Rules of Civil Procedure for the District Courts of the United States*, p. 441 (1946); 'Amendments to Federal Rules of Civil Procedure', 6 F.R.D. 229, 233.

⁹⁰ Pleadings themselves have been required in some cases to contain particulars (R.S.C. 1883, 0.19, r. 6; R.S.C. 1965, 0.18, r. 12(1)). Particulars and further particulars have been available. See R.S.C. 1965, 0.18, r. 12(3); R.S.C. 1883, 0.19, r. 7; Jacob, 'The English System of Civil Proceedings', p. 297; Committee on Supreme Court Practice and Procedure, p. 6. Accordingly, in England, when pleadings or particulars have been available to disclose contentions, it often understandably has been held that contentions are not subject to discovery. See *Sutherland (Duke)* v. *British Dominions Land Settlement Corp., Ltd.; Ingilby* v. *Shafto*, p. 42; *Edwards* v. *Wakefield*, p. 468; Committee on Supreme Court Practice and Procedure, p. 6; Wigram, pp. 285–6.

⁹¹ *Conley* v. *Gibson*, pp. 46–7; see *Sierocinski* v. *E.I. DuPont de Nemours & Co.; Hartsfield* v. *Gulf Oil Corp.*; Glaser, p. 29.

⁹² Advisory Committee on Rules of Civil Procedure, p. 524.

⁹³ Accord, *Shelak* v. *White Motor Co.* 581 F.2d 1155 (5th Cir. 1978); *Leumi Financial Corp.* v. *Hartford Accident & Indemnity Co.*, p. 543, n. 18; 8 Wright & Miller, s.2181, p. 578 (semble); 4A *Moore's Federal Practice*, ¶33.29[2], pp. 33–168–33–171; cf. *Allright, Inc.* v. *Yeager* 512 S.W.2d 731, 736–7 (Texas Court of Civil Appeals 1974); *Ruiz* v. *Hamburg-American Line* 478 F.2d 29 (9th Cir. 1973) (particularly n. 6, p. 33); but see *Freed* v. *Erie Lackawanna Ry. Co.*

⁹⁴ *Rogers* v. *Tri-State Materials Corp.*, pp. 242–5 (semble); see *Montecatini Edison* v. *Rexall Drug & Chemical Co.*, p. 491; cf. *Allright, Inc.* v. *Yeager*. But F.R.C.P. 26(e) does not assure an adversary that he may rely on the interrogatory answer, both because the sanction selected may not exclude the undisclosed contention and because Rule 26(e) depends on the state of mind of the party answering the interrogatory rather than on prejudicial reliance by his adversary.

⁹⁵ 4A *Moore's Federal Practice*, ¶33.29[2], pp. 33–170–1; cf. Advisory Committee on Rules of Civil Procedure, p. 533.

⁹⁶ James, Jr., *Civil Procedure*, s.6.12, p. 217.

⁹⁷ Accord, *Shelak* v. *White Motor Co.*; 8 Wright & Miller, s.2181, p. 578 (semble); 4A *Moore's Federal Practice*, ¶33.29[2], pp. 33–168–33–171; cf. *Allright, Inc.* v. *Yaeger*, pp. 736–7; *Ruiz* v. *Hamburg-American Line*, pp. 31–2. The essential principles of F.R.C.P. 15(b) already apply to limitation of issues through Rule 36 admissions by virtue of F.R.C.P. 36(b); however, 15(b) contains very useful operational details not found in 36(b).

⁹⁸ An interruption of trial always will cause additional time and expense. It will be especially uneconomical if the continuance is in a jury trial and for so long a period that the parties' right to have the case decided by a jury which considers all, and only, the evidence introduced at trial is jeopardized. When this is so, the conduct of the trial up to the point when the court allowed an amendment of contentions and granted a continuance will have to be duplicated. Nevertheless, these marginal costs of a continuance to the legal system as a whole, if not to the litigants in a particular case, will undoubtedly by counterbalanced by the marginal savings from freeing parties from the need to

prepare to meet other contentions than those disclosed by discovery, in view of the extremely general American federal pleading. Furthermore, equity between the litigants in a particular case may be achieved by exercise of the court's power to order the party who belatedly raised a contention to pay the expenses of his opponent entailed by the continuance and need for additional preparation. Cf. *Watson* v. *Cannon Shoe Co.* 165 F.2d 311 (5th Cir. 1948). A court will be inclined so to order in circumstances in which it would find the discovery statement of contentions 'in substance a knowing concealment' under F.R.C.P. 26(e)(2).

[99] See *Leumi Financial Corp.* v. *Hartford Accident & Indemnity Co.*, p. 542.

[100] The above proposal to tie admissions about contentions to the notion of F.R.C.P. 15(b) adds operational detail and flexibility to F.R.C.P. 36(b).

[101] Cf. *John Walker & Sons, Ltd.* v. *Henry Ost & Co., Ltd.* (1970) R.P.C. 151, 154 (CA).

[102] The most economical chronology would be to ask interrogatories first and then serve requests to admit that other contentions than those in interrogatory answers will not be raised.

[103] Cf. *Sherwood* v. *Lord Lonsdale* L.R. 5 C.P.D. 47, 49 (1879); *Allhusen* v. *Labouchère* 3 Q.B.D. 654 (1878); *Baker* v. *Newton* [1876] W.N. 8; *Finch* v. *Finch* 2 Ves. Sen. 491, 492 (1752).

[104] For example, an affidavit of documents is like an answer to an imaginary interrogatory; there is no distinction between them in principle. See *Daniel* v. *Ford*, 47 L.T. 575, 577 (1882); *Phillips* v. *Phillips* 40 L.T. 815, 821 (1879); Bray, *Digest*, p. 7.

[105] e.g. *Hickman* v. *Taylor*, p. 511; *Communist Party of United States* v. *Subversive Activities Control Board* 254 F.2d 314, 330 (D.C. Cir. 1958); *United States* v. *International Business Machines Corp.* 66 F.R.D. 215, 218–9 (S.D. N.Y. 1974); *DaSilva* v. *Moore-McCormack Lines, Inc.* 47 F.R.D. 364 (E.D. Pa. 1969); *Eaddy* v. *Little* 235 F. Supp. 1021 (E.D. S.C. 1964); *United States* v. *62.50 Acres of Land, More or Less* 23 F.R.D. 287 (N.D. Ohio 1959); *Barreca* v. *Penn. R.R. Co.* 5 F.R.D. 391 (E.D. N.Y. 1946); contra, e.g., *Wharton* v. *Lybrand, Ross Bros. & Montgomery* 41 F.R.D. 177, 179 (E.D. N.Y. 1966).

[106] Information of substantive as well as impeachment effect is considered subject to discovery. See 8 Wright & Miller, s.2015, p. 117; cf. R.S.C. 1965, 0.26, r. 1–(4).

[107] e.g. *Mort* v. *A/S D/S Svendborg* 41 F.R.D. 225 (E.D. Pa. 1966); *Stone* v. *Marine Transp. Lines, Inc.* 23 F.R.D. 222, 226 (D.C. Md. 1959); *Bogotay* v. *Montour R.R. Co.* 177 F. Supp. 269 (W.D. Pa. 1959); *Margeson* v. *Boston & Maine R.R.* 16 F.R.D. 200 (D.C. Mass. 1954) (semble); contra *Martin* v. *Long Island Railroad Co.* (collecting authorities).

[108] Cf. Section C of this Chapter.

[109] *Margeson* v. *Boston & Maine R.R.*, p. 201. The likelihood of success of such an effort 'to defeat the truth' can be minimized by providing that the impeaching information not be disclosed to the party or witness to be impeached until he himself has been committed to his position by interrogatory answer or deposition from him. See *Martin* v. *Long Island Railroad Co.*, p. 55.

[110] Cf. *Boldt* v. *Sanders* 111 N.W. 2d 225, 227–8 (Minn. 1961).

Chapter 9

[1] e.g. *Manchester Fire Ins. Co.* v. *Wykes* 33 L.T. 142, 23 W.R. 884 (1875); *Temperley* v. *Gye* 6 El. & Bl. 380, 382 (1856); *Balls* v. *Margrave* 3 Beav. 448, 449 (1841); *How* v. *Best* 5 Madd. 19 (1820); *Gibbons* v. *Waterloo Bridge Co.* 5 Price 491, 493 (1818) (dictum); *Dummer* v. *Chippenham* 14 Ves. 245, 252 (1807) (dictum); *Mayor of London* v. *Levy* 8 Ves. 398 (1803); *Fenton* v. *Hughes* 7 Ves. 287 (1802); *Plummer* v. *May* 1 Ves. Sen. 426 (1750); *Davers* v. *Davers*; 6 Wigmore, pp. 562, 576; Bray, *Principles of Discovery*, p. 270; Kerr, pp. 241–2; Daniell, Vol. II, p. 1410; Wigram, pp. 164, 315; but see 6 Holdsworth, p. 281; contra *Doe I. Morris* v. *Roe* 5 L. J. Ex. 105, 1 M. & W. 207, 1 Tyr. & G. 545, 1 Gale 367 (1836); *Harris* v. *Aldrit* 2 Chitty's Reports 229 (1814).

[2] *Penn-Texas Corp.* v. *Muralt Anstalt* (No. 2) [1964] 2 Q.B. 647, 667 (CA); *O'Shea* v. *Wood* [1891] P. 286 (CA); *Burstall* v. *Beyfus* 26 Ch. D. 35, 41–2 (1884) (CA); *Berry* v.

Keen 26 *Sol. Jour.* 312 (1882) (CA); *Heatley* v. *Newton*, pp. 336, 337; *Wilson* v. *Church* 9 Ch. Div. 552 (1878); *Radio Corp. of America* v. *Rauland Corp.* [1956] 1 All E.R. 549, 551 (dictum); *Amos* v. *Herne Bay Pavilion Promenade & Pier Co. Ltd.* 54 L.T. 264 (1886); 1 *Supreme Court Practice 1979*, ¶24/1/1; Jacob, 'The English System of Civil Proceedings', pp. 302, 303; Bray, *Digest*, p. 4; see *Burchard* v. *MacFarlane* [1891] 2 Q.B. 241, 251 (CA).

[3] Cf. id., p. 245.

[4] Cf. R.S.C. 1965, 0.26, r. 3.

[5] *Wilson* v. *Church*, pp. 555–7; *Amos* v. *Herne Bay Pavilion Promenade & Pier Co.*

[6] *Welsbach Incandescent Gas Lighting Co.* v. *New Sunlight Incandescent Co.* [1900] 2 Ch. 1; *Chaddock* v. *British South Africa Co.* [1896] 2 Q.B. 153 (CA); *Wilson* v. *Church*, p. 557; 1 *Supreme Court Practice 1979*, ¶26/2/1; Bray, *Principles of Discovery*, pp. 76, 79–80; cf. R.S.C. 1965, 0.26, r. 2.

[7] *Berkeley* v. *Standard Discount Co.* 13 Ch.D. 97 (1879); cf. Bray, *Principles of Discovery*, p. 83.

[8] *Orr* v. *Diaper* 4 Ch.D. 92 (1876); *Heathcote* v. *Fleete* 2 Vern 442 (1702); cf. *Morse* v. *Buckworth* 2 Vern 443 (1703); *Dineley* v. *Dineley* 2 Ath. 394 (1742); contra *Mayor of London* v. *Levy*, p. 405.

[9] *Norwich Pharmacal Co.* v. *Commissioners of Customs & Excise* [1973] 2 All E.R. 943 (dicta that non-party may have to be at least innocently involved with the wrongdoing in issue: 948, 951, 954, 957, 960, 966, 968, 970, 974, 975; but see 973–4, 975) (House of Lords); *Eyre* v. *Rodgers* 40 W.R. 137, 138 (1891); compare *Sebright* v. *Hanbury* [1916] 2 Ch. 245; cf. *Union Bank of London* v. *Manby* 13 Ch.D. 239, 241 (1879); *Hersom* v. *Bernett* [1954] 3 All E.R. 370, 372 (dictum); Bray, *Digest*, pp. 3–4, 41; but see 1 *Supreme Court Practice, 1970*, p. 444.

[10] *Perry* v. *Phosphor Bronze Co. Ltd.* 71 L.T. 854, 855 (1894) (CA).

[11] Contrast *Pollock* v. *Garle* [1898] 1 Ch. 1 (CA) with *Ironmonger & Co.* v. *Dyre* 44 T.L.R. 579, 580 (1928) (CA) and *South Staffordshire Tramways Co.* v. *Ebbsmith* [1895] 2 Q.B. 669, 674–5, 677–8 (CA).

[12] *Howard* v. *Beall* 23 Q.B.D. 1 (1889); See *South Staffordshire Tramways Co.* v. *Ebbsmith*, pp. 674–5, 676–8; *Arnott* v. *Hayes* 36 Ch.D. 731, 735, 737, 738 (1887) (CA). For the broader scope of discovery, see the cases and authorities cited in n. 37 of this Chapter.

[13] Accord, *James Nelson & Sons Ltd.* v. *Nelson Line Ltd.* [1906] 2 K.B. 217, 223, 227 (dicta) (CA); but see *Elder* v. *Carter* 25 Q.B.D. 194, 200 (1890) (dictum). The nominal plaintiff also may have to give discovery. See *Wilson* v. *Raffalovich* 7 Q.B.D. 553 (1881) (CA).

Although neither counsel nor the court is reported to have cited the House of Lords' contrary decision in *Portugal* v. *Glyn*, it does not appear distinguishable on its facts. See particularly id., pp. 472, 485. Hence *Willis & Co.* v. *Baddeley* is of questionable authority.

[14] Id., p. 326.

[15] Id., pp. 325–6.

In road-accident cases the parties usually are not impeded by the general rule against discovery from non-parties from learning what non-party witnesses saw of the accident if they were interviewed by the police. This is because the Home Office has recommended that, subject to the discretion of chief constables, the police should make available to a party statements made to the police by such witnesses even without their consent (64 *Law Society's Gazette* 418 (August 1967); see Committee on Personal Injuries Litigation, pp. 44, 49; Committee on Supreme Court Practice and Procedure, p. 119).

[16] See pp. 58, 84–6, 103–4 in this Report.

[17] Administration of Justice Act 1970, s.32(4).

[18] Id., s.32(1)(2). *Paterson* v. *Chadwick* 1 W.L.R. 890 (1974) wisely interpreted this statute as applicable to a malpractice action against solicitors who allegedly caused plaintiff to lose her claim for damages for personal injuries.

[19] Administration of Justice Act 1970, s.33(1).

[20] Id., s.33(2).

[21] R.S.C. 1965, 0.24, r. 7A–(1)(2)(4); 0.29, r. 7A–(2)(3); see 0.7, rr. 1, 2.

[22] R.S.C. 1965, 0.29, r. 7A–(3); 0.24, r. 7A–(3) (b).

[23] R.S.C. 1965, 0.24, r. 7A–(5); 0.29, r.7A–(5).

[24] Two additional possible exceptions to the general rule against discovery from non-parties have not yet materialized. The first concerns property inspection. Most authorities considered that the general rule applied to inspection of a non-party's property under R.S.C. 1883, 0.50, r. 3. See *Garand* v. *Edge* 37 W.R. 501, 502 (1889) (CA); *Shaw* v. *Smith* 18 Q.B.D. 193, 197 (1886) (dictum) (CA); *Reid* v. *Powers* 28 *Sol. Jour.* 653 (1884). However, Lord Esher, M.R., in *Shaw* v. *Smith*, p. 197 (dictum), and Roxburgh, J., in *Penfold* v. *Pearlberg* [1955] 3 All E.R. 120, 122 (dictum), did not think that 0.50, r. 3 expressly excluded property of a non-party; and the latter accordingly felt that a non-party might be joined in an action solely for the purpose of being ordered to permit inspection of his property (id., pp. 121, 122 (dictum)). Accord, *Coomer & Son* v. *Hayward* [1913] 1 K.B. 150 (dicta) (about the essentially identical County Court rule). The terms of the rule were ambiguous. They limited the power to authorize entry to 'any land or building in the possession of any party to…[an] action', but did not confine the power to authorize samples to be taken, observations to be made, and experiments to be conducted to the personal property of parties. R.S.C. 1965, 0.29, r. 3–(1)(2) has provided that to enable a sample to be taken, observation to be made, or experiments to be tried, the court may by order authorize entry 'upon any land or building in the possession of any party to the cause…' Thus, since 1965, the power to authorize entry to real estate for one of these purposes has been confined to the real estate of a party, just as has been the power to order inspection of real estate itself under R.S.C. 1965, 0.29 r. 2–(1)(2).

But R.S.C. 1965, 0.29, r. 3–(1) has continued not to prohibit ordering experiments and observations on and taking samples from a non-party's personal property. Such orders would be effective if they may be carried out without an order for entry on a non-party's real estate—for example, if the personal property in question were on public land or in a public building. In these limited instances R.S.C. 1965, 0.29, r. 3–(1) should be used to order discovery from a non-party for the same reasons, discussed in Section B of this Chapter, that discovery from non-parties in general is desirable.

Another rule might have been the instrument for entirely reversing the general rule against discovery of documents from non-parties had the courts been inclined to do so. R.S.C. 1883, 0.37, r. 7 and R.S.C. 1965, 0.38, r. 13 have provided that at any stage in a cause the Court may order any person to attend and produce any described document whose production appears necessary for the purpose of the cause. This rule was the successor to a number of statutes, including the Common Law Procedure Act 1854, s.46 (*Elder* v. *Carter*, pp. 198–9; *Straker* v. *Reynolds* 22 Q.B.D. 262, 264 (1889); *Central News Co.* v. *Eastern News Telegraph Co.* 53 L.J.Q.B. 236, 237, 238 (1884); J. Lely & W. Foulkes, *The Judicature Acts*, p. 269 (4th edn., London, 1883); see Bray, *Principles of Discovery*, p. 39; Statute Law Revision & Civil Procedure Act (46 & 47 Vict. c. 49) 1883 (repealing Common Law Procedure Act 1854, s.46)). This common-law statute as an exception to the absence of non-party discovery had been construed to empower the court to order discovery from non-parties in *Morgan* v. *Alexander*, L.R. 10 C.P. 184, 44 L.J.C.P. 167 (1875) and *Moline* v. *Tasmanian Railway Co.* 32 L.T. 828, 830 (1875).

Since this successor rule has not been limited to 'upon the hearing of any motion or summons', as was the common-law statute, this rule might have been employed even more liberally to order documentary discovery from non-parties than was the common-law statute. Lord Coleridge, C.J., thought that the rule did authorize ordering discovery by non-parties (*Central News Co.* v. *Eastern News Telegraph Co.*, pp. 237–8). *Rishdon* v. *White* 5 T.L.R. 59 (1888) so employed the rule, although the question of whether the rule empowered ordering a non-party to give documentary discovery is not reported to have been argued by counsel or discussed by the court. See *Straker* v. *Reynolds*, pp. 263, 264–5 (Wills, J., in this case explained his refusal to follow *Rishdon* v. *White* on the ground that he found the series of reports in which it is to be found 'not always accurate': id., p. 264). *Sub silentio*, of course, the court answered the question affirmatively. Afterwards, however, the rule has not been so employed, and the Court of Appeal has held that it does not empower ordering discovery by non-parties (*O'Shea* v. *Wood*, p. 288; *Elder* v. *Carter*; *Straker* v. *Reynolds*; see Committee on Personal Injuries Litigation, p. 87). The two reasons advanced by the Court of Appeal are unsatisfactory. One was that the power might be used oppressively (*Elder* v. *Carter*, p. 202). But there is no reason for oppressive discovery to be any less objectionable when sought from a non-party than when sought from a party. The power to order discovery by a non-party may coexist with the propriety of an objection against oppressive discovery. The court merely need not exercise its powers if it finds the discovery applied for to be oppressive. If it errs on this question and orders oppressive discovery from a non-party, he may be permitted to appeal, and so be protected from oppressive discovery. The second reason was that the power did not exist before the rule (*Elder* v. *Carter*, p. 199). In view of the applications of the Common Law Procedure Act 1854, s.46, in *Morgan* v. *Alexander* and *Moline* v. *Tasmanian Railway Co.*, this reason was inaccurate.

²⁵ *Norwich Pharmacal Co.* v. *Commissioners of Customs & Excise*, pp. 947, 951 (dicta); *Manchester Fire Ins. Co.* v. *Wykes* 33 L.T. 142, 144, 146, 23 W.R. 885; *How* v. *Best*; *Gibbons* v. *Waterloo Bridge Co.*; *Dummer* v. *Chippenham*; *Fenton* v. *Hughes*, p. 291; *Mayor of London* v. *Levy*, pp. 403, 405; *Plummer* v. *May*, p. 427; Mitford, p. 223 (1847 edn.), p. 188 (1827 edn.).

²⁶ See James & Hazard, pp. 172–3; Langdell, Part II, pp. 217–19.

²⁷ Evidence Act 1851, s.2.

²⁸ *Portugal* v. *Glyn*, p. 500 (dissenting judgment).

²⁹ *Fenton* v. *Hughes*, p. 291.

³⁰ *Rowell* v. *Pratt* [1938] A.C. 101, 116.

³¹ Cf. *Regina* v. *Inhabitants of Llanbaethly* 2 E. & B. 940 (1853).

³² *Wych* v. *Meal* 3 P. Wms. 310, 312 (1734).

³³ Cf. *Bettison* v. *Farringdon*, p. 364; Ragland, pp. 252–5.

³⁴ Cf. *Heatley* v. *Newton*, p. 338; *Potts* v. *Adair*; James, Jr., 'Discovery', p. 758.

³⁵ *Potts* v. *Adair*, p. 265, n.

³⁶ See Mitford, p. 223 (1847 edn.), p. 188 (1827 edn.); cf. James, Jr., 'Discovery', p. 755.

³⁷ e.g. *O'Rourke* v. *Darbishire*, pp. 616, 624, 630; *Osram Lamp Works, Ltd.* v. *Gabriel Lamp Co.* [1914] 2 Ch. 129 (CA); *Compagnie Financière Du Pacifique* v. *Peruvian Guano Co.* 11 Q.B.D. 55, 62, 63 (1882) (CA); *Radio Corp. of America* v. *Rauland Corp.*, pp. 550–1 (dictum); *Bustros* v. *White* 1 Q.B.D. 423, 425 (1876); *Nicholl* v. *Jones* 2 H. & M. 588, 593 (1865); *Hewitt* v. *Piggott*, p. 77; Jacob, 'The English System of Civil Proceedings', p. 301; Bray, *Principles of Discovery*, p. 142.

³⁸ Hare, p. 54 (2nd edn.), p. 68 (1st edn.); Accord, *Plummer* v. *May* (dictum).

³⁹ *Manchester Fire Ins. Co.* v. *Wykes* 33 L.T. 142, 145, 23 W.R. 855; *Portugal* v. *Glyn*, p. 490; *Kerr* v. *Rew* 5 My. & Cr. 154, 166, 9 L.J. (NS) 152.

⁴⁰ See James & Hazard, pp. 173–4.

⁴¹ Cf. *Kerr* v. *Rew* 5 My. & Cr. 166, 9 L.J. (NS) 152; *Portugal* v. *Glyn*, p. 499 (dissenting judgment).

⁴² Id., p. 501.

⁴³ See *Portugal* v. *Glyn*, p. 490; *Newman* v. *Godfrey*, pp. 333–4 (dictum); *Tooth* v. *Dean & Chapter of Canterbury*, p. 63; *Griffin* v. *Archer*.

⁴⁴ See *Norwich Pharmacal Co.* v. *Cmsrs. of Customs*, p. 973. The sanction for a non-party's discovery violation need, and should, not differ from the sanction for violating a trial subpoena, viz., punishment for contempt. Compare F.R.C.P. 45(d) (f).

⁴⁵ On the other hand, if the non-party's disclosure favours a party, his lawyer may conclude that the possibility of effecting a favourable compromise settlement before trial by disclosing the matter to his opponent through formal discovery subsequent to the interview outweighs the advantage of keeping the matter secret until producing it at trial.

⁴⁶ e.g. *O'Rourke* v. *Darbishire*, pp. 616, 624, 630; *Osram Lamp Works, Ltd.* v. *Gabriel Lamp Co.*; *Compagnie Financière Du Pacifique* v. *Peruvian Guano Co.*, pp. 62, 63; *Radio Corp.*

of America v. *Rauland Corp.*, pp. 550–1 (dictum); *Bustros* v. *White*, p. 425; *Nicholl* v. *Jones*, p. 593; *Hewitt* v. *Piggott*, p. 77; Jacob, 'The English System of Civil Proceedings', p. 301; Bray, *Principles of Discovery*, p. 142.

⁴⁷ Cf. Evershed Committee—*First Interim Report of the Committee on Supreme Court Practice and Procedure*, pp. 6–7, Part III (1949; Cmnd. 7764); see *Rishdon* v. *White*. To cultivate the goodwill of a non-party, a litigant may be expected to be solicitous of the non-party's convenience in arranging to secure discovery from him.

⁴⁸ *Penn-Texas Corp.* v. *Muralt Anstalt* (No. 2), p. 657 (dictum); *South Staffordshire Tramways Co.* v. *Ebbsmith*, p. 667 (dictum); *Arnott* v. *Hayes*, p. 739; Jacob and Wheatcroft, p. 15, Wigram, pp. 165–9; see *Zumbeck* v. *Biggs* 82 L.T. 654 (1900) (under what is now R.S.C. 1965, 0.38; r.13); R.S.C. 1965, 0.26, r.1–(3), 0.24, rr.8, 13–(1); 1 *Supreme Court Practice 1979*, ¶26/1/4, cf. *Reade* v. *Woodrooffe* 24 Beav. 421, 425 (1857).

Upon careful analysis it must be concluded that oppressiveness means that the burden on the person providing the discovery is inordinately disproportionate to the benefit the discovery may yield. Sometimes courts have used the misnomer of 'fishing' to describe oppressiveness.

⁴⁹ *Burchard* v. *Macfarlane*, p. 247 (dictum); *Lee* v. *Angas* L.R. 2 Eq. 59 (1866).

⁵⁰ The rules regulating documentary discovery from non-parties in death and personal-injuries cases do not impose on non-parties a duty to search all their documents for relevant ones. See R.S.C. 1965, 0.24, r.7A–(3)(b), (6)(b).

⁵¹ See Committee on Supreme Court Practice and Procedure, pp. 89–90.

⁵² See 8 Wright & Miller, ss.2131–3.

⁵³ See Administration of Justice Act 1970, s.32(1)(2), discussed in Section A5 of this Chapter; Committee on Personal Injuries Litigation, pp. 53, 84, 85, 86–7, 103–4, 113; Jacob and Wheatcroft, pp. 14, 15.

⁵⁴ F.R.C.P. 34(a) and 45(d)(1) call property other than real property 'tangible things'.

⁵⁵ See F.R.C.P. 45(d)(2). Concern for the non-party's convenience is reflected in the requirement that the examination take place in the county within the district in which the non-party resides, is employed, or was served, or 'such other convenient place as is fixed by an order of court' (ibid.).

⁵⁶ *Newmark* v. *Abul*; cf. *McLean* v. *Prudential Steamship Co., Inc.*; see Chapter 3, Section B1.

⁵⁷ Recall Chapter 3, Section B4.

⁵⁸ Persistent instances of illiteracy render compulsory interrogatories of non-parties inadvisable. A scheme, by which the discovering party rather than the non-party would pay the fee of the officer taking the non-party's oath to interrogatory answers, is sketched at the end of the preceding Section.

⁵⁹ Cf. Committee on Supreme Court Practice and Procedure, pp. 89–90.

⁶⁰ e.g. *Humphries* v. *Penn. R.R. Co.* 14 F.R.D. 177, 181 (N.D. Ohio 1953).

⁶¹ The frequency of inspections of non-parties' documents and movable property has not been studied empirically. But 29 per cent of parties have taken the deposition of non-parties (Glaser, p. 53).

⁶² Advisory Committee on Rules of Civil Procedure, p. 527.

⁶³ Recall Section A of this Chapter.

⁶⁴ Recall Section A5 of this Chapter.

⁶⁵ Advisory Committee on Rules of Civil Procedure, p. 527.

⁶⁶ Cf. 8 Wright & Miller, s.2209, p. 620.

⁶⁷ Compare *Ellenwood* v. *Marietta Chair Co.* 158 U.S. 105, 107 (1895) with *Stone* v. *United States* 167 U.S. 178, 182 (1897).

⁶⁸ See James & Hazard, pp. 172–3; Langdell, Part II, pp. 217–19.

⁶⁹ F.R.C.P. 35(a); *United States* v. *Dioguardi* 361 F. Supp. 954, 961, n. 20 (S.D. N.Y. 1973) (collecting authorities). The 1970 amendment to F.R.C.P. 35(a) extended it to those in the custody or under the legal control of parties (Advisory Committee on Rules

of Civil Procedure, p. 528). Thus 'a parent or guardian suing to recover for injuries to a minor may be ordered to produce the minor for examination' (id., p. 529). What other classes of non-parties are included by the amendment is unclear. See 8 Wright & Miller, s.2233, pp. 669–70.

Inasmuch as, before the promulgation of the F.R.C.P., the American federal courts were held to lack inherent power to order a physical examination of a party, it is extremely unlikely that they have such inherent power concerning a non-party (*Union Pacific Ry. Co.* v. *Botsford* 141 U.S. 250 (1891); 8 Wright & Miller, s.2233, p. 669; but see *Fong Sik Leung* v. *Dulles* 226 F.2d 74 (9th Cir. 1965); contra *Dinsel* v. *Penn. R.R.* 144 F. Supp. 880 (W.D. Pa. 1956) (dictum)).

[70] Cf. *Sibbach* v. *Wilson & Co., Inc.*, p. 18 (dissenting opinion).

[71] F.R.C.P. 35(b)(1) also protects the person to be examined by entitling him to a copy of a detailed written report by the examining physician.

[72] *Schlagenhauf* v. *Holder*, p. 118.

[73] Id., pp. 121, 116–22.

[74] 'Developments in the Law-Discovery', 74 *Harv. L. Rev.* 940, 1025 (1961).

This Act provides, 'The Supreme Court shall have the power to prescribe by general rules . . . the practice and procedure of the district courts . . . Such rules shall not abridge, enlarge or modify any substantive right . . .' (28 U.S.C. s.2072 (1948)).

[75] The Act then was essentially the same as it is now, as set forth in the preceding note. See 48 Stat. 1064 (1934).

[76] 312 U.S. at 16.

[77] Id., pp. 6–7.

[78] Id., p. 16.

[79] Ibid. Subsection (iv) of Rule 37(b)(2) then literally exempted refusal to obey a Rule 35 order only from 'arrest, not all punishment as for contempt' (see id., p. 9). But exemption from the latter was the negative implication of Rule 37(b)(1) as it then read (see id., p. 8).

[80] See id., pp. 8–9.

[81] Id., p. 14.

[82] Id., p. 9.

[83] The Court itself expressly affirmed the availability of these sanctions (id., p. 16).

[84] Id., p. 18.

[85] In this decision the Supreme Court also made it explicit that the propriety of examinations of the persons of plaintiffs is not based on a theory that plaintiffs waive claims to inviolability of their persons by invoking court action to secure relief (*Schlagenhauf* v. *Holder*, pp. 113–14). Such a theory is a second reason that the same commentator doubted whether extending Rule 35 to non-parties would be within the Rules Enabling Act ('Developments in the Law—Discovery', p. 1025). This commentator's final reason is that there has been no common-law tradition for examination of the persons of non-parties (ibid.). This reason need give little pause. The right to examine non-parties' documents and movable property and take their depositions for the purpose of discovery was created by the F.R.C.P. in the face of the absence of such common-law traditions (recall Section A of this Chapter). Yet no court has held this right unauthorized by the Rules Enabling Act.

[86] *Schlagenhauf* v. *Holder*, pp. 112–14; *Sibbach* v. *Wilson & Co., Inc.*, p. 17 (dissenting opinion agreeing with majority on this issue); but see *Roe* v. *Wade* 410 U.S. 113, 152 (semble as to citation of *Union Pacific Ry. Co.* v. *Botsford*). See the preceding note.

[87] *Union Pacific Ry. Co.* v. *Botsford*, p. 259 (dissenting opinion).

Chapter 10

[1] The less burdensome it is for a party to provide discovery, the less likely is it that he may successfully resist doing so by the objection of oppressiveness. See F.R.C.P. 26(c). Hence too the greater the quantity of information that he will furnish.

Chapter 11

[1] *Herbert* v. *Lando* 441 U.S. 153, 176 (1979).

[2] Segal, pp. 10–12, 67.

[3] e.g. Glaser, pp. vii, 35–6, and n. 13 (collecting authorities); Advisory Committee on Rules of Civil Procedure, p. 489; W. Speck, 'The Use of Discovery in United States District Courts', 60 *Yale L. J.* 1132, 1133, n. 3 (collecting authorities) (1951). Comment, pp. 121, 123–34, 130–1, 132, 137–8.

[4] Glaser, pp. 36–7, 42; Advisory Committee on Rules of Civil Procedure, p. 489; see ABA, 'Report of Pound Conference Follow-up Task Force', 74 F.R.D. 159, 192, n. 3 (1976).

[5] Glaser, pp. 201, 192, 197; see 4 *Moore's Federal Practice*, ¶26.02[3], p. 26–69 (2nd edn., New York, 1979).

[6] Glaser, p. 234.

[7] Advisory Committee on Rules of Civil Procedure, pp. 489–90; 398 U.S. 977 (1970); cf. ABA, p. 192, n. 3.

[8] Segal, pp. 10–11, 66, 67; see *Blue Chip Stamps* v. *Manor Drug Stores* 421 U.S. 723, 741 (1975).

[9] See Segal, pp. 68, 66.

[10] See 70 F.R.D. 79, 80.

[11] ABA, pp. 191–2. The Attorney-General of the United States endorsed this position of the Task Force. See G. B. Bell, 'The Pound Conference Follow-up: A Response from the United States Department of Justice', 76 F.R.D. 320, 328 (1977).

[12] Special Committee for the Study of Discovery Abuse, Section of Litigation, American Bar Association, *Report*, October 1977, pp. 1–25 (on file at Federal Judicial Center, 1520 H Street, N.W., Washington, D.C., U.S.A.).

[13] Id., pp. (iii)–(iv), 20.

[14] Id., pp. (iii)–(iv); S. Umin, 'Discovery Reform: A New Era Or Business as Usual?', 65 *American Bar Association Journal* 1050 (1979).

[15] Report of the Special Committee for the study of Discovery Abuse, pp. 3, 20, 24–5.

[16] Id., p. 2., cf. Ebersole, p. 53.

[17] Report of the Special Committee for the Study of Discovery Abuse, p. 18.

[18] Id., p. 24.

[19] 77 F.R.D. 613, 626.

[20] The Advisory Committee deemed another of the ABA Section's proposals, namely, a discovery conference, also to be directed at abuse of discovery, even though it does not *per se* restrict discovery (id., pp. 626–7).

[21] Id., p. 623.

[22] Id., p. 646.

[23] Id., p. 628.

[24] 74 F.R.D. 159, 192, n. 3.

[25] Id., p. 192.

[26] Connolly, Holleman, Kuhlman, pp. 1, 2, 85–90. This study primarily addressed the question of whether establishing cut-off dates for completing discovery saves time (id., pp. 1–3, 5, 36, 51–76, 80, 82). It does not bear on the extent to which discovery provides its intended benefits. Recall Sections A1 and 2 of Chapter 1.

[27] S. Flanders, *Case Management and Court Management in United States District Courts*, p. 27 (Federal Judicial Center, Washington, D.C., 1977); cf. id., pp. 128–30. This 1977 Federal Judicial Center conclusion was drawn from the same empirical data set forth in detail in the 1978 Center publication cited in the preceding note (id., pp. 1, 4–5, 17; Connolly, p. 2). Although a footnote to the quotation from page 27 in the 1977 Center publication indicates that this conclusion does not embrace discovery not docketed in court, the 1978 Center publication shows that this conclusion is reliable for all discovery, that which is not docketed as well as that which is docketed (id., pp. 27–8).

[28] Id., pp. 35, xi; cf. id., pp. 105–7.

[29] Id., p. 35.

[30] Id., p. 1. Only a summary and selective analysis of this empirical data had been published in 1977. Flanders, pp. 1, 4–5, 17, i.

[31] Advisory Committee, 'Revised Preliminary Draft of Proposed Amendments to the F.R.C.P.', 80 F.R.D. 323, 326, 330–2, 340–1, 344–7 (1979).

[32] Id., p. 332.

[33] See 48 F.R.D. 489–90. Apparently the penchant of practising trial lawyers to ignore empirical, systematic evidence that in general there is no abusive 'over-discovery' will not be stemmed by the Federal Judicial Center study. In the July 1979 *American Bar Association Journal*, a practising litigator and member of the ABA Discovery Abuse Committee reasserts that there is 'abusive overuse of discovery', laments the Advisory Committee's February 1979 withdrawal of its 1978 proposals to restrict discovery, and is conspicuously silent on the convincing 1963 and 1973–5 empirical studies (Umin, pp. 1051, 1050, 1052). A similar position was taken by the three Justices who dissented from the promulgation by the United States Supreme Court of 1980 Amendments to the federal discovery rules (—U.S.—, 64 L. Ed. 2d xlv–xlvii (1980)).

[34] 398 U.S. 977 (1970).

[35] —U.S.—, 64 L. Ed. 2d xli–xlv (1980).

[36] See 441 U.S., p. 176, n. 26, p. 204, n. 1. Some opinions by individual Justices, but not the majority opinion, in *Herbert* can be read as accepting the over-generalized allegations of discovery abuse. Cf. Umin, pp. 1050, 1052.

[37] 441 U.S. 176, n. 25.

[38] Connolly, pp. 28–32, 35; Glaser, pp. 191–2, 201.

[39] See Segal, pp. 10–12, 67.

[40] 441 U.S., p. 177; cf. id., p. 175 and 175, n. 24. The majority expressly rejected the dissenting position of Mr Justice Brennan that a defendant publisher should have a privilege against discovery of the editorial process unless a defamation plaintiff makes a prima-facie showing that the publication at issue constitutes defamatory falsehood (id., pp. 174, n. 23, 197–8; see Segal, p. 16; Rifkind, p. 107). Even the headiness of the Pound Conference did not propel Judge Rifkind's proposal to make a showing of 'probable merit' a prerequisite for discovery into acceptance by the ABA Discovery Abuse Committee or the Advisory Committee.

[41] 441 U.S., p. 177; see Ebersole, pp. 51, 52. Recent empirical evidence shows that the district courts have not hesitated to apply such powers, since they have granted the majority of motions under Rule 26 (c) and have overwhelmingly granted Rule 37 motions to compel discovery responses or for sanctions (Connolly, pp. 105–6, 20, 25). However, the same empirical study shows that lawyers have not invoked Rule 37 proceedings to compel nearly as often or as quickly as they are entitled to (id., pp. 18–26). (The data in this study did not permit a conclusion in this respect on invocation of Rule 37 sanctions or Rule 26(c): id., pp. 25, 106.) Invocation of powers to prevent abuse of discovery is facilitated, and so encouraged, by the Manual for Complex Litigation and by discovery conferences, which are discussed below. F.R.C.P. 26(f), which was added by the 1980 Amendments to the F.R.C.P., enables any party to bring about a discovery conference with the court.

[42] Accord, 4 *Moore's Federal Practice*, ¶26.02[3], pp. 26–69, 26–70; 'Advisory Committee Note', 77 F.R.D. 613, 649 (1978). All of these powers, except that under Rule 37, are available to check 'over-discovery' abuses, i.e. seeking too much discovery. Rule 37 and Rule 26(f) are available to check the other side of the abuse coin, 'avoidance', i.e. unjustifiably resisting discovery. Cf. Segal, pp. 10–12. See on Rule 37, *ACF Industries, Inc.* v. *Equal Employment Opportunity Commission* 439 U.S. 1081 (1979) (dissenting opinion); *National Hockey League* v. *Metropolitan Hockey Club, Inc.* See on Rule 26(f), Advisory Committee, 'Revised Preliminary Draft of Proposed Amendments to the F.R.C.P.', p. 332.

[43] Flanders, p. 27; 4 *Moore's Federal Practice*, ¶ 26.84; Glaser, pp. 190, 191, 193, 197; Preface to the 'Handbook of Recommended Procedures for the Trial of Protracted Cases', 25 F.R.D. 351, 359, 360 (1960); see Connolly, p. 35. Complex cases have been

generously estimated to constitute no more than 20 per cent of all civil litigation. Cf. Pollack, 'Pretrial Conferences', pp. 456, 460, 461.

44 See 'Manual for Complex Litigation', s.0.22, p. 7; 4 *Moore's Federal Practice*, ¶26.84; Glaser, pp. 189, 192.

45 4 *Moore's Federal Practice*, ¶26.84; Glaser, pp. 193, 197, 201.

46 Segal, pp. 10–11, 67, 68; Pollack, 'Discovery—Its Abuse and Correction', p. 222; Kirkham, pp. 202–4; Comment, pp. 126–7; cf. Glaser, p. 182.

47 Cf. 'Manual for Complex Litigation', para. 0.60.

48 Id., ss.1.00–4.70.

49 Id., s.2.50.

50 Id., ss.1.50, 2.30, 3.10, 3.11.

51 Id., ss.1.50, 1.70, 2.20, 2.30, 2.40, 3.10, 3.11, 4.30. Recall the empirical finding, set forth in note 55 of Chapter 1, that establishing cut-off dates for discovery reduces the time consumed by discovery but does not reduce the use of discovery. Cf. Connolly, p. 78.

52 77 F.R.D. 628.

53 80 F.R.D. 330–2; 77 F.R.D. 624–6, 628. Both the Manual and the discovery conference provide for enhanced judicial intrusion into federal discovery, which recent literature favours as an antidote against abuse. See 80 F.R.D. 332; Segal, p. 68; W.H. Becker, *Modern Discovery*, March 30, 1978 (unpublished paper on file at the University of Pennsylvania Law School and excerpted in Segal, p. App. B-4); but see Ebersole, p. 52.

54 Connolly, pp. 28–35; see Glaser, pp. 70–1, 192, 197, 201, 237, 241. Otherwise put, 'In most [cases]...discovery was abused primarily by non-use' (*Shelak* v. *White Motor Co.*, 1164 (dissenting opinion)).

55 Recall Chapter 1, Sections A1 and 2.

56 See *Herbert* v. *Lando*; 4 *Moore's Federal Practice*, ¶26.02[3], pp. 26–70–26–71; L. F. Powell, Jr., 'Reforms — Long Overdue', 33 *Record of the Association of the Bar of the City of New York* 458, 461 (1978); Connolly, p. 52; Pollack, p. 222; J. A. Stanley, 'President's Page', 62 *American Bar Association Journal* 1375 (1976); ABA, p. 192; cf. *Herbert* v. *Lando*, p. 176, n. 26; Segal, pp. 9, 67 (summarizing literature); Connolly, 59–62.

The survival and growth of discovery over the centuries bodes well for its future. See J.B. Levine, *Discovery in Civil Procedure, A Critical and Historical Study of the English Law* (July 1969) (unpublished D. Phil. thesis in Oxford University's Bodleian Library).

Bibliography

Abbott, Austin, 'The Co-Operation of "Law" and "Equity"; and the Engrafting of Equitable Remedies upon Common-Law Proceedings', 7 *Harv. L. Rev.* 76 (1893)

Advisory Committee on Rules of Civil Procedure, 'Proposed Amendments (and Notes thereto) to the Federal Rules of Civil Procedure Relating to Discovery (1970)', 48 F.R.D. 487

'Advisory Committee Note', 77 F.R.D. 613 (1978)

Advisory Committee, 'Revised Preliminary Draft of Proposed Amendments to the F.R.C.P.', 80 F.R.D. 323 (1979).

'Amendments to Federal Rules of Civil Procedure', 6 F.R.D. 229 (1946–7)

American Bar Association, 'Report of Pound Conference Follow-Up Task Force', 74 F.R.D. 159 (1976)

Annual Practice 1884–5

Annual Practice 1962, Vol. 1

Annual Practice 1963, Vols. 1 and 2

Barber, C., 'Statement on the Practice and Procedure of the Court of Chancery in England', Parl. Papers, Vol. XV, 1863

Barron, W. and A. Holtzoff, *Federal Practice and Procedure*, Vol. 2A (St. Paul, Minnesota, 1961)

Barton, C., *Historical Treatise of a Suit in Equity* (London, 1796)

Becker, *Modern Discovery*, March 30, 1978 (unpublished paper on file at the University of Pennsylvania Law School and excerpted in Segal, p. App. B–4)

Becker, W.H., 'A Modern, Efficient Use of the Bar and Other Parajudicial Personnel in Pretrial of Ordinary Civil Actions', 53 F.R.D. 159 (1971)

Bell, G.B., 'The Pound Conference Follow-Up: A Response from the United States Department of Justice', 76 F.R.D. 320 (1977)

Bentham, J., *Rationale of Judicial Evidence, Works*, Vol. VI (Bowing edn., Edinburgh, 1843)

Bowen, C., 'The Law Courts Under the Judicature Acts', 2 *L.Q.R.* 1 (1886)

Bray, E., *Principles of Discovery* (London, 1885)

Bray, E., *Digest of the Law of Discovery* (2nd edn., London, 1910)

Brennan, William J., Jr., Address to Round Table on Administration of Justice, San Juan, Puerto Rico, Feb. 5, 1962, quoted in Tauro, 'Improving the Quality of Justice in Massachusetts', 49 *Mass. Law Quarterly* (1964)

Buzzard, J., R. Amlot, and S. Mitchell, *Phipson on Evidence* (11th edn., 1970)

Chadbourn, James H., and A. Lee Levin, *Cases and Materials on Civil Procedure* (Brooklyn, New York, 1961)

Comment, 'Tactical Use and Abuse of Depositions Under the Federal Rules', 59 *Yale L.J.* 117 (1949)

Committee on Personal Injuries Litigation, *Report* (1968; Cmnd. 3691)

Committee on Supreme Court Practice and Procedure, *First Interim Report* (1949; Cmnd. 7764); *Second Interim Report* (1951; Cmnd. 8176); *Final Report* (1953; Cmnd. 8878)

Common Law Commission, 1853, *Second Report*, Parl. Papers, 1852–3, Vol. XL

Connolly, P.R., E.A. Holleman, and M.J. Kuhlman, *Judicial Controls and the Civil Litigative Process: Discovery* (District Court Study Series of Federal Judicial Center, Washington, D.C., 1978)

Cross, R., *Evidence* (2nd edn., 1963)

Daniell, E., *Chancery Practice*, Vols. 1 and 2 (5th edn., 1871)

Dawson, J., *A History of Lay Judges* (Cambridge, Mass., 1960)

Day, J. C., *Common Law Procedure Acts* (London, 1872)

'Developments in the Law—Discovery', 74 *Harv. L. Rev.* 940 (1961)

Devlin, P., *The Criminal Prosecution in England* (New Haven, 1958)

Diamond, A.S., *The New Summons for Directions* (The Law Society, Notes of a Lecture, London 1954)

Diamond, A.S., 'The Summons for Directions', 75 *B.Q.R.* 43 (1959)

Diamond, A.S., 'Changes in High Court Procedure', *Notes of a Lecture Given at The Law Society's Hall on 5 December 1963* (The Solicitor's Law Stationery Society, Ltd., Oyez House, Breams Bldg., London, E.C. 4)

Doskow, A., 'Procedural Aspects of Discovery', 45 F.R.D. 498 (1968)

Ebersole, J., 'Discovery Problems. Is Help on the Way?', 66 *American Bar Association Journal* 50 (1980)

Field, R.H., and V.L. McKusick, *Maine Civil Practice* (Boston, 1959)

Field, R.H., and B. Kaplan, *Materials for a Basic Course in Civil Procedure* (temporary 2nd edn., Mineola, New York, 1968)

Field, R.H., B. Kaplan, and K.M. Clermont, *Materials for a Basic Course in Civil Procedure* (4th edn., Mineola, New York, 1978)

Flanders, S., *Case Management and Court Management in United States District Courts* (Federal Judicial Center, Washington, D.C., 1977)

Form No. PF 62, 2 *Supreme Court Practice 1979*

Freund, F., 'Work Product', 45 F.R.D. 493

Glaser, W.A., *Pretrial Discovery and the Adversary System* (New York, 1968)

Halsbury's Laws of England, Vol. 15 (3rd edn., 1956)

'Handbook of Recommended Procedures for the Trial of Protracted Cases', 25 F.R.D. 351 (1960)

Hanworth Committee on the Business of the Courts, *Interim Report* (1933; Cmnd. 4265)

Hare, T., *Discovery of Evidence* (1st edn., 1836 and 2nd edn., 1876, London)

Hazard, Jr., G.C., *Research in Civil Procedure* (Walter E. Meyer Institute of Law, 1963)

Holdsworth, W., *A History of English Law*, Vols. I, V, VI, and IX (1926)

Israel, J., and W. La Fave, *Criminal Procedure in a Nutshell* (2nd edn., 1975)

Jacob, I., 'The Rules of the Supreme Court (Revision), 1962', *The Legal Executive* 263 (November 1963)

Jacob, I., 'The English System of Civil Proceedings', 1 *Common Market Law Review* 294 (1963–4)

Jacob, I., 'The Rules of the Supreme Court (Revision) 1965', (Lecture before the Institute of Legal Executives, Maltravers House, Arundel Street, Strand, London, W.C. 2), (available at University of London Institute of Advanced Legal Studies, 25 Russell Square, London, W.C. 2)

Jacob, I., and G. Wheatcroft, *Courts and Methods of Administering Justice, Third Commonwealth and Empire Law Conference, Sydney, 1965* (available at University of London Institute of Advanced Legal Studies, 25 Russell Square, London, W.C. 2)

James, Jr., F., 'Discovery', 38 *Yale L.J.* 746 (1929)

James, Jr., F., *Civil Procedure* (Boston, 1965)

James, Jr., F., and G. Hazard, *Civil Procedure* (2nd edn., 1977)

Karlen, D., *Appellate Courts in the United States and England* (New York, 1963)

Karlen, D., *Judicial Administration: The American Experience* (New York, 1970)

Kelley, J., *Roman Litigation* (Oxford, 1966)

Kerr, W., *Treatise on the Law of Discovery* (London, 1870)

Kirkham, F.R., 'Complex Civil Litigation — have Good Intentions gone awry?', 70 F.R.D. 199 (1976)

Langdell, C., 'Discovery Under the Judicature Acts, 1873, 1875, Part I.', 11 *Harv. L. Rev.* 137, 'Part II', *Harv. L. Rev.* 205, 'Part III', 12 *Harv. L. Rev.* 151 (1897–8)

Langdell, C., *Development of Equity Pleading from Canon Law Procedure*, in *Select Essays in Anglo-American Legal History*, compiled by Association of American Law Schools, Vol. 2 (Cambridge, 1908)

Law Reform Committee, *Sixteenth Report — Privilege in Civil Proceedings* (1967; Cmnd. 3472)

64 *Law Society's Gazette* 418 (August 1967)

Lely, J., and W. Foulkes, *The Judicature Acts* (4th edn., London, 1883)

Levin, A., and E. Wooley, *Dispatch and Delay* (University of Pennsylvania Institute of Legal Research, 1961)

Levine, J.B., *Discovery in Civil Procedure, A Critical and Historical Study of the English Law* (July 1969) (unpublished D. Phil. thesis in Oxford University's Bodleian Library)

'Manual for Complex Litigation', 1 *Moore's Federal Practice — Part 2* (2nd edn., 1979)

McCormick, C., *Law of Evidence* (St. Paul, Minn., 1954)

Millar, R., 'The Mechanism of Fact-Discovery', 32 *Northwestern Law Rev.* 261 (1937)

Millar, R., *Civil Procedure of the Trial Court in Historical Perspective* (New York, 1952)

Mitford, J. (later, Lord Redesdale), *Pleadings in Chancery* (4th edn., 1827, 5th edn., 1847, London)

Moore, W., and J. Lucas, *Moore's Federal Practice*, Vols. 4 and 4A (2nd edn., New York, 1979)

National Conference on the Causes of Popular Dissatisfaction with the Administration of Justice (Pound Conference), Addresses, 70 F.R.D. 79 (1976)

Note, 'The Emerging Deterrence Orientation in the Imposition of Discovery Sanctions', 91 *Harv. L.R.* 1032 (1978)

Odgers on Pleading and Practice (19th edn. by Giles F. Harwood, 1966, London)

Park, W.D., *Notes on Discovery and Inspection of Documents in Civil Procedure* (London, 1967)

Parliamentary Papers 1830, Vol. XI, Second Report of Common Law Commission, 1830; 1851, Vol. XXII, First Report of Common Law Commission, 1851; 1852, Vol. XXI, Chancery Commission of 1850; 1860, Vol. XXXI, Third Report of Common Law Commission, 1860; 1868–9, Vol. XXV, First Report of Judicature Commission, 1869

Petheran, W.C., *Interrogatories Under the Common Law Procedure Act 1854* (London, 1861)

Petitioner's Brief for Certiorari, *National Hockey League* v. *Metropolitan Hockey Club, Inc.*, 427 U.S. 639 (1976)

Pollack, M., 'Pretrial Conferences', 50 F.R.D. 451 (1970)

Pollack, M., 'Pretrial Procedures More Effectively Handled', 65 F.R.D. 475 (1974)

Pollack, M., 'Discovery — Its Abuse and Correction', 80 F.R.D. 219 (1978)

Pollock, C., *Power of Courts of Common Law to Compel Production of Documents for Inspection* (London, 1851)

Pomeroy, J., *Equity Jurisprudence*, Vol. 1 (4th edn. by John W. Pomeroy, Jr., San Francisco, 1918)

Powell, Jr., L.F., 'Reforms — Long Overdue', 33 *Record of the Association of the Bar of the City of New York* 458 (1978)

'Preliminary Draft of Proposed Amendments to F.R.C.P.', 77 F.R.D. 613 (1978)

'Preliminary Draft of Proposed Amendments to Rules of Civil Procedure for the United States District Courts, Rule 26(e) and Note', 43 F.R.D. 228 (1967)

Project for Effective Justice, Columbia University, Field Survey of Federal Pretrial Discovery V–1–10· (1965) (Unpublished Report to the American Federal Advisory Committee on Rules of Civil Procedure)

Ragland, Jr., G., *Discovery Before Trial* (Chicago, 1932)

'Report of Council of Judges', 36 *Sol. Jour.* 716 (1892)

'Report of Lord Chancellor's Legal Procedure Committee', 25 *Sol. Jour.* 911 (1881)

Report of Proposed Amendments to Rules of Civil Procedure for the District Courts of the United States (1946)

Report of the Royal Commission on the Despatch of Business at Common

Law (1936; Cmnd. 5065)

Report of the Special Committee for the Study of Discovery Abuse, Section of Litigation, American Bar Association, October 1977 (on file at Federal Judicial Center, 1520 H Street, N.W., Washington, D.C.)

Respondents' Brief in Opposition to Certiorari, *National Hockey League* v. *Metropolitan Hockey Club, Inc.*, 427 U.S.–639 (1976)

Rifkind, S., 'Are we asking too much of our courts?', 70 F.R.D. 96 (1976)

Rosenbaum, S., 'Studies in English Civil Procedure, II', 63 *Univ. of Penn. Law Rev.* 182 (1915)

Rosenberg, M., *The Pretrial Conference and Effective Justice* (Columbia University Press, 1964)

Rosenberg, M., 'Changes Ahead in Federal Pretrial Discovery', 45 F.R.D. 479 (1969)

Ross, R.E., *Law of Discovery* (London, 1912)

Scott, A., and R. Kent, *Cases and Other Materials on Civil Procedure* (Boston, 1967)

Segal, D., *Survey of Literature on Discovery from 1970 to the Present* (Federal Judicial Center, Washington, D.C., 1978)

Sichel, W.S., and W. Chance, *Discovery* (London, 1883)

26 *Sol. Jour.* 69 (1881)

38 *Sol. Jour.* 74 (1894)

81 *Sol. Jour.* 109 (1937)

Speck, W., 'The Use of Discovery in United States District Courts', 60 *Yale L.J.* 1132 (1951)

Spence, G., *The Equitable Jurisdiction of the Courts of Chancery*, Vol. 1 (London, 1845)

Stanley, J.A., 'President's Page', 62 *American Bar Association Journal* 1375 (1976)

Story, J., *Commentaries on Equity Jurisprudence*, Vol. 1 (London, 1839)

Story, Mr Justice, *Commentaries on Equity Jurisprudence* (1st and 2nd English edns., 1884 and 1892, by W.S. Grigsby, London)

Sunderland, E.R., 'An Appraisal of English Procedure', 24 *Mich. L.R.* 109 (1925)

Sunderland, E.R., 'Scope and Method of Discovery Before Trial', 42 *Yale L.J.* 863 (1933)

Supreme Court Practice 1979, Vol. 1 (London, 1978)

Supreme Court Practice 1967, Vols. 1 and 2 (London, 1966)

Sutton, R., *Personal Actions at Common Law* (London, 1929)

Tauro, G.J., 'Improving the Quality of Justice', 49 *Mass. Law Quarterly* 7 (1964)

Tauro, G.J., 'Oral Discovery and the Plaintiff's Tort Bar', 16 *The Legalite* 216 (1965)

Tauro, G.J., 'The State of the Judiciary', 56 *Mass. Law Quarterly* 207 (1971)

Umin, S., 'Discovery Reform: A New Era or Business as Usual?', 65 *American Bar Association Journal* 1050 (1979)

Weinstein, J., E. Gleit, and J. Kay, 'Procedures for Obtaining Information Before Trial', 35 *Texas L.R.* 481 (1957)

Wigmore, J., *Evidence*, Vol. 6 (3rd edn., 1940 and Chadbourn rev., 1976) and Vol. 8 (McNaughton rev., 1961)

Wigram, J., *Points in the Law of Discovery* (2nd edn., 1840, London)

Williston, S., *Life and Law* (Boston, 1940)

Wilson, A., *Supreme Court of Judicature Acts, 1873 and 1875* (London, 1875)

Wilson, G., 'Book Review', 82 *Harv. L. Rev.* 1408

Wright, C., H. Wegner, and L. Richardson, Jr., 'Practicing Attorney's View of the Utility of Discovery', 12 F.R.D. 97 (1952)

Wright, C.A., *Law of Federal Courts* (3rd edn., 1976)

Wright and Miller, *Federal Practice and Procedure*, Vol. 9 (1971)

Yale, D. E. C., Introduction to Lord Nottingham's 'Manual of Chancery Procedure' and 'Prolegemena of Chancery and Equity' (Cambridge, 1965)

Appendix: Major Discovery Rules
Federal Rules of Civil Procedure

Rule 26.

GENERAL PROVISIONS GOVERNING DISCOVERY

(a) Discovery Methods. Parties may obtain discovery by one or more of the following methods: depositions upon oral examination or written questions; written interrogatories; production of documents or things or permission to enter upon land or other property, for inspection and other purposes; physical and mental examinations; and requests for admission. Unless the court orders otherwise under subdivision (c) of this rule, the frequency of use of these methods is not limited.

(b) Scope of Discovery. Unless otherwise limited by order of the court in accordance with these rules, the scope of discovery is as follows:

(1) *In General*. Parties may obtain discovery regarding any matter, not privileged, which is relevant to the subject matter involved in the pending action, whether it relates to the claim or defense of the party seeking discovery or to the claim or defense of any other party, including the existence, description, nature, custody, condition and location of any books, documents, or other tangible things and the identity and location of persons having knowledge of any discoverable matter. It is not ground for objection that the information sought will be inadmissible at the trial if the information sought appears reasonably calculated to lead to the discovery of admissible evidence.

(2) *Insurance Agreements*. A party may obtain discovery of the existence and contents of any insurance agreement under which any person carrying on an insurance business may be liable to satisfy part or all of a judgment which may be entered in the action or to indemnify or reimburse for payments made to satisfy the judgment. Information concerning the insurance agreement is not by reason of disclosure admissible in evidence at trial. For purposes of this paragraph, an application for insurance shall not be treated as part of an insurance agreement.

(3) *Trial Preparation: Materials.* Subject to the provisions of subdivision (b) (4) of this rule, a party may obtain discovery of documents and tangible things otherwise discoverable under subdivision (b) (1) of this rule and prepared in anticipation of litigation or for trial by or for another party or by or for that other party's representative (including his attorney, consultant, surety, indemnitor, insurer, or agent) only upon a showing that the party seeking discovery has substantial need of the materials in the preparation of his case and that he is unable without undue hardship to obtain the substantial equivalent of the materials by other means. In ordering discovery of such materials when the required showing has been made, the court shall protect against disclosure of the mental impressions, conclusions, opinions, or legal theories of an attorney or other representative of a party concerning the litigation.

A party may obtain without the required showing a statement concerning the action or its subject matter previously made by that party. Upon request, a person not a party may obtain without the required showing a statement concerning the action or its subject matter previously made by that person. If the request is refused, the person may move for a court order. The provisions of Rule 37(a) (4) apply to the award of expenses incurred in relation to the motion. For purposes of this paragraph, a statement previously made is (A) a written statement signed or otherwise adopted or approved by the person making it, or (B) a stenographic, mechanical, electrical, or other recording, or a transcription thereof, which is a substantially verbatim recital of an oral statement by the person making it and contemporaneously recorded.

(4) *Trial Preparation: Experts.* Discovery of facts known and opinions held by experts, otherwise discoverable under the provisions of subdivision (b) (1) of this rule and acquired or developed in anticipation of litigation or for trial, may be obtained only as follows:

(A) (i) A party may through interrogatories require any other party to identify each person whom the other party expects to call as an expert witness at trial to state the subject matter on which the expert is expected to testify, and to state the substance of the facts and opinions to which the expert is expected to testify and a summary of the grounds for each opinion. (ii) Upon motion, the court may order further discovery by other means, subject to such restrictions as to scope and such provision, pursuant to subdivision (b) (4) (C) of this rule, concerning fees and expenses as the court may deem appropriate.

(B) A party may discover facts known or opinions held by an expert who has been retained or specially employed by another party in anticipation of litigation or preparation for trial and who is not expected to be called as a witness at trial, only as provided in Rule 35(b) or upon a showing of exceptional circumstances under which it is impracticable for the party seeking discovery to obtain facts or opinions on the same subject by other means.

(C) Unless manifest injustice would result, (i) the court shall require that the party seeking discovery pay the expert a reasonable fee for time spent in responding to discovery under subdivisions (b) (4) (A) (ii) and (b) (4) (B) of this rule; and (ii) with respect to discovery obtained under subdivision (b) (4) (A) (ii) of this rule the court may require, and with respect to discovery obtained under subdivision (b) (4) (B) of this rule the court shall require, the party seeking discovery to pay the other party a fair portion of the fees and expenses reasonably incurred by the latter party in obtaining facts and opinions from the expert.

(c) Protective Orders. Upon motion by a party or by the person from whom discovery is sought, and for good cause shown, the court in which the action is pending or alternatively, on matters relating to a deposition, the court in the district where the deposition is to be taken may make any order which justice requires to protect a party or person from annoyance, embarrassment, oppression, or undue burden or expense, including one or more of the following: (1) that the discovery not be had; (2) that the discovery may be had only on specified terms and conditions, including a designation of the time or place; (3) that the discovery may be had only be a method of discovery other than that selected by the party seeking discovery; (4) that certain matters not be inquired into, or that the scope of the discovery be limited to certain matters; (5) that discovery be conducted with no one present except persons designated by the court; (6) that a deposition after being sealed be opened only by order of the court; (7) that a trade secret or other confidential research, development, or commercial information not be disclosed or be disclosed only in a designated way; (8) that the parties simultaneously file specified documents or information enclosed in sealed envelopes to be opened as directed by the court.

If the motion for a protective order is denied in whole or in part, the court may, on such terms and conditions as are just, order that any party or person provide or permit discovery. The provisions of Rule 37(a) (4) apply to the award of expenses incurred in relation to the motion.

(d) Sequence and Timing of Discovery. Unless the court upon motion, for the convenience of parties and witnesses and in the interests of justice, orders otherwise, methods of discovery may be used in any sequence and the fact that a party is conducting discovery, whether by deposition or otherwise, shall not operate to delay any other party's discovery.

(e) Supplementation of Responses. A party who has responded to a request for discovery with a response that was complete when made is under no duty to supplement his response to include information thereafter acquired, except as follows:

(1) A party is under a duty seasonably to supplement his response with respect to any question directly addressed to (A) the identity and location of persons having knowledge of discoverable matters, and (B) the identity of each person expected to be called as an expert witness at trial, the subject matter on which he is expected to testify, and the substance of his testimony.

(2) A party is under a duty seasonably to amend a prior response if he obtains information upon the basis of which (A) he knows that the response was incorrect when made, or (B) he knows that the response though correct when made is no longer true and the circumstances are such that a failure to amend the response is in substance a knowing concealment.

(3) A duty to supplement responses may be imposed by order of the court, agreement of the parties, or at any time prior to trial through new requests for supplementation of prior responses.

(f) Discovery Conference. — At any time after commencement of an action the court may direct the attorneys for the parties to appear before it for a conference on the subject of discovery. The court shall do so upon motion by the attorney for any party if the motion includes:

(1) A statement of the issues as they then appear;

(2) A proposed plan and schedule of discovery;

(3) Any limitations proposed to be placed on discovery;

(4) Any other proposed orders with respect to discovery; and

(5) A statement showing that the attorney making the motion has made a reasonable effort to reach agreement with opposing attorneys on the matters set forth in the motion. Each party and his attorney are under a duty to participate in good faith in the framing of a discovery plan if a plan is proposed by the attorney for any party. Notice of the motion shall be served on all parties. Objections or additions to matters set forth in the motion shall be served not later than 10 days after service of the motion.

Following the discovery conference, the court shall enter an order tentatively identifying the issues for discovery purposes, establishing a plan and schedule for discovery, setting limitations on discovery, if any; and determining such other matters, including the allocation of expenses, as are necessary for the proper management of discovery in the action. An order may be altered or amended whenever justice so requires.

Subject to the right of a party who properly moves for a discovery conference to prompt convening of the conference, the court may combine the discovery conference with a pretrial conference authorized by Rule 16.

As amended April 29, 1980, eff. Aug. 1, 1980.

Rule 27.

DEPOSITIONS BEFORE ACTION OR PENDING APPEAL

(a) Before Action.

(1) *Petition.* A person who desires to perpetuate his own testimony or that of another person regarding any matter that may be cognizable in any court of the United States may file a verified petition in the United States district court in the district of the residence of any expected adverse party. The petition shall be entitled in the name of the petitioner and shall show: 1, that the petitioner expects to be a party to an action cognizable in a court of the United States but is presently unable to bring it or cause it to be brought, 2, the subject matter of the expected action and his interest therein, 3, the facts which he desires to establish by the proposed testimony and his reasons for desiring to perpetuate it, 4, the names or a description of the persons he expects will be adverse parties and their addresses so far as known, and 5, the names and addresses of the persons to be examined and the substance of the testimony which he expects to elicit from each, and shall ask for an order authorizing the petitioner to take the depositions of the persons to be examined named in the petition, for the purpose of perpetuating their testimony.

(2) *Notice and Service.* The petitioner shall thereafter serve a notice upon each person named in the petition as an expected adverse party, together with a copy of the petition, stating that the petitioner will apply to the court, at a time and place named therein, for the order described in the petition. At least 20 days before the date of hearing the notice shall be served either within or without the district or state in the manner provided in Rule 4(d) for service of summons; but if such service cannot with due diligence be made upon any expected adverse party named in the petition, the court may make such order as is just for service by publication or otherwise, and shall appoint, for persons not served in the manner provided in Rule 4(d), an attorney who shall represent them, and, in case they are not otherwise represented, shall cross-examine the deponent. If any expected adverse party is a minor or incompetent the provisions of Rule 17(c) apply.

(3) *Order and Examination.* If the court is satisfied that the perpetuation of the testimony may prevent a failure or delay of justice, it shall make an order designating or describing the persons whose depositions may be taken and specifying the subject matter of the examination and whether the despositions shall be taken upon oral examination or written interrogatories. The depositions may then be taken in accordance with these rules; and the court may make orders of the character provided for by Rules 34 and 35. For the purpose of applying these rules to depositions for perpetuating testimony, each reference therein to the court in which the action is pending shall be deemed to refer to the court in which the petition for such deposition was filed.

(4) *Use of Deposition.* If a deposition to perpetuate testimony is taken under these rules or if, although not so taken, it would be admissible in evidence in the courts of the state in which it ís taken, it may be used in any action involving the same subject matter subsequently brought in a United States district court, in accordance with the provisions of Rule 32(a).

(b) Pending Appeal. If an appeal has been taken from a judgment of a district court or before the taking of an appeal if the time therefor has not expired, the district court in which the judgment was rendered may allow the taking of the depositions of witnesses to perpetuate their testimony for use in the event of further proceedings in the district court. In such case the party who desires to perpetuate the testimony may make a motion in the district court for leave to take the depositions, upon the same notice and service thereof as if the action was pending in the district court. The motion shall show (1) the names and addresses of persons to be examined and the substance of the testimony which he expects to elicit from each; (2) the reasons for perpetuating their testimony. If the court finds that the perpetuation of the testimony is proper to avoid a failure or delay of justice, it may make an order allowing the depositions to be taken and may make orders of the character provided for by Rules 34 and 35, and thereupon the depositions may be taken and used in the same manner and under the same conditions as are prescribed in these rules for depositions taken in actions pending in the district court.

(c) Perpetuation by Action. This rule does not limit the power of a court to entertain an action to perpetuate testimony.
As amended Dec. 27, 1946, eff. March 19, 1948; Dec. 29, 1948, eff. Oct. 20, 1949; March 1, 1971, eff. July 1, 1971.

Rule 28.

PERSONS BEFORE WHOM DEPOSITIONS MAY BE TAKEN

(a) Within the United States. — Within the United States or within a territory or insular possession subject to the jurisdiction of the United States, depositions shall be taken before an officer authorized to administer oaths by the laws of the United States or of the place where the examination is held, or before a person appointed by the court in which the action is pending. A person so appointed has power to administer oaths and take testimony. The term officer as used in Rules 30, 31 and 32 includes a person appointed by the court or designated by the parties under Rule 29.

(b) In Foreign Countries. In a foreign country, depositions may be taken (1) on notice before a person authorized to administer oaths in the place in which the examination is held, either by the law thereof or by the law of the United States, or (2) before a person commissioned by the court, and a person so commissioned shall have the power by virtue of his commission to administer any necessary oath and take testimony, or (3) pursuant to a letter rogatory. A commission or a letter rogatory shall be issued on application and notice and on terms that are just and appropriate. It is not requisite to the issuance of a commission or a letter rogatory that the taking of the deposition in any other manner is impracticable or inconvenient; and both a commission and a letter rogatory may be issued in proper cases. A notice or commission may designate the person before whom the deposition is to be taken either by name or descriptive title. A letter rogatory may be addressed. 'To the Appropriate Authority in [here name the country]'. Evidence obtained in response to a letter rogatory need not be excluded merely for the reason that it is not a verbatim transcript or that the testimony was not taken under oath or for any similar departure from the requirements for depositions taken within the United States under these rules.

(c) Disqualification for Interest. No deposition shall be taken before a person who is a relative or employee or attorney or counsel of any of the parties, or is a relative or employee of such attorney or counsel, or is financially interested in the action.
As amended Dec. 27, 1946, eff. March 19, 1948; Jan. 21, 1963, eff. July 1, 1963; April 29, 1980, eff. Aug. 1, 1980.

Rule 29.

STIPULATIONS REGARDING DISCOVERY PROCEDURE

Unless the court orders otherwise, the parties may by written stipulation (1) provide that depositions may be taken before any person, at any time or place, upon any notice, and in any manner and when so taken may be used like other depositions, and (2) modify the procedures provided by these rules for other methods of discovery, except that stipulations extending the time provided in Rules 33, 34, and 36 for responses to discovery may be made only with the approval of the court.

As amended March 30, 1970, eff. July 1, 1970.

Rule 30.

DEPOSITIONS UPON ORAL EXAMINATION

(a) When Depositions May be Taken. After commencement of the action, any party may take the testimony of any person, including a party, by deposition upon oral examination. Leave of court, granted with or without notice, must be obtained only if the plaintiff seeks to take a deposition prior to the expiration of 30 days after service of the summons and complaint upon any defendant or service made under Rule 4(e), except that leave is not required (1) if a defendant has served a notice of taking deposition or otherwise sought discovery, or (2) if special notice is given as provided in subdivision (b) (2) of this rule. The attendance of witnesses may be compelled by subpoena as provided in Rule 45. The deposition of a person confined in prison may be taken only by leave of court on such terms as the court prescribes.

(b) Notice of Examination: General Requirements; Special Notice; Non-stenographic Recording; Production of Documents and Things; Deposition of Organization; Deposition by Telephone.

(1) A party desiring to take the deposition of any person upon oral examination shall give reasonable notice in writing to every other party to the action. The notice shall state the time and place for taking the deposition and the name and address of each person to be examined, if known, and, if the name is not known, a general description sufficient to identify him or the particular class or group to which he belongs. If a subpoena duces tecum is to be served on the person to be examined, the designation of the materials to be produced as set forth in the subpoena shall be attached to or included in the notice.

(2) Leave of court is not required for the taking of a deposition by plaintiff if the notice (A) states that the person to be examined is about to go out of the district where the action is pending and more than 100 miles from the place of trial, or is about to go out of the United States, or is bound on a voyage to sea, and will be unavailable for examination unless his deposition is taken before expiration of the 30-day period, and (B) sets forth facts to support the statement. The

plaintiff's attorney shall sign the notice, and his signature constitutes a certification by him that to the best of his knowledge, information, and belief the statement and supporting facts are true. The sanctions provided by Rule 11 are applicable to the certification.

If a party shows that when he was served with notice under this subdivision (b) (2) he was unable through the exercise of diligence to obtain counsel to represent him at the taking of the deposition, the deposition may not be used against him.

(3) The court may for cause shown enlarge or shorten the time for taking the deposition.

(4) The parties may stipulate in writing or the court may upon motion order that the testimony at a deposition be recorded by other than stenographic means. The stipulation or order shall designate the person before whom the deposition shall be taken, the manner of recording, preserving and filing the deposition, and may include other provisions to assure that the recorded testimony will be accurate and trustworthy. A party may arrange to have a stenographic transcription made at his own expense. Any objections under subdivision (c), any changes made by the witness, his signature identifying the deposition as his own or the statement of the officer that is required if the witness does not sign, as provided in subdivision (e), and the certification of the officer required by subdivision (f) shall be set forth in a writing to accompany a deposition recorded by non-stenographic means.

(5) The notice to a party deponent may be accompanied by a request made in compliance with Rule 34 for the production of documents and tangible things at the taking of the deposition. The procedure of Rule 34 shall apply to the request.

(6) A party may in his notice and in a subpoena name as the deponent a public or private corporation or a partnership or association or governmental agency and describe with reasonable particularity the matters on which examination is requested. In that event, the organization so named shall designate one or more officers, directors, or managing agents, or other persons who consent to testify on its behalf, and may set forth, for each person designated, the matters on which he will testify. A subpoena shall advise a non-party organization of its duty to make such a designation. The persons so designated shall testify as to matters known or reasonably available to the organization. This subdivision (b) (6) does not preclude taking a deposition by any other procedure authorized in these rules.

(7) The parties may stipulate in writing or the court may upon motion order that a deposition be taken by telephone. For the purposes of this rule and Rules 28(a), 37(a)(1), 37(b)(1) and 45(d), a deposition taken by telephone is taken in the district and at the place where the deponent is to answer questions propounded to him.

(c) Examination and Cross-Examination; Record of Examination; Oath; Objections. Examination and cross-examination of witnesses may proceed as permitted at the trial under the provisions of the Federal Rules of Evidence. The officer before whom the deposition is to be taken shall put the witness on oath and shall personally, or by someone acting under his direction and in his presence, record the testimony of the witness. The testimony shall be taken stenographically or recorded by any other means ordered in accordance with subdivision (b) (4) of this rule. If requested by one of the parties, the testimony shall be transcribed. All objections made at time of the examination to the qualifications of the officer taking the deposition, or to the manner of taking it, or to the evidence presented, or to the conduct of any party, and any other objection to the proceedings, shall be noted by the officer upon the deposition. Evidence objected to shall be taken subject to the objections. In lieu of participating in the oral examination, parties may serve written questions in a sealed envelope on the party taking the deposition and he shall transmit them to the officer, who shall propound them to the witness and record the answers verbatim.

(d) Motion to Terminate or Limit Examination. At any time during the taking of the deposition, on motion of a party or of the deponent and upon a showing that the examination is being conducted in bad faith or in such manner as unreasonably to annoy, embarrass, or oppress the deponent or party, the court in which the action is pending or the court in the district where the deposition is being taken may order the officer conducting the examination to cease forthwith from taking the deposition, or may limit the scope and manner of the taking of the deposition as provided in Rule 26(c). If the order made terminates the examination, it shall be resumed thereafter only upon the order of the court in which the action is pending. Upon demand of the objecting party or deponent, the taking of the deposition shall be suspended for the time necessary to make a motion for an order. The provisions of Rule 37(a) (4) apply to the award of expenses incurred in relation to the motion.

(e) Submission to Witness; Changes; Signing. When the testimony is fully transcribed the deposition shall be submitted to the witness for examination and shall be read to or by him, unless such examination and reading are waived by the witness and by the parties. Any changes in form or substance which the witness desires to make shall be entered upon the deposition by the officer with a statement of the reasons given by the witness for making them. The deposition shall then be signed by the witness, unless the parties by stipulation waive the signing or the witness is ill or cannot be found or refuses to sign. If the deposition is not signed by the witness within 30 days of its submission to him, the officer shall sign it and state on the record the fact of the waiver or of the illness or absence of the witness or the fact of the refusal to sign together with the reason, if any, given therefor; and the deposition may then be used as fully as though signed unless on a motion to suppress under Rule 32(d) (4) the court holds that the reasons given for the refusal to sign require rejection of the deposition in whole or in part.

(f) Certification and Filing by Officer; Exhibits; Copies; notice of Filing.

(1) The officer shall certify on the deposition that the witness was duly sworn by him and that the deposition is a true record of the testimony given by the witness. Unless otherwise ordered by the court, he shall then securely seal the deposition in an envelope indorsed with the title of the action and marked "Deposition of [here insert name of witness]' and shall promptly file it with the court in which the action is pending or send it by registered or certified mail to the clerk thereof for filing.

Documents and things produced for inspection during the examination of the witness, shall, upon the request of a party, be marked for identification and annexed to the deposition and may be inspected and copied by any party, except that if the person producing the materials desires to retain them he may (A) offer copies to be marked for identification and annexed to the deposition and to serve thereafter as originals if he affords to all parties fair opportunity to verify the copies by comparison with the originals, or (B) offer the originals to be marked for identification, after giving to each party an opportunity to inspect and copy them, in which event the materials may then be used in the same manner as if annexed to the deposition. Any party may move for an order that the original be annexed to and returned with the deposition to the court, pending final disposition of the case.

(2) Upon payment of reasonable charges therefor, the officer shall furnish a copy of the deposition to any party or to the deponent.

(3) The party taking the deposition shall give prompt notice of its filing to all other parties.

(g) Failure to Attend or to Serve Subpoena; Expenses.

(1) If the party giving the notice of the taking of a deposition fails to attend and proceed therewith and another party attends in person or by attorney pursuant to the notice, the court may order the party giving the notice to pay to such other party the reasonable expenses incurred by him and his attorney in attending, including reasonable attorney's fees.

(2) If the party giving the notice of the taking of a deposition of a witness fails to serve a subpoena upon him and the witness because of such failure does not attend, and if another party attends in person or by attorney because he expects the deposition of that witness to be taken, the court may order the party giving the notice to pay to such other party the reasonable expenses incurred by him and his attorney in attending, including reasonable attorney's fees.

As amended Jan. 21, 1963, eff. July 1, 1963; March 30, 1970, eff. July 1, 1970; March 1, 1971, eff. July 1, 1971; April 29, 1980, eff. Aug. 1, 1980.

Rule 31.

DEPOSITIONS UPON WRITTEN QUESTIONS

(a) Serving Questions; Notice. After commencement of the action, any party may take the testimony of any person, including a party, by deposition upon written questions. The attendance of witnesses may be compelled by the use of subpoena as provided in Rule 45. The deposition of a person confined in prison may be taken only by leave of court on such terms as the court prescribes.

A party desiring to take a deposition upon written questions shall serve them upon every other party with a notice stating (1) the name and address of the person who is to answer them, if known, and if the name is not known, a general description sufficient to identify him or the particular class or group to which he belongs, and (2) the name or descriptive title and address of the officer before whom the deposition is to be taken. A deposition upon written questions may be taken of a public or private corporation or a partnership or association or governmental agency in accordance with the provisions of Rule 30(b)(6).

Within 30 days after the notice and written questions are served, a party may serve cross questions upon all other parties. Within 10 days after being served with cross questions, a party may serve redirect questions upon all other parties. Within 10 days after being served with redirect questions, a party may serve recross questions upon all other parties. The court may for cause shown enlarge or shorten the time.

(b) Officer to Take Responses and Prepare Record. A copy of the notice and copies of all questions served shall be delivered by the party taking the deposition to the officer designated in the notice, who shall proceed promptly, in the manner provided by Rule 30(c), (e), and (f), to take the testimony of the witness in response to the questions and to prepare, certify, and file or mail the deposition, attaching thereto the copy of the notice and the questions received by him.

(c) Notice of Filing. When the deposition is filed the party taking it shall promptly give notice thereof to all other parties.
As amended March 30, 1970, eff. July 1, 1970.

Rule 32.

USE OF DEPOSITIONS IN COURT PROCEEDINGS

(a) Use of Depositions. At the trial or upon the hearing of a motion or an interlocutory proceeding, any part or all of a deposition, so far as admissible under the rules of evidence applied as though the witness were then present and testifying, may be used against any party who was present or represented at the taking of the deposition or who had reasonable notice thereof, in accordance with any of the following provisions:

(1) Any deposition may be used by any party for the purpose of contradicting or impeaching the testimony of deponent as a witness or for any other purpose permitted by the Federal Rules of Evidence.

(2) The deposition of a party or of anyone who at the time of taking the deposition was an officer, director, or managing agent, or a person designated under Rule 30(b) (6) or 31(a) to testify on behalf of a public or private corporation, partnership or association or governmental agency which is a party may be used by an adverse party for any purpose.

(3) The deposition of a witness, whether or not a party, may be used by any party for any purpose if the court finds: (A) that the witness is dead; or (B) that the witness is at a greater distance than 100 miles from the place of trial or hearing, or is out of the United States, unless it appears that the absence of the witness was procured by the party offering the deposition; or (C) that the witness is unable to attend or testify because of age, illness, infirmity, or imprisonment; or (D) that the party offering the deposition has been unable to procure the attendance of the witness by subpoena; or (E) upon application and notice, that such exceptional circumstances exist as to make it desirable, in the interest of justice and with due regard to the importance of presenting the testimony of witnesses orally in open court, to allow the deposition to be used.

(4) If only part of a deposition is offered in evidence by a party, an adverse party may require him to introduce any other party which ought in fairness to be considered with the party introduced, and any party may introduce any other parts.

Substitution of parties pursuant to Rule 25 does not affect the right to use depositions previously taken; and, when an action in any court of the United States or of any State has been dismissed and another action involving the same subject matter is afterward brought between the same parties or their representatives or successors in interest, all depositions lawfully taken and duly filed in the former action may be used in the latter as if originally taken therefor. A deposition previously taken may also be used as permitted by the Federal Rules of Evidence.

(b) Objections to Admissibility. Subject to the provisions of Rule 28(b) and subdivision (d) (3) of this rule, objection may be made at the trial or hearing to receiving in evidence any deposition or part thereof for any reason which would require the exclusion of the evidence if the witness were then present and testifying.

(c) Effect of Taking or Using Depositions. (Abrogated effective July 1, 1975.)

(d) Effect of Errors and Irregularities in Depositions.

(1) *As to Notice.* All errors and irregularities in the notice for taking a deposition are waived unless written objection is promptly served upon the party giving the notice.

(2) *As to Disqualification of Officer.* Objection to taking a deposition because of disqualification of the officer before whom it is to be taken is waived unless made before the taking of the deposition begins or as soon thereafter as the disqualification becomes known or could be discovered with reasonable diligence.

(3) *As to Taking of Deposition.*
(A) Objections to the competency of a witness or to the competency, relevancy, or materiality of testimony are not waived by failure to make them before or during the taking of the deposition, unless the ground of the objection is one which might have been obviated or removed if presented at that time.
(B) Errors and irregularities occurring at the oral examination in the manner of taking the deposition, in the form of the questions or answers, in the oath or affirmation, or in the conduct of parties, and errors of any kind which might be obviated, removed, or cured if promptly presented, are waived unless seasonable objection thereto is made at the taking of the deposition.
(C) Objections to the form of written questions submitted under Rule 31 are waived unless served in writing upon the party propounding them within the time allowed for serving the succeeding cross or other questions and within 5 days after service of the last questions authorized.

(4) *As to Completion and Return of Deposition.* Errors and irregularities in the manner in which the testimony is transcribed or the deposition is prepared, signed, certified, sealed, indorsed, transmitted, filed, or otherwise dealt with by the officer under Rules 30 and 31 are waived unless a motion to suppress the deposition or some part thereof is made with reasonable promptness after such defect is, or with due diligence might have been, ascertained.

As amended March 30, 1970, eff. July 1, 1970; April 29, 1980, eff. Aug. 1, 1980.

Rule 33.

INTERROGATORIES TO PARTIES

(a) Availability; Procedures for Use. Any party may serve upon any other party written interrogatories to be answered by the party served or, if the party served is a public or private corporation or a partnership or association or governmental agency, by any officer or agent, who shall furnish such information as is available to the party. Interrogatories may, without leave of court, be served upon the plaintiff after commencement of the action and upon any other party with or after service of the summons and complaint upon that party.

Each interrogatory shall be answered separately and fully in writing under oath, unless it is objected to, in which event the reasons for objection shall be stated in lieu of an answer. The answers are to be signed by the person making them, and the objections signed by the attorney making them. The party upon whom the interrogatories have been served shall serve a copy of the answers, and objections if any, within 30 days after the service of the interrogatories, except that a defendant may serve answers or objections within 45 days after service of the summons and complaint upon that defendant. The court may allow a shorter or longer time. The party submitting the interrogatories may move for an order under Rule 37(a) with respect to any objection to or other failure to answer an interrogatory.

(b) Scope; Use at Trial. Interrogatories may relate to any matters which can be inquired into under Rule 26(b), and the answers may be used to the extent permitted by the rules of evidence.

An interrogatory otherwise proper is not necessarily objectionable merely because an answer to the interrogatory involves an opinion or contention that relates to fact or the application of law to fact, but the court may order that such an interrogatory need not be answered until after designated discovery has been completed or until a pre-trial conference or other later time.

(c) Option to Produce Business Records. Where the answer to an interrogatory may be derived or ascertained from the business records of the party upon whom the interrogatory has been served or from an examination, audit or inspection of such business records, or from a compilation, abstract or summary based thereon, and the burden of deriving or ascertaining the answer is substantially the same for the party serving the interrogatory as for the party served, it is a sufficient answer to such interrogatory to specify the records from which the answer may be derived or ascertained and to afford to the party serving the interrogatory reasonable opportunity to examine, audit or inspect such records and to make copies, compilations, abstracts or summaries. A specification shall be in sufficient detail as to permit the interrogating party to locate and to identify as readily as can the party served, the records from which the answer may be ascertained.
As amended April 29, 1980, eff. Aug. 1 1980.

Rule 34.

PRODUCTION OF DOCUMENTS AND THINGS AND ENTRY UPON LAND FOR INSPECTION AND OTHER PURPOSES

(a) Scope. Any party may serve on any other party a request (1) to produce and permit the party making the request, or someone acting on his behalf, to inspect and copy, any designated documents (including writings, drawings, graphs, charts, photographs, phonorecords, and other data compilations from which information can be obtained, translated, if necessary, by the respondent through detection devices into reasonably usable form), or to inspect and copy, test, or sample any tangible things which constitute or contain matters within the scope of Rule 26(b) and which are in the possession, custody or control of the party upon whom the request is served; or (2) to permit entry upon designated land or other property in the possession or control of the party upon whom the request is served for the purpose of inspection and measuring, surveying, photographing, testing, or sampling the property or any designated object or operation thereon, within the scope of Rule 26(b).

(b) Procedure. The request may, without leave of court, be served upon the plaintiff after commencement of the action and upon any other party with or after service of the summons and complaint upon that party. The request shall set forth the items to be inspected either by individual item or by category, and describe each item and category with reasonable particularity. The request shall specify a reasonable time, place, and manner of making the inspection and performing the related acts.

The party upon whom the request is served shall serve a written response within 30 days after the service of the request, except that a defendant may serve a response within 45 days after service of the summons and complaint upon that defendant. The court may allow a shorter or longer time. The response shall state, with respect to each item or category, that inspection and related activities will be permitted as requested, unless the request is objected to, in which event the reasons for objection shall be stated. If objection is made to part of an item or category, the part shall be specified. The party submitting the request may move for an order under Rule 37(a) with respect to any objection to or other failure to respond to the request or any part thereof, or any failure to permit inspection as requested.

A party who produces documents for inspection shall produce them as they are kept in the usual course of business or shall organize and label them to correspond with the categories in the request.

(c) Persons Not Parties. This rule does not preclude an independent action against a person not a party for production of documents and things and permission to enter upon land.
As amended April 29, 1980, eff. Aug. 1, 1980.

Rule 35.

PHYSICAL AND MENTAL EXAMINATION OF PERSONS

(a) Order for Examination. When the mental or physical condition (including the blood group) of a party, or of a person in the custody or under the legal control of a party, is in controversy, the court in which the action is pending may order the party to submit to a physical or mental examination by a physician or to produce for examination the person in his custody or legal control. The order may be made only on motion for good cause shown and upon notice to the person to be examined and to all parties and shall specify the time, place, manner, conditions, and scope of the examination and the person or persons by whom it is to be made.

(b) Report of Examining Physician.
(1) If requested by the party against whom an order is made under Rule 35(a) or the person examined, the party causing the examination to be made shall deliver to him a copy of a detailed written report of the examining physician setting out his findings, including results of all tests made, diagnoses and conclusions, together with like reports of all earlier examinations of the same condition. After delivery the party causing the examination shall be entitled upon request to receive from the party against whom the order is made a like report of any examination, previously or thereafter made, of the same condition, unless,

in the case of a report of examination of a person not a party, the party shows that he is unable to obtain it. The court on motion may make an order against a party requiring delivery of a report on such terms as are just, and if a physician fails or refuses to make a report the court may exclude his testimony if offered at the trial.

(2) By requesting and obtaining a report of the examination so ordered or by taking the deposition of the examiner, the party examined waives any privilege he may have in that action or any other involving the same controversy, regarding the testimony of every other person who has examined or may thereafter examine him in respect of the same mental or physical condition.

(3) This subdivision applies to examinations made by agreement of the parties, unless the agreement expressly provides otherwise. This subdivision does not preclude discovery of a report of an examining physician or the taking of a deposition of the physician in accordance with the provisions of any other rule.

As amended March 30, 1970, eff. July 1, 1970.

Rule 36.

REQUESTS FOR ADMISSION

(a) **Request for Admission.** A party may serve upon any other party a written request for the admission, for purposes of the pending action only, of the truth of any matters within the scope of Rule 26(b) set forth in the request that relate to statements or opinions of fact or of the application of law to fact, including the genuineness of any documents described in the request. Copies of documents shall be served with the request unless they have been or are otherwise furnished or made available for inspection and copying. The request may, without leave of court, be served upon the plaintiff after commencement of the action and upon any other party with or after service of the summons and complaint upon that party.

Each matter of which an admission is requested shall be separately set forth. The matter is admitted unless, within 30 days after service of the request, or within such shorter or longer time as the court may allow, the party to whom the request is directed serves upon the party requesting the admission a written answer or objection addressed to the matter, signed by the party or by his attorney, but, unless the court shortens the time, a defendant shall not be required to serve answers or objections before the expiration of 45 days after service of the summons and complaint upon him. If objection is made, the reasons therefor shall be stated. The answer shall specifically deny the matter or set forth in detail the reasons why the answering party cannot truthfully admit or deny the matter. A denial shall fairly meet the substance of the requested admission, and when good faith requires that a party qualify his answer or deny only a part of the matter of which an admission is requested, he shall specify so much of it as is true and qualify or deny the remainder. An answering party may not give lack of information or knowledge as a reason for failure to admit or deny unless he states that he has made reasonable inquiry and that the information known or readily obtainable by him is insufficient to enable him to admit or deny. A party who considers that a matter of which an admission has been requested presents a genuine issue for trial may not, on that ground alone, object to the request; he may, subject to the provisions of Rule 37(c), deny the matter or set forth reasons why he cannot admit or deny it.

The party who has requested the admissions may move to determine the sufficiency of the answers or objections. Unless the court determines that an objection is justified, it shall order that an answer be served. If the court determines that an answer does not comply with the requirements of this rule, it may order either that the matter is admitted or that an amended answer be served. The court may, in lieu of these orders, determine that final disposition of the request be made at a pre-trial conference or at a designated time prior to trial. The provisions of Rule 37(a) (4) apply to the award of expenses incurred in relation to the motion.

(b) Effect of Admission. Any matter admitted under this rule is conclusively established unless the court on motion permits withdrawal or amendment of the admission. Subject to the provisions of Rule 16 governing amendment of a pre-trial order, the court may permit withdrawal or amendment when the presentation of the merits of the action will be subserved thereby and the party who obtained the admission fails to satisfy the court that withdrawal or amendment will prejudice him in maintaining his action or defense on the merits. Any admission made by a party under this rule is for the purpose of the pending action only and is not an admission by him for any other purpose nor may it be used against him in any other proceeding. As amended Dec. 27, 1946, eff. March 19, 1948; March 30, 1970, eff. July 1, 1970.

Rule 37.

FAILURE TO MAKE OR COOPERATE IN DISCOVERY: SANCTIONS

(a) Motion for Order Compelling Discovery. A party, upon reasonable notice to other parties and all persons affected thereby, may apply for an order compelling discovery as follows:

(1) *Appropriate Court.* An application for an order to a party may be made to the court in which the action is pending, or, on matters

relating to a deposition, to the court in the district where the deposition is being taken. An application for an order to a deponent who is not a party shall be made to the court in the district where the deposition is being taken.

(2) *Motion.* If a deponent fails to answer a question propounded or submitted under Rules 30 or 31, or a corporation or other entity fails to make a designation under Rule 30(b) (6) or 31(a), or a party fails to answer an interrogatory submitted under Rule 33, or if a party, in response to a request for inspection submitted under Rule 34, fails to respond that inspection will be permitted as requested or fails to permit inspection as requested, the discovering party may move for an order compelling an answer, or a designation, or an order compelling inspection in accordance with the request. When taking a deposition on oral examination, the proponent of the question may complete or adjourn the examination before he applies for an order.

If the court denies the motion in whole or in part, it may make such protective order as it would have been empowered to make on a motion made pursuant to Rule 26(c).

(3) *Evasive or Incomplete Answer.* For purposes of this subdivision an evasive or incomplete answer is to be treated as a failure to answer.

(4) *Award of Expenses of Motion.* If the motion is granted, the court shall, after opportunity for hearing, require the party or deponent whose conduct necessitated the motion or the party or attorney advising such conduct or both of them to pay to the moving party the reasonable expenses incurred in obtaining the order, including attorney's fees, unless the court finds that the opposition to the motion was substantially justified or that other circumstances make an award of expenses unjust.

If the motion is denied, the court shall, after opportunity for hearing, require the moving party or the attorney advising the motion or both of them to pay to the party or deponent who opposed the motion the reasonable expenses incurred in opposing the motion, including attorney's fees, unless the court finds that the making of the motion was substantially justified or that other circumstances make an award of expenses unjust.

If the motion is granted in part and denied in part, the court may apportion the reasonable expenses incurred in relation to the motion among the parties and persons in a just manner.

(b) Failure to Comply with Order.

(1) *Sanctions by Court in District Where Deposition is Taken.* If a deponent fails to be sworn or to answer a question after being directed to do so by the court in the district in which the deposition is being taken, the failure may be considered a contempt of that court.

(2) *Sanctions by Court in Which Action is Pending.* If a party or an officer, director, or managing agent of a party or a person designated under Rule 30(b) (6) or 31(a) to testify on behalf of a party fails to obey an order to provide or permit discovery, including an order made under subdivision (a) of this rule or Rule 35, or if a party fails to obey an order entered under Rule 26(f), the court in which the action is pending may make such orders in regard to the failure as are just, and among others the following:

(A) An order that the matters regarding which the order was made or any other designated facts shall be taken to be established for the purposes of the action in accordance with the claim of the party obtaining the order;

(B) An order refusing to allow the disobedient party to support or oppose designated claims or defenses, or prohibiting him from introducing designated matters in evidence;

(C) An order striking out pleadings or parts thereof, or staying further proceedings until the order is obeyed, or dismissing the action or proceeding or any part thereof, or rendering a judgment by default against the disobedient party;

(D) In lieu of any of the foregoing orders or in addition thereto, an order treating as a contempt of court the failure to obey any orders except an order to submit to a physical or mental examination;

(E) Where a party has failed to comply with an order under Rule 35(a) requiring him to produce another for examination, such orders as are listed in paragraphs (A), (B), and (C) of this subdivision, unless the party failing to comply shows that he is unable to produce such person for examination.

In lieu of any of the foregoing orders or in addition thereto, the court shall require the party failing to obey the order or the attorney advising him or both to pay the reasonable expenses, including attorney's fees, caused by the failure, unless the court finds that the failure was substantially justified or that other circumstances make an award of expenses unjust.

(c) Expenses on Failure to Admit.

If a party fails to admit the genuineness of any document or the truth of any matter as requested under Rule 36, and if the party requesting the admissions thereafter proves the genuineness of the document or the truth of the matter, he may apply to the court for an order requiring the other party to pay him the reasonable expenses incurred in making that proof, including reasonable attorney's fees. The court shall make the order unless it finds that (1) the request was held objectionable pursuant to Rule 36(a), or (2) the admission sought was of no substantial importance, or (3) the party failing to admit had reasonable ground to believe that he might prevail on the matter, or (4) there was other good reason for the failure to admit.

(d) Failure of Party to Attend at Own Deposition or Serve Answers to Interrogatories or Respond to Request for Inspection. If a party or an officer, director, or managing agent of a party or a person designated under Rule 30(b) (6) or 31(a) to testify on behalf of a party fails (1) to appear before the officer who is to take his deposition, after being served with a proper notice, or (2) to serve answers or objections to interrogatories submitted under Rule 33, after proper service of the interrogatories, or (3) to serve a written response to a request for inspection submitted under Rule 34, after proper service of the request, the court in which the action is pending on motion may make such orders in regard to the failure as are just, and among others it may take any action authorized under paragraphs (A), (B), and (C) of subdivision (b) (2) of this rule. In lieu of any order or in addition thereto, the court shall require the party failing to act or the attorney advising him or both to pay the reasonable expenses, including attorney's fees, caused by the failure, unless the court finds that the failure was substantially justified or that other circumstances make an award of expenses unjust.

The failure to act described in this subdivision may not be excused on the ground that the discovery sought is objectionable unless the party failing to act has applied for a protective order as provided by Rule 26(c).

(e) Abrogated April 29, 1980, eff. Aug. 1, 1980.

(f) Expenses against United States. Except to the extent permitted by statute, expenses and fees may not be awarded against the United States under this rule.

(g) Failure to Participate in the Framing of a Discovery Plan. If a party or his attorney fails to participate in good faith in the framing of a discovery plan by agreement as is required by Rule 26(f), the court may, after opportunity for hearing, require such party or his attorney to pay any other party the reasonable expenses, including attorney's fees, caused by the failure.

As amended April 29, 1980, eff. Aug. 1, 1980.

Rule 45.

SUBPOENA

(a) For Attendance of Witnesses; Form; Issuance. Every subpoena shall be issued by the clerk under the seal of the court, shall state the name of the court and the title of the action, and shall command each person to whom it is directed to attend and give testimony at a time and place therein specified. The clerk shall issue a subpoena, or a subpoena for the production of. documentary evidence, signed and sealed but otherwise in blank, to a party requesting it, who shall fill it in before service.

(b) For Production of Documentary Evidence. A subpoena may also command the person to whom it is directed to produce the books, papers, documents, or tangible things designated therein; but the court, upon motion made promptly and in any event at or before the time specified in the subpoena for compliance therewith, may (1) quash or modify the subpoena if it is unreasonable and oppressive or (2) condition denial of the motion upon the advancement by the person in whose behalf the subpoena is issued of the reasonable cost of producing the books, papers, documents, or tangible things.

(c) Service. A subpoena may be served by the marshal, by his deputy, or by any other person who is not a party and is not less than 18 years of age. Service of a subpoena upon a person named therein shall be made by delivering a copy thereof to such person and by tendering to him the fees for one day's attendance and the mileage allowed by law. When the subpoena is issued on behalf of the United States or an officer or agency thereof, fees and mileage need not be tendered.

(d) Subpoena for Taking Depositions; Place of Examination.
(1) Proof of service of a notice to take a deposition as provided in Rules 30(b) and 31(a) constitutes a sufficient authorization for the issuance by the clerk of the district court for the district in which the deposition is to be taken of subpoenas for the persons named or described therein. Proof of service may be made by filing with the clerk of the district court for the district in which the deposition is to be taken a copy of the notice together with a statement of the date and manner of service and of the names of the persons served, certified by the person who made service. The subpoena may command the person to whom it is directed to produce and permit inspection and copying of designated books, papers, documents, or tangible things which

constitute or contain matters within the scope of the examination permitted by Rule 26(b), but in that event the subpoena will be subject to the provisions of Rule 26(c) and subdivision (b) of this rule.

The person to whom the subpoena is directed may, within 10 days after the service thereof or on or before the time specified in the subpoena for compliance if such time is less than 10 days after service, serve upon the attorney designated in the subpoena written objection to inspection or copying of any or all of the designated materials. If objection is made, the party serving the subpoena shall not be entitled to inspect and copy the materials except pursuant to an order of the court from which the subpoena was issued. The party serving the subpoena may, if objection has been made, move upon notice to the deponent for an order at any time before or during the taking of the deposition.

(2) A resident of the district in which the deposition is to be taken may be required to attend an examination only in the county wherein he resides or is employed or transacts his business in person, or at such other convenient place as is fixed by an order of court. A nonresident of the district may be required to attend only in the county wherein he is served with a subpoena, or within 40 miles from the place of service, or at such other convenient place as is fixed by an order of court.

(e) Subpoena for a Hearing or Trial.

(1) At the request of any party subpoenas for attendance at a hearing or trial shall be issued by the clerk of the district court for the district in which the hearing or trial is held. A subpoena requiring the attendance of a witness at a hearing or trial may be served at any place within the district, or at any place without the district that is within 100 miles of the place of the hearing or trial specified in the subpoena or at a place within the state where a state statute or rule of court permits service of a subpoena issued by a state court of general jurisdiction sitting in the place where the district court is held; and, when a statute of the United States provides therefor, the court upon proper application and cause shown may authorize the service of a subpoena at any other place.

(2) A subpoena directed to a witness in a foreign country shall issue under the circumstances and in the manner and be served as provided in Title 28, U.S.C., § 1783.

(f) Contempt. Failure by any person without adequate excuse to obey a subpoena served upon him may be deemed a contempt of the court from which the subpoena is issued.

As amended Dec. 27, 1946, eff. March 19, 1948; Dec. 29, 1948, eff. Oct. 20, 1949; March 30, 1970, eff. July 1, 1970; April 29, 1980, eff. Aug. 1, 1980.

Rules of the Supreme Court

Order 24
(R. S. C. 1965)

DISCOVERY AND INSPECTION OF DOCUMENTS

MUTUAL DISCOVERY OF DOCUMENTS (O. 24, r. 1).

1.—(1) After the close of pleadings in an action begun by writ there shall, subject to and in accordance with the provisions of this Order, be discovery by the parties to the action of the documents which are or have been in their possession, custody or power relating to matters in question in the action.

(2) Nothing in this Order shall be taken as preventing the parties to an action agreeing to dispense with or limit the discovery of documents which they would otherwise be required to make to each other.

Take from O. 24, r. 1, of 1962 without alteration. Till then discovery of documents and interrogatories were dealt with in one Order (O. 31).

DISCOVERY BY PARTIES WITHOUT ORDER (O. 24, r. 2).

2.—(1) Subject to the provisions of this rule and of rule 4, the parties to an action between whom pleadings are closed must make discovery by exchanging lists of documents and, accordingly, each party must, within 14 days after the pleadings in the action are deemed to be closed as between him and any other party, make and serve on that other party a list of the documents which are or have been in his possession, custody or power relating to any matter in question between them in the action.

Without prejudice to any directions given by the Court under Order 16, rule 4, this paragraph shall not apply in third party proceedings, including proceedings under that Order involving fourth or subsequent parties.

(2) Unless the Court otherwise orders, a defendant to an action arising out of an accident on land due to a collision or opprehended collision involving a vehicle shall not make discovery of any documents to the plaintiff under paragraph (1).

(3) Paragraph (1) shall not be taken as requiring a defendant to an action for the recovery of any penalty recoverable by virtue of any enactment to make discovery of any documents.

(4) Paragraphs (2) and (3) shall apply in relation to a counterclaim as they apply in relation to an action but with the substitution, for the reference in paragraph (2) to the plaintiff, of a reference to the party making the counterclaim.

(5) On the application of any party required by this rule to make discovery of documents, the Court may—

(*a*) order that the parties to the action or any of them shall make discovery under paragraph (1) of such documents or classes of documents only, or as to such only of the matters in question, as may be specified in the order, or

(*b*) if satisfied that discovery by all or any of the parties is not necessary, or not necessary at the stage of the action, order that there shall be no discovery of documents by any or all of the parties either at all or at that stage;

and the Court shall make such an order if and so far as it is of opinion that discovery is not necessary either for disposing fairly of the action or for saving costs.

(6) An application for an order under paragraph (5) must be by summons, and the summons must be taken out before the expiration of the period within which by virtue of this rule discovery of documents in the action is required to be made.

(7) Any party to whom discovery of documents is required to be made under this rule may, at any time before the summons for directions in the action is taken out, serve on the party required to make such discovery a notice requiring him to make an affidavit verifying the list he is required to make under paragraph (1), and the party on whom such a notice is served must, within 14 days after service of the notice, make and file an affidavit in compliance with the notice and serve a copy of the affidavit on the party by whom the notice was served.

Reproduces O. 24, r. 2, of 1962, which was new, with amendments made by R.S.C. (Amendment) 1969 (S.I. 1969 No. 1105) consequent on the abolition by section 16 1 (*a*) of the Civil Evidence Act 1968 of the privilege against exposure to forfeiture.

ORDER FOR DISCOVERY (O. 24, r. 3).

3. (1) Subject to the provisions of this rule and of rules 4 and 8, the Court may order any party to a cause or matter (whether begun by writ, originating summons or otherwise) to make and serve on any other party a list of the documents which are or have been in his possession, custody or power relating to any matter in question in the cause or matter, and may at the same time or subsequently also order him to make and file an affidavit verifying such a list and to serve a copy thereof on the other party.

(2) Where a party who is required by rule 2 to make discovery of documents fails to comply with any provision of that rule, the Court,

on the application of any party to whom the discovery was required to be made, may make an order against the first-mentioned party under paragraph (1) of this rule or, as the case may be, may order him to make and file an affidavit verifying the list of documents he is required to make under rule 2 and to serve a copy thereof on the applicant.

(3) An order under this rule may be limited to such documents or classes of document only, or to such only of the matters in question in the cause or matter, as may be specified in the order.

Reproduces O. 24, r. 3, of 1962.

ORDER FOR DETERMINATION OF ISSUE, ETC., BEFORE DISCOVERY (O. 24, r. 4).

4. — (1) Where on an application for an order under rule 2 or 3 it appears to the Court that any issue or question in the cause or matter should be determined before any discovery of documents is made by the parties, the Court may order that that issue or question be determined first.

(2) Where in an action begun by writ an order is made under this rule for the determination of an issue or question, Order 25, rules 2 to 7, shall, with the omission of so much of rule 7 (1) as requires parties to serve a notice specifying the orders and directions which they desire and with any other necessary modifications, apply as if the application on which the order was made were a summons for directions.

Reproduces O. 24, r. 4, of 1962.

FORM OF LIST AND AFFIDAVIT (O. 24, r. 5).

5. — (1) A list of documents made in compliance with rule 2 or with an order under rule 3 must be in Form No. 26 in Appendix A, and must enumerate the documents in a convenient order and as shortly as possible but describing each of them or, in the case of bundles of documents of the same nature, each bundle, sufficiently to enable it to be identified.

(2) If it is desired to claim that any documents are privileged from production, the claim must be made in the list of documents with a sufficient statement of the grounds of the privilege.

(3) An affidavit made as aforesaid verifying a list of documents must be in Form No. 27 in Appendix A.

Taken from O. 24, r. 5, of 1962.

DEFENDANT ENTITLED TO COPY OF CO-DEFENDANT'S LIST (O. 24, r. 6).

6. — (1) A defendant who has pleaded in an action shall be entitled to have a copy of any list of documents served under any of the forego-

ing rules of this Order on the plaintiff by any other defendant to the action; and a plaintiff against whom a counterclaim is made in an action begun by writ shall be entitled to have a copy of any list of documents served under any of those rules on the party making the counterclaim by any other defendant to the counterclaim.

(2) A party required by virtue of paragraph (1) to supply a copy of a list of documents must supply it free of charge on a request made by the party entitled to it.

(3) Where in an action begun by originating summons the Court makes an order under rule 3 requiring a defendant to the action to serve a list of documents on the plaintiff, it may also order him to supply any other defendant to the action with a copy of that list.

(4) In this rule "list of documents" includes an affidavit verifying a list of documents.

This rule was new in 1962.

ORDER FOR DISCOVERY OF PARTICULAR DOCUMENTS (O. 24, r. 7).

7. — (1) Subject to rule 8, the Court may at any time, on the application of any party to a cause or matter, make an order requiring any other party to make an affidavit stating whether any document specified or described in the application or any class of document so specified or described is, or has at any time been, in his possession, custody or power, and if not then in his possession, custody or power when he parted with it and what has become of it.

(2) An order may be made against a party under this rule notwithstanding that he may already have made or been required to make a list of documents or affidavit under rule 2 or rule 3.

(3) An application for an order under this rule must be supported by an affidavit stating the belief of the deponent that the party from whom discovery is sought under this rule has, or at some time had, in his possession, custody or power the document, or class of document, specified or described in the application and that it relates to one or more of the matters in question in the cause or matter.

Reproduced from O. 24, r. 7, of 1962.

APPLICATION UNDER SS. 31 OR 32 (1) OF ADMINISTRATION OF JUSTICE ACT 1970 (O. 24, r. 7A).

7A. — (1) An application for an order under section 31 of the Administration of Justice Act 1970 for the disclosure of documents before the commencement of proceedings shall be made by originating summons and the person against whom the order is sought shall be made defendant to the summons.

(2) An application after the commencement of proceedings for an order under section 32 (1) of the said Act for the disclosure of docu-

ments by a person who is not a party to the proceedings shall be made by summons, which must be served on that person personally and on every party to the proceedings other than the applicant.

(3) A summons under paragraph (1) or (2) shall be supported by an affidavit which must—

(*a*) in the case of a summons under paragraph (1), state the grounds on which it is alleged that the applicant and the person against whom the order is sought are likely to be parties to subsequent proceedings in the High Court in which a claim for personal injuries is likely to be made;

(*b*) in any case, specify or describe the documents in respect of which the order is sought and show, if practicable by reference to any pleading served or intended to be served in the proceedings, that the documents are relevant to an issue arising or likely to arise out of a claim for personal injuries made or likely to be made in the proceedings and that the person against whom the order is sought is likely to have or have had them in his possession, custody or power.

(4) A copy of the supporting affidavit shall be served with the summons on every person on whom the summons is required to be served.

(5) An order under the said section 31 or 32 (1) for the disclosure of documents may be made conditional on the applicant's giving security for the costs of the person against whom it is made or on such other terms, if any, as the Court thinks just, and shall require the person against whom the order is made to make an affidavit stating whether any documents specified or described in the order are, or at any time have been, in his· possession, custody or power and, if not then in his possession, custody or power, when he parted with them and what has become of them.

(6) No person shall be compelled by virtue of such an order to produce any documents which he could not be compelled to produce—

(*a*) in the case of a summons under paragraph (1), if the subsequent proceedings had already been begun, or

(*b*) in the case of a summons under paragraph (2), if he had been served with a writ of *subpoena duces tecum* to produce the documents at the trial.

(7) In this rule "a claim for personal injuries" means a claim in respect of personal injuries to a person or in respect of a person's death.

(8) For the purposes of rules 10 and 11 an application for an order under the said section 31 or 32 (1) shall be treated as a cause or matter between the applicant and the person against whom the order is sought.

Added by R.S.C. (Amendment No. 4) 1971 (S.I. 1971 No. 1269) with effect from 31, August 1971, and amended by R.S.C. (Amendment No. 2) 1975 (S.I. 1975 No. 911).

DISCOVERY TO BE ORDERED ONLY IF NECESSARY (O. 24, r. 8).

8. On the hearing of an application for an order under rule 3, 7 or 7A the Court, if satisfied that discovery is not necessary, or not necessary at that stage of the cause or matter, may dismiss or, as the case may be, adjourn the application and shall in any case refuse to make such an order if and so far as it is of opinion that discovery is not necessary either for disposing fairly of the cause or matter or for saving costs.

Reproduces O. 24, r. 8, of 1962, as amended by R.S.C. (Amendment No. 4) 1971 (S.I. 1971, 1269).

INSPECTION OF DOCUMENTS REFERRED TO IN LIST (O. 24, r. 9).

9. A party who has served a list of documents on any other party, whether in compliance with rule 2 or with an order under rule 3, must allow the other party to inspect the documents referred to in the list (other than any which he objects to produce) and to take copies thereof and, accordingly, he must when he serves the list on the other party also serve on him a notice stating a time within 7 days after the service thereof at which the said documents may be inspected at a place specified in the notice.

This Rule (then r. 10) was new in 1962.

INSPECTION OF DOCUMENTS REFERRED TO IN PLEADINGS AND AFFIDAVITS (O .24, r. 10).

10.— (1) Any party to a cause or matter shall be entitled at any time to serve a notice on any other party in whose pleadings or affidavits reference is made to any document requiring him to produce that document for the inspection of the party giving the notice and to permit him to take copies thereof.

(2) The party on whom a notice is served under paragraph (1) must, within 4 days after service of the notice, serve on the party giving the notice a notice stating a time within 7 days after the service thereof at which the documents, or such of them as he does not object to produce, may be inspected at a place specified in the notice, and stating which (if any) of the documents he objects to produce and on what grounds.

Reproduces O. 24, r. 11, of 1962.

ORDER FOR PRODUCTION FOR INSPECTION (O. 24, r. 11).

11.— (1) If a party who is required by rule 9 to serve such a notice as is therein mentioned or who is served with a notice under rule 10 (1)—

(*a*) fails to serve a notice under rule 9 or, as the case may be, rule 10 (2), or

(*b*) objects to produce any document for inspection, or

(*c*) offers inspection at a time or place such that, in the opinion of the Court, it is unreasonable to offer inspection then or, as the case may be, there,

then, subject to rule 13 (1), the Court may, on the application of the party entitled to inspection, make an order for production of the documents in question for inspection at such time and place, and in such manner, as it thinks fit.

(2) Without prejudice to paragraph (1), but subject to rule 13 (1) the Court may, on the application of any party to a cause or matter, order any other party to permit the party applying to inspect any documents in the possession, custody or power of that other party relating to any matter in question in the cause or matter.

(3) An application for an order under paragraph (2) must be supported by an affidavit specifying or describing the documents of which inspection is sought and stating the belief of the deponent that they are in the possession, custody or power of the other party and that they relate to a matter in question in the cause or matter.

Taken from O. 24, r. 12, of 1962

ORDER FOR PRODUCTION TO COURT (O. 24, r. 12).

12. At any stage of the proceedings in any cause or matter the Court may, subject to rule 13 (1), order any party to produce to the Court any document in his possession, custody or power relating to any matter in question in the cause or matter and the Court may deal with the document when produced in such manner as it thinks fit.

Taken from O. 24, r. 13, of 1962.

PRODUCTION TO BE ORDERED ONLY IF NECESSARY, ETC. (O. 24, r. 13).

13. — (1) No order for the production of any documents for inspection or to the Court shall be made under any of the foregoing rules unless the Court is of opinion that the order is necessary either for disposing fairly of the cause or matter or for saving costs.

(2) Where on an application under this Order for production of any document for inspection or to the Court privilege from such production is claimed or objection is made to such production on any other ground, the Court may inspect the document for the purpose of deciding whether the claim or objection is valid.

Taken from O. 24, r. 14, of 1962.

PRODUCTION OF BUSINESS BOOKS (O. 24, r. 14).

14. — (1) Where production of any business books for inspection is applied for under any of the foregoing rules, the Court may, instead of ordering production of the original books for inspection, order a copy of any entries therein to be supplied and verified by an affidavit of some person who has examined the copy with the original books.

(2) Any such affidavit shall state whether or not there are in the original book any and what erasures, interlineations or alterations.

(3) Notwithstanding that a copy of any entries in any book has been supplied under this rule, the Court may order production of the book from which the copy was made.

Reproduces O. 24, r. 16, of 1962.

DOCUMENT DISCLOSURE OF WHICH WOULD BE INJURIOUS TO PUBLIC INTEREST: SAVING

15. The foregoing provisions of this Order shall be without prejudice to any rule of law which authorises or requires the withholding of any document on the ground that the disclosure of it would be injurious to the public interest.

New in 1965.

FAILURE TO COMPLY WITH REQUIREMENT FOR DISCOVERY, ETC. (O. 24, r. 16).

16. — (1) If any party who is required by any of the foregoing rules, or by any order made thereunder, to make discovery of documents or to produce any documents for the purpose of inspection or any other purpose fails to comply with any provision of that rule or with that order, as the case may be, then, without prejudice, in the case of a failure to comply with any such provision, to rules 3 (2) and 11 (1), the Court may make such order as it thinks just including, in particular, an order that the action be dismissed or, as the case may be, an order that the defence be struck out and judgment be entered accordingly.

(2) If any party against whom an order for discovery or production of documents is made fails to comply with it, then, without prejudice to paragraph (1), he shall be liable to committal.

(3) Service on a party's solicitor of an order for discovery or production of documents made against that party shall be sufficient service to found an application for committal of the party disobeying the order, but the party may show in answer to the application that he had no notice or knowledge of the order.

(4) A solicitor on whom such an order made against his client is served and who fails without reasonable excuse to give notice thereof to his client shall be liable to committal.

Taken from O. 24, r. 16, of 1962; amended in 1965.

REVOCATION AND VARIATION OF ORDERS (O. 24, r. 17).

17. Any order made under this Order (including an order made on appeal) may, on sufficient cause being shown, be revoked or varied by a subsequent order or direction of the Court made or given at or before the trial of the cause or matter in connection with which the original order was made.

Repeats O. 24, r. 18, of 1962.

Order 26
(R. S. C. 1965)

INTERROGATORIES

DISCOVERY BY INTERROGATORIES (O. 26, r. 1).

1. — (1) A party to any cause or matter may apply to the Court for an order —

   (*a*) giving him leave to serve on any other party interrogatories relating to any matter in question between the applicant and that other party in the cause of matter, and

   (*b*) requiring that other party to answer the interrogatories on affidavit within such period as may be specified in the order.

(2) A copy of the proposed interrogatories must be served with the summons, or the notice under Order 25, rule 7, by which the application for such leave is made.

(3) On the hearing of an application under this rule, the Court shall give leave as to such only of the interrogatories as it considers necessary either for disposing fairly of the cause or matter or for saving costs; and in deciding whether to give leave the Court shall take into account any offer made by the party to be interrogated to give particulars or to make admissions or to produce documents relating to any matter in question.

(4) A proposed interrogatory which does not relate to such a matter as is mentioned in paragraph (1) shall be disallowed notwithstanding that it might be admissible in oral cross-examination of a witness.

Taken from O. 26, r. 1, of 1962.

INTERROGATORIES WHERE PARTY IS A BODY OF PERSONS (O. 26, r. 2).

2. Where a party to a cause or matter is a body of persons, whether corporate or unincorporate, being a body which is empowered by law to sue or be sued whether in its own name or in the name of an officer or other person, the Court may, on the application of any other party,

make an order allowing him to serve interrogatories on such officer or member of the body as may be specified in the order.

Reproduces O. 26, r. 2, of 1962.

STATEMENT AS TO PARTY, ETC., REQUIRED TO ANSWER (O. 26, r. 3).

3. Where interrogatories are to be served on two or more parties or are required to be answered by an agent or servant of a party, a note at the end of the interrogatories shall state which of the interrogatories each party or, as the case may be, an agent or servant is required to answer, and which agent or servant.

Reproduces O. 26, r. 3, of 1962.

OBJECTION TO ANSWER ON GROUND OF PRIVILEGE (O. 26, r. 4).

4. Where a person objects to answering any interrogatory on the ground of privilege he may take the objection in his affidavit in answer.

Taken from O. 26, r. 4, of 1962.

INSUFFICIENT ANSWER (O. 26, r. 5).

5. If any person on whom interrogatories have been served answers any of them insufficiently, the Court may make an order requiring him to make a further answer, and either by affidavit or on oral examination as the Court may direct.

Reproduces O. 26, r. 5, of 1962.

FAILURE TO COMPLY WITH ORDER (O. 26, r. 6).

6. — (1) If a party against whom an order is made under rule 1 or 5 fails to comply with it, the Court may make such order as it thinks just including, in particular, an order that the action be dismissed or, as the case may be, an order that the defence be struck out and judgment be entered accordingly.

(2) If a party against whom an order is made under rule 1 or 5 fails to comply with it, then, without prejudice to paragraph (1), he shall be liable to committal.

(3) Service on a party's solicitor of an order to answer interrogatories made against the party shall be sufficient service to found an application for committal of the party disobeying the order, but the party may show in answer to the application that he had no notice or knowledge of the order.

(4) A solicitor on whom an order to answer interrogatories made against his client is served and who fails without reasonable excuse to give notice thereof to his client shall be liable to committal.

Taken from O. 26, r. 6, of 1962.

USE OF ANSWERS TO INTERROGATORIES AT TRIAL (O. 26, r. 7).

7. A party may put in evidence at the trial of a cause or matter, or of any issue therein, some only of the answers to interrogatories, or part only of such an answer, without putting in evidence the other answers or, as the case may be, the whole of that answer, but the Court may look at the whole of the answers and if of opinion that any other answer or other part of an answer is so connected with an answer or part thereof used in evidence that the one ought not to be so used without the other, the Court may direct that that other answer or part shall be put in evidence.

Reproduces O. 26, r. 7, of 1962.

REVOCATION AND VARIATION OF ORDERS (O. 26, r. 8).

8. Any order made under this Order (including an order made on appeal) may, on sufficient cause being shown, be revoked or varied by a subsequent order or direction of the Court made or given at or before the trial of the cause or matter in connection with which the original order was made.

Repeats the former O. 31, r. 31, introduced in 1956.

Order 27
(R. S. C. 1965)

ADMISSIONS

ADMISSION OF CASE OF OTHER PARTY (O. 27, r. 1).

1. Without prejudice to Order 18, rule 13, a party to a cause or matter may give notice, by his pleading or otherwise in writing, that he admits the truth of the whole or any part of the case of any other party.

Reproduces O. 27, r. 1, of 1962.

NOTICE TO ADMIT FACTS (O. 27, r. 2).

2.—(1) A party to a cause or matter may not later than 21 days after the cause or matter is set down for trial serve on any other party a notice requiring him to admit, for the purpose of that cause or matter only, the facts specified in the notice.

(2) An admission made in compliance with a notice under this rule shall not be used against the party by whom it was made in any cause or matter other than the cause or matter for the purpose of which it was made or in favour of any person other than the person by whom the notice was given, and the Court may at any time allow a party to

amend or withdraw an admission so made by him on such terms as may be just.

Reproduces O. 27, r. 2 of 1962, as amended by R.S.C. (Amendment) 1969 (S.I. 1969 No. 1105).

JUDGMENT ON ADMISSIONS OF FACTS (O. 27, r. 3).

3. Where admissions of fact are made by a party to a cause or matter either by his pleadings or otherwise, any other party to the cause or matter may apply to the Court for such judgment or order as upon those admissions he may be entitled to, without waiting for the determination of any other question between the parties, and the Court may give such judgment, or make such order, on the application as it thinks just.

An application for an order under this rule may be made by motions or summons.

Taken from O. 27, r. 3, of 1962.

ADMISSION AND PRODUCTION OF DOCUMENTS SPECIFIED IN LIST OF DOCUMENTS (O. 27, r. 4).

4.—(1) Subject to paragraph (2) and without prejudice to the right of a party to object to the admission in evidence of any document, a party on whom a list of documents is served in pursuance of any provision of Order 24 shall, unless the Court otherwise orders, be deemed to admit—

(*a*) that any document described in the list as an original document is such a document and was printed, written, signed or executed as it purports respectively to have been, and

(*b*) that any document described therein as a copy is a true copy.

This paragraph does not apply to a document the authenticity of which the party has denied in his pleading.

(2) If before the expiration of 21 days after inspection of the documents specified in a list of documents or after the time limited for inspection of those documents expires, whichever is the later, the party on whom the list is served serves on the party whose list it is a notice stating, in relation to any document specified therein, that he does not admit the authenticity of that document and requires it to be proved at the trial, he shall not be deemed to make any admission in relation to that document under paragraph (1).

(3) A party to a cause or matter by whom a list of documents is served on any other party in pursuance of any provision of Order 24 shall be deemed to have been served by that other party with a notice requiring him to produce at the trial of the cause or matter such of the documents specified in the list as are in his possession, custody or power.

(4) The foregoing provisions of this rule apply in relation to an affidavit made in compliance with an order under Order 24, rule 7, as they apply in relation to a list of documents served in pursuance of any provision of that Order.

Reproduces O. 27, r. 4, of 1962 (then new), as amended by R.S.C. (Amendment) 1969 (S.I. 1969 No. 1105).

NOTICES TO ADMIT OR PRODUCE DOCUMENTS (O. 27, r. 5).

5.— (1) Except where rule 4 (1) applies, a party to a cause or matter may within 21 days after the cause or matter is set down for trial serve on any other party a notice requiring him to admit the authenticity of the documents specified in the notice.

(2) If a party on whom a notice under paragraph (1) is served desires to challenge the authenticity of any document therein specified he must, within 21 days after service of the notice, serve on the party by whom it was given a notice stating that he does not admit the authenticity of the document and requires it to be proved at the trial.

(3) A party who fails to give a notice of non-admission in accordance with paragraph (2) in relation to any document shall be deemed to have admitted the authenticity of that document unless the Court otherwise orders.

(4) Except where rule 4 (3) applies, a party to a cause or matter may serve on any other party a notice requiring him to produce the documents specified in the notice at the trial of the cause or matter.

Reproduces O. 27, r. 5, of 1962, as amended by R.S.C. (Amendment) 1969 (S.I. 1969 No. 1105).

Order 29

DETENTION, PRESERVATION, ETC., OF SUBJECT-MATTER OF CAUSE OR MATTER (O. 29, r. 2).

2.— (1) On the application of any party to a cause or matter the Court may make an order for the detention, custody or preservation of any property which is the subject-matter of the cause or matter, or as to which any question may arise therein, or for the inspection of any such property in the possession of a party to the cause or matter.

(2) For the purpose of enabling any order under paragraph (1) to be carried out the Court may by the order authorise any person to enter upon any land or building in the possession of any party to the cause or matter.

(3) Where the right of any party to a specific fund is in dispute in a cause or matter, the Court may, on the application of a party to the cause or matter, order the fund to be paid into court or otherwise secured.

(4) An order under this rule may be made on such terms, if any, as the Court thinks just.

(5) An application for an order under this rule must be made by summons or by notice under Order 25, rule 7.

(6) Unless the Court otherwise directs, an application by a defendant for such an order may not be made before he enters an appearance.

POWER TO ORDER SAMPLES TO BE TAKEN, ETC. (O. 29, r. 3).

3. — (1) Where it considers it necessary or expedient for the purpose of obtaining full information or evidence in any cause or matter, the Court may, on the application of a party to the cause or matter, and on such terms, if any, as it thinks just, by order authorise or require any sample to be taken of any property which is the subject-matter of the cause or matter or as to which any question may arise therein, any observation to be made on such property or any experiment to be tried on or with such property.

(2) For the purpose of enabling any order under paragraph (1) to be carried out the Court may by the order authorise any person to enter upon any land or building in the possession of any party to the cause or matter.

(3) Rule 2 (5) and (6) shall apply in relation to an application for an order under this rule as they apply in relation to an application for an order under that rule.

Rules 2 and 3 are taken from the former O. 50, rr. 2, 3 and 4.

INSPECTION ETC. OF PROPERTY UNDER S. 21 OF ADMINISTRATION OF JUSTICE ACT 1969 OR S 32 (2) OF ADMINISTRATION OF JUSTICE ACT 1970 (O. 29, r. 7A).

7A. — (1) An application for an order under section 21 (1) of the Administration of Justice Act 1969 in respect of property which may become the subject-matter of subsequent proceedings in the High Court or as to which any question may arise in any such proceedings shall be made by originating summons and the person against whom the order is sought shall be made defendant to the summons.

(2) An application after the commencement of proceedings for an order under section 32 (2) of the Administration of Justice Act 1970 in respect of property which is not the property of or in the possession of any party to the proceedings shall be made by summons, which must be served on the person against whom the order is sought and on every party to the proceedings other than the applicant.

(3) A summons under paragraph (1) or (2) shall be supported by affidavit which must specify or describe the property in respect of which the order is sought and show, if practicable by reference to any pleading served or intended to be served in the proceedings or subse-

quent proceedings, that it is property which is or may become the subject-matter of the proceedings or as to which any question arises or may arise in the proceedings.

(4) A copy of the supporting affidavit shall be served with the summons on every person on whom the summons is required to be served.

(5) An order made under the said section 21 or 32 (2) may be made conditional on the applicant's giving security for the costs of the person against whom it is made or on such other terms, if any, as the Court thinks just.

(6) No such order shall be made if it appears to the Court—

(*a*) that compliance with the order, if made, would result in the disclosure of information relating to a secret process, discovery or invention not in issue in the proceedings, and

(*b*) that the application would have been refused on that ground if—

(i) in the case of a summons under paragraph (1), the subsequent proceedings had already been begun, or

(ii) in the case of a summons under paragraph (2), the person against whom the order is sought were a party to the proceedings.

Added by R.S.C. (Amendment No. 4) 1971 (S.I. 1971 No. 1269) and amended by R.S.C. (Amendment No. 5) 1971 (S.I. 1971 No. 1955).

Order 38

ORDER TO PRODUCE DOCUMENT AT PROCEEDING OTHER THAN TRIAL (O. 38, r. 13).

13.—(1) At any stage in a cause or matter the Court may order any person to attend any proceedings in the cause or matter and produce any document, to be specified or described in the order, the production of which appears to the Court to be necessary for the purpose of that proceeding.

(2) No person shall be compelled by an order under paragraph (1) to produce any document at a proceeding in a cause or matter which he could not be compelled to produce at the trial of that cause or matter.

This Rule was taken from the former O. 37, r. 7.

Summary of Contents

1   INTRODUCTION   1

A.   The intended benefits of American federal discovery are the same as those of discovery in England.   1

    1. Results of a national field-study about the effects of American federal discovery.   3

    2. The American evidence is that, although expensive and dilatory, discovery promotes just adjudication.   5

B.   Discussion of the different mechanisms by which the English and American federal legal systems seek the same benefits.   8

2   INTERROGATORIES UNDER F.R.C.P. 33 and R.S.C. 1965, O. 26   12

A.   The requirement of leave of court in England; the method of objection to interrogatories in the U.S.A.   12

B.   F.R.C.P. 33(c) should be amended so that its purpose of shifting the burden to the party seeking information about documents from interrogatories is fulfilled; and so that it has a wider application than just to 'business records of the party.'   15

3   DOCUMENTS   17

A.   Documents under F.R.C.P. 34; R.S.C. 1965, O. 24.   17

    1. American federal mechanisms for production of documents upon request.   17

    2. In contrast to English mandatory documentary disclosure, the American federal request must 'describe' documents 'with reasonable particularity'; therefore, obtaining disclosure of documents under F.R.C.P. 30, 31, or 33 sometimes will be necessary before securing their production under F.R.C.P. 34, although the American courts should try to avoid requiring two separate steps to secure production.   18

3. In both jurisdictions discovery extends to documents in a party's possession, custody, or control-power.   25

4. F.R.C.P. 34 should be amended so that American federal courts will have mandatory, self-executing disclosure and production of documents, as do the English courts.   28

B.   Documents under F.R.C.P. 45   31

1. Mechanisms for production by subpoena duces tecum incident to depositions upon oral examination or written questions.   31

2. Because F.R.C.P. 34 and 45 are read as integrated discovery devices, obtaining disclosure of documents under F.R.C.P. 30, 31, or 33 sometimes will be necessary before securing their production under F.R.C.P. 45.   34

3. As in England and under F.R.C.P. 34, discovery under F.R.C.P. 45 extends to documents in a person's possession, custody, or control-power.   36

4. Production of documents from parties under F.R.C.P. 45 should be eliminated, for production under F.R.C.P. 34 is preferable.   37

4   DISCLOSURE AND INSPECTION OF REAL AND PERSONAL PROPERTY UNDER F.R.C.P. 34, 45; R.S.C. 1965, O. 29, rr. 2–(1) (2) (4) (6), 3–(1)(2)(3)   40

A.   Disclosure and inspection of real and personal property should be made mandatory in both systems; at least, they should be made available extrajudicially in England.   40

B.   Instructive examples of enlightened, flexible inspection orders by English courts.   40

C.   Discovery inspections of property and documents by experts should trigger exchange of experts' reports.   41

D.   Inspection of methods of operation should be available in England, as it is in the U.S.A.   42

5   ADMISSIONS OF DOCUMENTS AND FACTS UNDER F.R.C.P. 36 and R.S.C. 1965, O. 27, rr. 2, 4, 5, O. 62, r. 3; PROPOSALS TO ENCOURAGE THEIR USE IN THE AMERICAN FEDERAL AND ENGLISH CIVIL LEGAL SYSTEMS (DISCOVERY SANCTIONS IN GENERAL)   45

6   IN ENGLAND ORAL EXAMINATION
         SHOULD BE MADE AVAILABLE AS AN
         ALTERNATIVE OR SUPPLEMENT TO
         INTERROGATORIES EVEN IF
         INTERROGATORIES HAVE NOT BEEN
         ANSWERED INSUFFICIENTLY; THE
         AMERICAN FEDERAL ORAL DEPOSITION
         IS A MODEL   61

7   THE ENGLISH COURTS HAVE BEEN
         BRINGING ABOUT DISCOVERY BY
         MEDICAL EXAMINATIONS ONLY IN
         LIMITED CLASSES OF CASES; THEY.
         SHOULD HAVE POWER TO DO SO IN ALL
         CIVIL LITIGATION, AS AMERICAN
         FEDERAL COURTS DO UNDER F.R.C.P. 35   68

8   THE 'OWN CASE' RULE, ALTHOUGH NO
         LONGER PERVASIVE, STILL RESTRICTS
         DISCOVERY   75

A.   In England the rule continues to apply to
         inspection of property and interrogatories, although 75
         1. In the case of interrogatories, in some instances
            this rule has been superseded by a rule that all
            facts, but no evidence, are subject to discovery,
            and   75
         2. The restrictive effect has been curtailed because
            a party's allegations negativing or impeaching
            his opponent's case, even though not specifying
            a defect in it, have been considered part of the
            party's own case.   76
B.   Thus in England a party has not had to disclose
         whom he plans to call as witnesses at trial.   76
C.   The rationales for the 'own case' rule do not justify
         it; the rule should be wholly abrogated in England,
         including its application to the disclosure of
         witnesses; the same is true of the 'fact-evidence'
         rule.   76
         1. If the 'own case' rule is not abrogated in.
            England, it should continue to be construed to
            permit discovery of what negatives or impeaches
            an opponent's case without requiring the party
            seeking discovery to specify defects in it. Courts
            should be wary of objections phrased in terms of

'fishing' which are a disguise for the 'own case'
rule. 84

D. Under the F.R.C.P. the 'own case' rule has been
abrogated for all discovery mechanisms, unlike in
England. 84

   1. Yet a vestige of the 'own case' rule may linger in
the unwillingness of most American federal
courts to require disclosure of witnesses planned
to be called at trial. 85

   2. The 'own case' rule has been extirpated to the
extent that a party's contentions are subject to
discovery, although the American federal
practice concerning contentions should be
improved. It is especially important that issues
be narrowed or illuminated through discovery of
contentions in view of the notice nature of
pleadings and the absence of bills of particulars
in the U.S.A. 87

E. The American federal law on discovery of
information solely impeaching the credibility of
witnesses adheres to the 'own case' rule more
precisely than the English law. 93

9 DISCOVERY FROM NON-PARTIES 95

A. In England as a general rule there is no discovery
from non-parties. 95

   1. Exception to the general rule for a member or
officer of a corporate party. 95

   2. Exception to the general rule for discovery to
determine from whom relief should be sought. 95

   3. Exception to the general rule of Banker's Books
Evidence Act 1879, s. 7. 95

   4. Exception to the general rule requiring discovery
from a real plaintiff in interest who sues by a
nominal party. 96

   5. Exception to the general rule for inspection of
documents and real and personal property in
personal-injuries cases of Administration of
Justice Act 1970, s. 32(1) (2). 96

B. Discovery from non-parties should be available
generally in England rather than only in
exceptional categories. 97

C. In American federal practice there is discovery
from non-parties except for inspection of their real

property and their physical and mental
examination; non-party discovery should be
extended to these two forms and improved in
respect to the other forms.   103

10   SUMMARY OF DISCOVERY LAW REFORM
        PROPOSALS IN TERMS OF THE CENTRAL
        PURPOSES OF DISCOVERY LAW   112
11   EPILOGUE: ANTICIPATED AMERICAN
        FEDERAL OPPOSITION TO PROPOSALS TO
        EXPAND DISCOVERY (THE CONTINUING
        SAGA OF UNFOUNDED ALLEGATIONS OF
        DISCOVERY ABUSE IN THE FACE OF
        CONVINCING EVIDENCE TO THE
        CONTRARY AND AMPLE F.R.C.P. POWERS
        TO CURB ABUSE)   115

Index

Abuse ✓
  allegations 115–20
  overuse 115, 118, n. 11–33, 119, 121
Adjournment 77, 99–100
  see also Continuances; Stay of action
Admissibility 49, 53, 78–9, 99
  establishment of 45, 46, 101; *see also*
    Best evidence rule; Documents,
    authentication of; Property,
    admissions of authenticity
  objections to 49
  see also Evidence
Admissions 45, 113
  contentions (American) 88–93
  documents (American) 8, 45, 47, 54;
    (English) 45–6, 48–9, 52
  effect 48, 53–4, 88
  extrajudicial operation 50–1
  fact (American) 8, 47–8, 51, 52;
    (English) 8, n. 1–60, 46, 48–9, 52,
    53, 54–5, 75
  objections and denials (American)
    47–8, 50, 55, 56–7, 59–60; (English)
    46, 47, 55–6, 59–60
  order (English, proposed) 55–6
  refusal to admit 51, 52, 59
  withdrawal and amendment 48–9, 113
Adversary Function vi, 10–11, 30
  see also 'Sporting theory'
Adverse comment 73–4
Answers
  amendment 86, 91–2
  sufficiency 12, 47–8, 50
  see also Admissions; Interrogatories

Banker's books 95–6
Best evidence rule 46
Bills of particulars 6, 89
Business records of party 15–16

Collateral use 28, 48
Complaint and summons 108
Compromise settlements 1, 4–5, 6, 51, n.
    5–47, 79, 98, n. 9–45, 101
  fairness 5, 6–7, 115
Contempt 50, 58–9, n. 5–78, 60, 108–10
  failure to obey subpoena 32, 98, 106

proposed uses 55–7, 74, 113
  see also Sanctions, constitutionality
Contentions 3–4, 5–6, 87–93, 114
Continuance 91
  see also Adjournment
Convenience 102–3, n. 9–55, 104
Corporate officers 95
Costs of discovery 6, 8, 9, 25, 30, 52, n.
    5–45, 64–7, 80, 116
Costs of litigation 53, 66–7, 80, 98, 115
Costs of proof-sanction 49–51, n. 5–45, 56
Costs-sanction 13, 17, 18, 23, 38, 47,
    49–50
'Custody or legal control' 68, 107–8
  see also Documents, 'possession, custody
    or power'

Defamation (American) n. 11–40
Delay 9, 20, n. 8–98, 99
Depositions
  (American) 8, 9–10, 31, 61–2, 63–4
  (English) 9, 61, 62, 64, 66
  cost 64–6
  and documents (American) 21, 25,
    31–4, 37, 103–4
  effect of answers 53–4
  non-party (American) 8, 103, 104, 106
  objections (English) 61
  subpoena 31
  on written questions (American) 31, 38
  see also Recording and transcription
Discoverable information, admissions 52
Discovery
  benefits 1–2, 7–8, 98, 112; empirical
    evidence (American) 3–7, 62–3,
    115–16; *see also* Compromise
    settlements; Evidence; Facts, full
    presentation of; Issues, narrowing of;
    Strength of case, evaluation
  mechanisms available (American) 8,
    9–10, 31, 40, 68; (English) 8, 9,
    10–11, 40, 61, 68–9; proposed 40, 42,
    52, 112–14; *see also* Admissions;
    Depositions; Documents;
    Interrogatories; Non-parties;
    Property
  use and effectiveness (American) 9,

29–30, 31, 40, 51, 61–2, n. 6–10, n.
6–14, 63–4, 68, 116, 118, 121;
(English) 40
Dismissal and default 50, n. 5–78
constitutionality (American) 56–9
proposed use 55, 56–7, 59–60, 74,
109
Disrespect for system 7–8, 30, 86, 110
Documents
(American) 10, 17, 21, 29–30, 37, 112,
120
authentication (American) 45, 54, 113;
(English) 46
description (American) 17, 19, 21–3,
24–5, 34–6, 103, 114; (English
non-party) 102
designation: *see* description (American)
disclosure (American) 18, 24
mandatory discovery (English) 8, 10–11,
19–20, 21, 27, 28–9, 30, 45, 46, 52,
75, 76–7, 78; exceptions 20–1, 28–9,
113; grounds for resistance 11, 20,
27–8
non-party (American) 26–7, 36–7,
n. 3–73, 103–5, 112; (English) 26,
27–8, 95–7, n. 9–24, 102
'possession, custody or control'
(American) 18, 19, 25–7, 36–7
'possession, custody or power'
(English) 26, n. 3–41, 27–8, 95–6,
96–7
production and inspection (American)
16, 17–19, 27, 33, 38–9; court order
(American) 17–18, 19, 23–4;
(English) 20–1
'reasonable particularity': *see*
description (American)
relevance (American) 21, 23–4
subpoena duces tecum (American)
31–7
see also Admissions; Banker's books;
Business records of party;
Depositions; Extrajudicial request;
Interrogatories
Due process (American) 57–9, n. 5–76

Equity, merger with law 1, n. 5–73, 75
Ethical considerations 66, 99–100
Evaluation: *see* Strength of case,
evaluation
Evidence
and admissions 45–6, 49, 53
concealment 5–6, 7, 30, 80
effective use 2, 4–5, 46, 63, 98
evaluation 51, 63

false or misleading 2, 77–9, 99
irrelevant 6
laws of 49, 78
presentation and preparation 2, 46,
80–1, 98
provision 2, 4, 6, 7, 41, 62, 63, 82
relevance 49, 78
see also Admissibility; 'Fact-evidence'
rule; Hearsay; Impeachment;
Surprise; Witnesses
Expense: *see* Costs of discovery;
Oppression, undue burden or expense
Experts, reports 41–2, 113
Extrajudicial request (American) 8, 10
documents 17–18
inspection of property 40
see also Informal agreement; Informal
interview, non-party

'Fact-evidence' rule (English) n. 6–31, 75,
81–4, 101, 113
Facts, full presentation of vi, 2, 7, 8–9, 10,
30, 52, 71, 72, 84, 102, 112, 119, 121–2
Fairness of result 7, 71, 81, 102, 112
see also Compromise settlements; Facts,
full presentation of
'Fishing' 76, n. 8–14, 84
see also 'Own case' rule

Hearsay 27, 98–9

Identity of defendant 95
Illiteracy n. 9–58
Impeachment
allegations 76
evidence 2, 77, 78–9, 81, 83–4
witnesses 93–4
Informal agreement 18, 29, 42, 68
Informal interview, non-party (English)
100–1
Inherent power (English) 69–72
see also Stay of action
Inspection: *see* Documents; Property
Integration of discovery devices n. 3–27,
34–5, 36
Interrogatories
(American) 12–13, 62–4, 92
(English) 9, 13, 14, 27–8, 61, 63–4,
n. 6–31, 75, 76–7, 78, 81, 82
answers (American) 6, 12, 15–16, 25,
87, 89–91, 114; effect 6, 53–4, 88–93
and documents (American) 15–16, 21,
25, 34, 113–14; (English) 27–8
leave of court (American) n. 1–61,
13–14, 117, 118–19; (English) 9,

n. 1–60, 13–14, n. 2–12, 15, 66, 82, 83, 93
non-party (American) 104; (English) 95, 102
objections (American) 12; (English) 13, 82, 83
quality 13–14, 98
see also Answers
Issues 47, 62, 78
narrowing of 1, 6, n. 1–40, 79, 88–92

Judicial economy 7–8, 9, 10, 23, 66–7, 112, 113
Juries 2, 51, n. 8–98
Jurisdiction 105–6, 107
Just adjudication: *see* Fairness of result

Legal professional privilege (English) 11, 81, 82
see also Work product privilege
Liberty of subject (English) 9, 72–3, 73–4
see also Privacy and sensibilities

Mental examination: *see* Physical or mental examination
Methods of operation 42–4

New trials 77, 98
Nominal parties 96, 100
see also Real plaintiff in interest
Non-parties
costs 97, 102–3
discovery from (American) 36, 37, 103–8, 110–11, 114; (English) 9, 28, 95–103, 105
notice 36, 37, n. 3–73, 107–8
objections (American) 103, 106, 108; (English) 97, 102
summons and affidavit (English) 96, 106–7
summons and complaint (American) 107, 108
see also Banker's books; Corporate officers; Depositions; Documents; Identity of defendant; Interrogatories; Liberty of subject; Property; Real plaintiff in interest; Subpoenas

Objections: *see* Admissibility; Oppression, undue burden or expense; Privilege
Opinions 88–9
see also Contentions
Oppression, undue burden or expense 19, 23, 32, 47, 82, n. 9–24, 102, 119–20

Oral examination: *see* Depositions
'Own case' rule n. 6–31, 75–85, 87, 93–4, 99, 100–1
see also 'Fact-evidence' rule; 'Fishing'

Patent actions (English) n. 4–21
Paternalism 29, 54
Paternity 71–2
Perjury 77, 78, 93–4, 99
Personal injuries (English) 70, 71, 96, 105, 106
Physical or mental examination
(American) 9–10, 41–2, 68, n. 9–85
(English) 9, 68–74
non-party (American) 107–11
see also Contempt; 'Custody or legal control'; Liberty of subject; Paternity; Privacy and sensibilities; Writs de ventre inspiciendo
Pleadings
(American) 24–5, 35, 36
(English) n. 1–60, 52
generality 6, 52, 89, 91
see also Bills of particulars; Statement of claim
Prejudice 91–2
see also Reliance
Pre-trial conference (American) n. 1–55, 53, 85, 120–1
see also Summons for directions
Privacy and sensibilities (American) 10, 107–8, 109–10
see also Liberty of subject
Privacy, non-party (English) 9, 100–3
Privilege 11, 42, 47, 102, 103, 106, n. 11–40
see also Legal professional privilege; Self-incrimination; Work product privilege
Pro confesso 55, 58–60, 74, 109, 110
Production: *see* Documents; Property
Property 73
(American) 40, 44
(English) 40, 75, 76–7, 78
personal 41, 42, 98
real n. 9–24
authenticity 54–5
court order (English) 9, 40–1
non-parties (American) 103–7; (English) 96–7, n. 9–24, 105, 106–7
third persons, inspection by (English) 41
see also Subpoenas
Protective orders (American) 23, 32, 103, 119–20

Protracted or complex cases 14, n. 3–28,
n. 5–52, 65, 120–1

Questions, order to answer (English) 61,
65

Real plaintiff in interest 96, 100
see also Nominal parties
Recording and transcription 25, 31, 61,
65–6, 100–1, 102, 103
Reliance
admissions 48–9, 92
answers to interrogatories 89–93
see also Prejudice

Sanctions 88, 98
abuse of discovery (American) 117,
118–19
constitutionality (American) 57–9
disobedience of discovery orders 50–1
refusal to admit 49–51, 52, 55–7, 59–60
refusal to submit to physical
examination 74
unjustified motions and objections
(American) 12–13, 18, 23, 38, 47
use and effectiveness (American) 50–1,
n. 11–41
see also Adjournment; Contempt; Costs
of proof; Costs; Dismissal and
default; Due process; New trial; Pro
confesso; Stay of action
Scope of discovery
(American) 6, 21, 35–6, 44, 45,
n. 6–31, 84–6, 87, 92, 93–4, 117
(English) 27–8, 42–3, n. 6–31, 75, 76,
79, 81, 84, 93, 95–6, 99
see also Contentions; 'Fact-evidence'
rule; 'Fishing'; Hearsay;
Impeachment; Opinions; Physical or
mental examination; Privilege;
Witnesses
Scope of proof 90–2
Self-incrimination 37, n. 3–73
Service 19–20, 25, 31, 37–8, 97
Settlement: *see* Compromise settlements
Slander (English) 76

Special verdicts 51
'Sporting theory' of justice 2, 5, 7, 10,
79–80, 81, 83–4
State courts (American) 1, 62–3
Stay of action (English) 69–71, 96
Strength of case, evaluation 1, 4, 79, 98
Subpoenas
(American) 31, 32, 33, n. 3–64
duces tecum 22–3, 31–7, 54, 97, 98,
102, 103, 104, 106; objections
(American) 32
non-party (American) 104, 105–6
trial (English) 28, 98, 100
see also Contempt; Depositions;
Documents; Physical or mental
examination; Property
Summons for directions (English)
n. 2–11, 53, n. 5–51, 64, 80
see also Pre-trial conference
Surprise 2, 3–4, 5–6, 98
contentions 3–4, 5–6, 93
evidence vi, 2, 5, 77, 80–1
see also 'Sporting theory' of justice

Time limitations
(American) n. 1–55, 12, 25, 38, 50
(English) 19, 53
Time, place and manner 17–18, 33, 38,
101, 108
Third party practice 107
Trade secrets 41
Transcription: *see* Recording and
transcription

Vehicular accidents 20, 71, n. 9–15

Witnesses
identity 5, 76, 81, 85–7, n. 8–71
location 62, 63, 81–2, 85
testimony 80–1, 99, 100
Work product privilege (American) 11,
27, n. 8–64, n. 8–79
see also Legal professional privilege
Writs de ventre inspiciendo 43, 68–9,
72–3